Ye Heart of a Ma

YE HEART OF A MAN

The Domestic Life of Men in Colonial New England

LISA WILSON

Yale University Press   New Haven and London

Published with assistance from the Annie Burr Lewis Fund.

Set in Caslon type.
Printed in the United States of America.

Library of Congress Cataloging-in-Publication Data
Wilson, Lisa, 1957-
Ye heart of a man : the domestic life of men in colonial
New England / Lisa Wilson.
p.   cm.
Includes bibliographical references and index.
ISBN 0-300-07546-4 (cloth : alk. paper)
ISBN 0-300-08550-8 (pbk. : alk. paper)
1. New England — Social life and customs — To 1775.   2. Men — New
England — Social life and customs — 18th century.   3. Sex role — New
England — History — 18th century.   4. Family — New England —
History — 18th century.   5. Man-woman relationships — New England —
History — 18th century.   I. Title.
F7.C36   1999
305.31'0974 — dc21   98-37095

A catalogue record for this book is
available from the British Library.

The paper in this book meets the guidelines
for permanence and durability of the Committee
on Production Guidelines for Book Longevity of
the Council on Library Resources.

10 9 8 7 6 5 4 3 2

To Dave and Alex

~~The great secret therefore, the main~~ The primary Endeavour therefore, should be to distinguish between Useful and unuseful, to pursue the former with unwearied Industry, and to neglect with much Contempt all the Rest.

John Adams, 1758

Contents

PREFACE

Firmly entrenched in women's history, I have struggled with the subject of gender more broadly conceived. Men's history, at first, seemed a silly concept—wasn't most history about men? My change of heart began when I saw Ava Baron present a paper in the mid-1980s. Some of this material appeared later in her edited volume, *Work Engendered: Toward a New History of American Labor.* Also mind-opening was a question put to me during an interview for a fellowship. I was then finishing my dissertation on widowed women in early Pennsylvania. An impertinent interrogator dared to ask, "What about widowers?" After my initial grumbling, I kept returning to that question, "What about widowers?" I knew their story was different; for example, men remarried more quickly after losing a spouse, whereas women, who seemed most financially in need of a partner, shunned remarriage. I began to think about gender as a two-sided coin. Later, as I did more reading, I realized that the historical study of men as a gendered group had barely begun. The scholarship that did exist focused almost exclusively on the nineteenth century.

I began my research locally. I lived and worked in New Haven for a year, one semester of which was a sabbatical from Connecticut College funded by a Sherman Fairchild Grant. To my great good fortune, I received both an Andrew W. Mellon Faculty Fellowship and a Charles Warren Center for Studies in American History Fellowship, both from Harvard University, for the following academic year, 1990–91. My colleagues at

Harvard provided much-needed guidance and support, particularly Deborah J. Coon, Philip J. Ethington, Nancy L. Green, Karen V. Hansen, Janet A. Headley, Deborah J. Lyons, Peter C. Mancall, and Mary E. Odem. Other Cambridge colleagues on whom I counted for friendship as well as historical insights were Barbara DeWolfe and Nancy Bernard.

During the year I spent exploring the rich archival and library resources of the Boston area, the staff at the Massachusetts Historical Society, particularly Catherine Craven, Peter Drummey, Richard A. Ryerson, and Virginia Smith, were most helpful and generous with material and even an occasional ride home. I am also thankful for the help of the staff members of the Boston Public Library, the Congregational Library, the Houghton and Widner libraries at Harvard University, and the Harvard University Archives. In addition, I took advantage of the critical mass of scholars in the Boston area, presenting part of my work at Boston University, the Charles Warren Center, and the Boston Area Seminar in Early American History.

When I returned to full-time teaching, I finished my local research, often setting up camp at the Manuscripts and Archives division of the Yale University Library. I hounded Kenneth P. Minkema, executive editor of *The Works of Jonathan Edwards,* at Yale Divinity School. He was extraordinarily helpful and hospitable. Also helpful were the staff members of the Connecticut Historical Society, the Connecticut State Archives, the American Antiquarian Society, and the Beinecke and Sterling libraries at Yale University. During this final stretch of research I was aided in my travels by the R. F. Johnson Faculty Development Fund at Connecticut College.

At Connecticut College, two colleagues in the history department, Catherine McNichol Stock and Marc R. Forster, and one in the government department, MaryAnne Borelli, read and commented on a draft manuscript. I am very grateful for their comments and their support. Also at the college, I gained from the insights of my students, particularly in my fall 1996 senior seminar entitled "Puritan New England." Many students skillfully commented on various draft chapters; among them were Tom Betzig, Leila Edwards, Chase Eschauzier, Laura Gardner, Hillary Hanscom, Brendan Jones, Valerie Martin, K. K. McGregor, Dan Melia, Jon Patton, Randy Smith, Keith Snow, Julie Soto, Robin Spruce, and Elizabeth Wood. I was privileged to have the help of Elizabeth Wood, an honors student of real talent, in the final editing of the manuscript. Finally, I benefited from the unfailing and good-humored aid of the library staff at Connecticut College.

Outside the college, I have continued to lean heavily on my Philadelphia roots. My graduate mentor, P. M. G. Harris of Temple University, still finds time to critique my work and bolster my spirits. My fellow Temple graduate Jean Soderlund also provided me with her intellectual insights, for which I am most grateful. Michael Zuckerman and Shan Holt read and reread the manuscript at different stages and proved to be two of my toughest critics. Mike also asked me to present part of the material for this book in the informal seminar he runs from his West Philadelphia home. Their comments forced me to think, rework, and defend my findings. I thank them for their friendship and their honesty.

I have previously published some of the material in this book. A part of chapter 3 was included in *"A Shared Experience": Men, Women, and the History of Gender,* a collection edited by Laura McCall and Donald Yacovone. Chapter 5 was published as an article entitled, " 'Ye Heart of a Father': Male Parenting in Colonial New England." This piece appeared in the *Journal of Marriage and the Family* as part of a special 1999 issue on fatherhood, edited by Robert L. Griswold. I am grateful for the insights of these editors.

In addition, I would like to thank a group of scholars who, in the best tradition of the profession, read a draft of this manuscript simply because they were asked. Christopher Collier, John Demos, and E. Anthony Rotundo, read the manuscript and lent me their expertise. Chuck Grench at Yale University Press deserves thanks for his enthusiasm and his deft shepherding of the manuscript through the publication process.

On a personal note, I would like to thank James Connolly for his wise counsel and friendship. Equally essential to my equilibrium have been Pam, Terry, Andy, and Emily Taylor, my surrogate family in Connecticut. Long talks, free dinners, child care, and love marked their invaluable contribution.

Finally, I have dedicated this book to the two men with whom I live in twentieth-century New England. My son, Alexander Waciega, has been my constant companion through this project. He has even come to like the lullaby of my computer keys clacking at night. My husband, David P. Kanen, has a confounding faith in me. His patient and gentle nature sustained me through it all.

Introduction

Colonial New England men, like Peter Thatcher of Milton Massachusetts, spent their days "Ingaged in domestick concernes."[1] Samuel Sewall of Boston delineated his "domestick Concerns" in a letter to colonial agent Jeremiah Dummer in 1719—the recent deaths of two grandchildren, his remarriage, the prolonged disability of his daughter Hannah and the recent engagement of another daughter, Judith.[2] In 1709, John Winthrop, great-grandson and namesake of the first governor of Massachusetts, wrote to his father, Wait Winthrop, then in New London, Connecticut, "Domestick news is of such variety yt I know not where to begin." He informed him about recent sicknesses, deaths, marriages, comings and goings, greetings from common acquaintances, and troubles with servants.[3] When Cotton Mather thanked God for the "undeserved Enjoyments in my domestic Circumstances" he included in his list, "An amiable Consort, agreeable Children, most accomodated Habitation, a plentiful Table: the Respects of kind Neighbours, a flourishing Auditory."[4] All these men felt an unshakable connection to something they labeled the "domestic" world.

Men and women in colonial America spent most of their time working and living together in the same space.[5] The domestic world was inhabited by families. Family members were interdependent: all members contributed to the welfare of the whole. Individual autonomy in such a system was secondary to mutual obligation and responsibility; each family member contributed their share according to gender, age, and ability.[6] A man demonstrated his worth in the domestic context of service to his family and community.[7] Such "serviceableness" or "usefulness" secured him his place and status as an adult man.

The nineteenth-century ideology of separate spheres—the private for women, the public for men—fails to capture the essence of this kind of interdependent world.[8] Recently, Mary Beth Norton, in *Founding Mothers and Fathers: Gendered Power and the Forming of American Society*, proposed a remodeling of the public-private dichotomy for early America. Specifically, she preserves the idea of a private sphere but divides the public sphere into the formal and the informal. In her framework, the informal public consisted of a community of familiars rather than the more distant political and clerical authorities of the formal public. Roughly, the domestic world of early New England men examined here includes Norton's notion of the private as well as her informal public.[9]

Many scholars have shifted their focus from the careful contouring of separate spheres to a subtle exposing of power relations. Colonial society, in this scholarship, was a world governed by various systems of gender, race, and class inequalities. The language of gender difference, in fact, exposes these patterns of race and class disparities in the colonial past.[10] Although pathbreaking in many ways, this scholarship does little to help uncover the lives of men. Men appear in this literature as one-dimensional power brokers rather than flesh and blood people with complex and contested relationships. Studying power does not allow for a nuanced portrait of colonial manhood.

The concept of patriarchy, like the more general notion of power, likewise needs some careful recasting to make sense of male identity constructed in a domestic world. Gerda Lerner has defined patriarchy as "the manifestation and institutionalization of male dominance over women and children in the family and the extension of male dominance over women in society in general."[11] Women's history has carefully analyzed the struggles of women to work within such a system. Implicit in any discussion of patriarchy is the perhaps logical assumption that men treasured, or at the very least tacitly accepted, their superior position. The writings of colonial New England men suggest, however, a more nuanced view of patriarchy, particularly in the domestic realm.[12] Independence, interdependence, and dependence or, to use words more familiar to these men, "to be of use," "usefulness," and "the specter of uselessness" more accurately capture the shifting, relational interactions they describe.[13] A man saw his power, such as it was, wax and wane over a lifetime.[14] In addition, he positioned himself within a system of obligation and duty. Edmund Morgan, in his classic examination of the Puritan family, focused on dual relationships—parent-child, husband-wife, master-servant.[15] These relationships were uneven, but nonetheless reciprocal.[16] The family tied men and women together in a complex series of mutual dependencies. Everyone was not equal, but neither was anyone autonomous.

Research on the gendered history of North American men has so far focused primarily on the nineteenth and twentieth centuries.[17] The colonial period has too often been neglected or described as simply an "agrarian patriarchy."[18] The literature on men in colonial New England is indeed spare, but research on women has flourished. The publication of Laurel Thatcher Ulrich's *Good Wives: Image and Reality in the Lives of Women in Northern New England, 1650–1750* in 1982 marked the beginning of a new interest in colonial New England women's history.[19] Ulrich's creative use of limited sources allowed a new and intimate view of colonial New England women's lives. I have chosen to use Ulrich's book as a model in part to provide opportunity for comparison. Significantly, men were given the title "Goodmen" not "Goodhusbands." As their title suggests, men were allowed a more complex base for self-definition, but cultural expectations also shaped the contours of their lives.

Ulrich's methodology—role analysis, rather than the newer idea of gender as a "performance"—better fits the colonial New England context. Judith Butler, who put forward the notion of gender performance in her influential book *Gender Trouble: Feminism and the Subversion of Identity,* would no doubt see me as overly concerned with the "materiality" of the body or, in layman's terms, with the inherent component of gender not mediated by culture.[20] I would have to plead guilty. Gender in colonial New England was a cultural and social category, but it was also a biological reality of great power. Marriage and parenthood were the only alternatives for adult men and women. Single people could not legally live outside family government.[21] Society punished sexual difference with the threat and sometimes the reality of execution.[22] With marriage came children in a society without effective birth control. Men and women performed their gender roles, but constant childbirth set the limits of what was possible.

Colonial New England society broadly agreed on male domestic roles; men, in turn, played the roles assigned them.[23] For example, they were expected to become husbands, fathers, and providers, and most men fulfilled these expectations with varying degrees of success.[24] In addition, a man continually reconfigured his sense of himself and his place. Such transitions were often marked by events—marriage, birth, spouse loss—not necessarily chronological age. When making such generalizations it must be remembered, of course, that roles were negotiated in the real world and responded to individual needs and desires as well as the expectations of others.[25] Also roles themselves shifted and changed over time.[26]

Massachusetts and Connecticut between 1620 and the Revolution provide the setting for this book.[27] Both these colonies were heavily influenced by Puritanism. Although Puritan orthodoxy itself changed, evolved, and withered by the end of this period, even in these colonies, Puritan concepts of family government and male behavior remained influential.[28] This book ends with the birth of the new nation and the glimmer of coming industrialization in the 1780s. The last two decades of the eighteenth century saw changes, economic and political, that altered the way men defined themselves. No longer did a man look to the domestic realm to find his sense of self; rather, he increasingly looked to the newly defined "public sphere" for validation and meaning.[29]

My hope for this project from the start has been to recover the voices of men in the domestic world. As in all historical inquiry dependent on written sources, the experiences of some kinds of men were easier to establish than the experiences of others. No history is complete without the lives of the inarticulate; but digging out detail for more ordinary individuals is frustrating at best. Although there does exist, for example, quite a few diaries for farmers, these men often simply recorded weather and remarkable local events with little personal commentary. Combing the court, town, and church records still leaves the evidence weighted heavily toward the elite. All these sources have been consulted, but with no illusion or claim that the final product reflects the circumstances of all men in this place and time. Eighteenth-century, privileged, white men are overrepresented in the relevant documents and, therefore, in this study. Nonetheless, the opinions that articulate men had about their lives set a cultural pattern that inarticulate men could look to, imitate, or boldly reject. Like women's history, the gendered history of men must begin with this paradigm to understand the less visible alternatives.

Self-revelatory records are remarkably silent about African and Native American manhood as well. Interpreting a lack of evidence is tricky at best, but the shards of material that do survive and the useful work of other scholars are suggestive. Kathleen M. Brown has argued for colonial Virginia that gender identity emerged from the crucible of colonization. Colonial men, in other words, birthed themselves through contact with the Native American and African "other."[30] Her argument is very persuasive for the slave society of Virginia. New England, however, was different. It was, to use Philip D. Morgan's terminology, a "slave-owning society" not a "slave society."[31]

If there was a male "other" for New England men, he was Native American. Native American men served as a reminder that if civilized norms were jettisoned, savagery loomed.[32] To be a proper man was to be a hard-working Christian. Native American men, however, insisted that their women do the farming and at the same time boldly rebuffed colonial efforts to convert them to Protestant Christianity.[33] Puritan condescension and even repulsion for this Native American other could also turn to titillation. Exotic tales of capture, enslavement, and even marriage fascinated New England readers.[34] What could be more horrifying and intriguing than a white man or woman willingly living with Indians?[35] Even a calculated or jocular imitation of Native American style threatened gender foundations. Hair, for example, had to be properly shorn to distinguish colonial manhood from the unruliness of the alternative.[36] The image of a trader in Native American garb or a Native American in European finery was both daring and shocking.[37] Perhaps this alluring, frightful, Native American other was so threatening that strict adherence to form, and silence about alternatives, was the only viable defense. Gender distinctions had to remain clear or chaos loomed.[38]

I have organized this book with an eye to the delicate balance men tried to maintain in the domestic realm between affection and power. The first section of this book deals with coming of age and declaring independence from childhood: a man first found work and then a wife. The second section focuses on the interdependent roles of men within their families—husband, provider, and father. The third and final section explores the changes of later life with a discussion of the widower, forced retirement, and lurking dependency.

In chapter 1 I shall explore the process of finding a calling. A woman's careful choice of a mate determined her future, but a man had to secure a career as well as a spouse. The right calling could insure his status and his financial and personal independence, make him a useful member of his community, and help him find a wife. A wrong choice could lead to penury, dependence, and uselessness. Work defined a man for good or evil in ways that women's work rarely did. As the eighteenth century came to an end, the search for a profession increasingly hinged on individualistic goals. Some traditional notions of public service survived, nonetheless, even as the century turned.

In chapter 2 I shall examine the next step in an adult man's life—choosing a wife. A man had the freedom to pursue and court, but a woman had a right to reject an admirer. This ability to turn down a proposal could be devastating. As the more public actor, the man put himself on the line and suffered rejection as the community judged his progress. By the end of the eighteenth century, this emotional pain was exacerbated by a new emphasis on romantic love. When a man was rejected it was clear that *he* was insufficient, not just his estate.

Young suitors began to speak of beauty and riches as much if not more than piety and character as essential qualities for a wife. Along with this change came a new freedom for men to pursue and sometimes openly exploit women in their sexual adventures. This transformation may have resulted from a new cultural milieu, which allowed more open expression of such desires, or more simply it may have represented a response to the changing marriage market. As men moved west, the bachelors who remained behind could afford to be choosy in the face of abundance.

A man began his own interdependent family after selecting his career and wife. He became a husband, the subject of chapter 3. For men, this role entailed love and companionship, but also financial responsibility and a vulnerable reputation. Men openly expressed their strong feelings for their wives throughout the period studied. An unhappy marriage, however, could be a devastating blow to a man's name. Public quarrels and family disunity exposed a man to ridicule. If he were beaten or cuckolded by his wife, the damage to his character was irreparable. For some men this caused professional ruin as their respect in the community waned.

A good husband, as illustrated in chapter 4, provided for his family. He had to take on this responsibility by law. In divorce, separation, determinations of illegitimacy, and inheritance the concept of proper and adequate providing prevailed. A family required what was "needful." This varied according to status and community norms. A man's obligations increased along with the size of his family. For most men, however, providing depended on contributions from a wife and children. A woman's careful management and income were crucial. Children also gave their labor to the family enterprise. Nonetheless, a man alone felt the burden of failure. To fail as a provider brought on the contempt of the community.

In chapter 5 I shall examine the nearly inevitable next step for an adult man: fatherhood. A look at the fathering of young children reveals the hallmarks of "tender" male parenting. Like their wives, men concerned themselves with the development of their children. The special task for men, however, was the religious and secular education of their offspring. Feelings were often masked by diligence in this realm. Finally, when sickness or death threatened a child, a man bargained with God for his child's life. For some fathers, a son's or daughter's suffering seemed the outcome of their own sin. They blamed themselves and mourned the innocent victim of their thoughtlessness.

The loss of a spouse, explored in chapter 6, marked a new life stage, one that threatened the all-important domestic world. Men grieved, but at the same time tried frantically to mend the breach. Some circumstances of spouse loss were unique for men. For instance, only men lost a spouse to childbirth. The poignant combination of life and death was theirs alone to witness. Few men suffered such a calamity. Widows, in fact, greatly outnumbered widowers in colonial New England. The few unfortunate widowers quickly remedied their situation through remarriage. Distinct from their widowed counterparts, they risked little financially or legally in remarrying. Meanwhile, unlike women, men found life alone intolerable. Family obligations and loneliness weighed heavily and found remedy only in a new wife.

Men likewise dreaded "retirement," as chapter 7 illustrates. The delicate balance of family duty and obligation required that all members contribute to the family coffers. When a man lost this capacity he became useless, dependent, and even emasculated. This fear of dependency combined with the uniquely healthy demographic environment of early New England created a special urgency for men to remain productive. To this end, as a man aged he kept his family intact, sacrificing the independence of the younger generation. The young restlessly waited for their delayed inheritance. The increasingly negative image of the old as the eighteenth century progressed further fueled a man's sense of insecurity. Dependency was accepted only under duress and with great trepidation.

A man operated in the domestic world as a key member of an interdependent family. A man's sense of self came from performing adequately in his family and in his community. "Usefulness" in the domestic realm defined an adult man. Independence was merely a temporary stage that freed him from the subordination of childhood and allowed him to begin a family of his own. Autonomy was not the goal; in fact, it was quickly ameliorated by marriage. Likewise, dependency or "uselessness" was to be avoided at all costs. A kind of relational and fluctuating patriarchal power framed the domestic lives of these "goodmen."

To Be of Use

I

A "Business for Life"

Simeon Baldwin, in college during the Revolution, faced a
difficult decision about his future when his father ran out of
funds for his tuition due to "deprecian of our money." He faced
leaving the "pleasing path of litterature."

> Shall I entirely lay aside all hopes of furthering my-
> self ~~myself~~ in the pleasing path of litterature this
> is a disagreeable thought—but if I should what
> should I do next—~~shall~~ must I without further
> ceremony become a rusty farmer? this was ever
> my aversion.—shall I go to keeping school? this is
> no business for life nor would the same prospect
> arise from it, of finding business as there would
> be, had I finished the Collegiate part of my Edu-
> cation—shall I go into the Army and try that for
> a livelyhood? surely no not under the preasent en-
> couragements.—perhaps you will advise ~~the~~ me to
> try my luck on the Seas & become a privateers-
> man—I confess this best suits my inclination but
> ~~I should not Like [illegible] there~~ is the difficulty
> of procuring a birth in the way—well you may try
> merchandizing since the merchant is quick to make
> an estate—but this requires preasent money as well
> as my present employment; & if you propose the
> use of physic the same answer may be given—&
> in short I can almost say with Cato "Im wearly of
> Conjectures Death must end them" but I believe

you are weary of hearing my Complaints & perhaps you do not think them so great as I do but
no heavyer than they are when—joined to a mind
hardly able to support itself the consequences must
be bad.[1]

Farming was below his station. School keeping was a transi-
tional career for young college graduates waiting for a pulpit.
Baldwin rightly thought such a position was lowly paid and
difficult to find without finishing college. The army during
the Revolution was a dangerous option. The sea beckoned but
positions were hard to find. Merchandizing and medicine were
unlikely without financial resources. Finally, he did settle for
the position of schoolmaster to support himself and maintain
some social respectability. Ultimately, Baldwin completed his
education at Yale and found a "business for life" as a lawyer.[2]

At least Baldwin and other elite young men had options.
Jeremiah Dummer of Boston recorded in his memoranda book
in 1709 his thankfulness for the "wonderful mercys" of God.
"He made me a man & not of ye other Sex, whereby I have
greater opportunitys to glorify him & do Service in ye World."[3]
He had the blessings of his birth—a healthy body, Godly parents, and his manhood. Doing service in the world applied
to men and women, but men had more "opportunitys."[4] Not
all men had choices. Farming was the main occupation of most
men in what became the United States until the late nineteenth century. Nonetheless, for the men that could and did
take advantage of alternative careers, their range of options was
limited only by ability and economic privilege.

Women had no such freedom. The careers open to them,
away from farm and home, were few and poorly paid. A woman
was, however, crucial to a man's economic success.[5] In fact, men
like Elisha Niles, of Colchester, Connecticut, felt that farming

demanded marriage. He found himself in 1782, at the tender age of nineteen, in possession of a farm. "Not having any Stock or Tools to Enter on farming to any advantage added to my being single" made it impossible for him to exploit his inheritance. He eventually took up farming, but only after military service and school teaching provided the funds and the Lord provided a wife.[6]

Once a man found a career he could claim his freedom from the dependence of childhood and become an adult. Work, marriage, and inevitably children—the trappings of adult life—came in quick succession.[7] For example, Ebenezer Parkman received his master's degree on 1 July 1724 and married Mary Champney on 7 July 1724. He was ordained in Westborough, Massachusetts, in October. His daughter Mary was born the following fall. Likewise, Joseph Pease of Suffield, Connecticut, "Set up Trading" in 1755, bought a house by the following spring, and by summer he was married to Mindwell King. In 1757 his first child was born.[8]

Much remains to be done to uncover the link between manhood and work in the colonial period. For early New England, there is an extensive literature on the idea of the calling.[9] A man's calling was to a Christian life as well as to a profession that would glorify God. Ideally, a good man worked hard at his divinely ordained labor and gained status in the effort rather than the outcome.[10] By the end of the eighteenth century, this cultural imperative began to change. Hard work had become a virtue in its own right.[11] Puritans had evolved into Yankees.[12] The new self-made man of the nineteenth century defined himself by his success in the marketplace.[13] Outcome rather than process became the focus.

In addition, men in colonial New England saw their success, or lack thereof, in terms of their contribution to the domestic world. Men spoke of their work in terms of serviceableness or usefulness to their community as well as duty to their family. A young man in the seventeenth century focused on his potential for service to God, family, and community. As the eighteenth century came to a close, career goals became more secular, but service still had its place. Aspects of the traditional concept of Christian calling remained vital—the imperative to exercise God-given talent, the importance of providing service to one's community, the pursuit of wealth within the context of traditional notions of comfortable subsistence.[14]

Puritan ideology clearly stated that a "calling" came from God. Ministers entered their profession only if "called."[15] One also received a "call" from a particular church. William Bradford's *Of Plymouth Plantation* included a description of the selection process in choosing leaders for the newly formed Salem church in 1629. He distinguished between an "inward" and an "outward" calling. "They [the candidates] acknowledged there was a twofold calling, the one an inward calling when the Lord moved the heart of a man to take that calling upon him and fitted him with gifts for the same; the second was an outward calling which was from the people, when a company of believers are joined together in covenant to walk together in all the ways of God."[16] Other careers, however, also required a calling. When Stephen Winthrop wrote his father from the West Indies in 1645 he discussed his brother Samuel's calling to merchandizing. "We had not beene longe heare before my brother Samuell expressed to me some thoughts he had of staying heere, wth some mercht to be perfected in yt calling."[17]

In 1712, Boston merchant, Samuel Sewall admonished his wayward cousin to be "diligent in General and particular Calling."[18] Besides the inward and outward calling there was also the "particular" and "general."[19] A general calling referred to the search for God's grace and any sign of personal redemption; a particular calling referred to a chosen profession ideally dedicated to the glory of God. The Puritan divine, Increase Mather, in 1677, "resolved not to allow my selfe above 7 hours in 24 (if so much) for sleep, and to spend the rest of my Time in attending to the duties of my general and particular calling."[20]

Once a man found his calling, the dogged pursuit of work—diligence—was required.[21] In the seventeenth century, industry was a legal as well as a religious necessity.[22] Richard Norcross found this out when he faced the selectmen of Watertown, Massachusetts, in 1684 for "His time Being Cumplained of for negligence in his Calling." His contrition and a neighbor's willingness to take him in saved the slacker further punishment. His neighborly advocate promised to "take ceare that He did atend family ordour: and dilygently follow His calling or if He did not then He would acquaint The select men with it."[23] Thomas Oddingsall was "presented for idleness" in Salem Court in 1641. He promised to improve and keep "a weekly account of his employment."[24] An idle church member could receive admonishment from his congregation. John Martin, in 1671, faced the charge that "in the space of a year's time he had been observed not to do so much as might amount to a penny a day taking one day with another throughout the year." Although he tried to excuse himself through references to his "inability," the church had dealt with similar complaints against him before and felt less than generous. The congregation "unanamously voted that he was guilty of willful idleness and neglect of a particular calling or any employments suitable to his ability and that he should be publicly admonished therefore."[25]

What has not been examined in the literature thus far is the relation between the idea of the calling and the concept of "serviceableness."[26] In choosing a career, men often referred to their need to be serviceable to God, their families, and their generation. Service defined a man's work and his place in the broader community. Career options were evaluated according to relative serviceableness. This idea continued to have resonance for men in the late colonial period even as service to oneself found a place in the job search. Conversely, becoming "unfit" for service threatened a man's place in the world.

An adult man by definition was serviceable. Boston minister Cotton Mather struggled to help a "Candidate of the Ministry" in 1713/14 who found himself still without a church at the age of thirty. "I am in distress for him; full of Sollicitudes, that he may find acceptance with the People of God, and be serviceable. I do for him all that I can; but I would particularly endeavour to reconcile his Mind unto Serviceableness at a further Distance, and procure him an Offer of Opportunities."[27] To be without serviceableness meant to be without a sense of identity. A man of thirty without a settled career was an object of pity. Even if settled, a man's serviceableness could still be threatened. Cotton Mather himself feared that gossip concerning a forward, overly young, female admirer could hurt his serviceableness in 1703. In fact, he claimed to have turned her down over such concerns.[28] With financial difficulties and a laity reluctant to help, Increase Mather similarly claimed in 1672 stressful circumstances threatened to hinder his serviceableness. "I can not express how much my spirit was broken with those miseries, and it is a wonder that I was not thereby nearly overthrown and made unfitt for service."[29]

Early on, many men spoke of serviceableness in the context of service to God and the call to the ministry. In 1709, Jeremiah Dummer considered becoming a colonial agent rather than a minister. He recorded his struggle to make a "choice as may make me most Serviceable to his glory wch. ought to be the ultimate end of all my actions."[30] Michael Wigglesworth, when considering a call to preach in Malden, Massachusetts, recorded in his diary in 1655, "God requireth and I desire to do service as my strength will bear."[31] Josiah Cotton, schoolmaster of Plymouth, Massachusetts, recorded that in the 1690s the friends of his brother Roland "had great expectation of his serviceableness" to the church.[32] This is not to suggest that men in the seventeenth century thought only of God and not of their own advantage. Embarking on a career in medicine in 1672, the young Joseph Pynchon wrote to his father, a man of great financial power in western Massachusetts, for help and fatherly advice. His father responded generously with both and included an injunction "to be really serviceable to your generation and advantageous to yourself."[33]

As the eighteenth century progressed, service did, however, become more a social than a divine mandate. As William Samuel Johnson of Stratford, Connecticut, struggled to convince his father that he preferred the law to the ministry in 1747, he summarized, "I must Consider not in what profession the greatest Good *May* be Done to Mankind, but in what Station I with these Dispositions, these Abilities and Acquirements which I possess are most likely to Serve them."[34] Still, in 1778, there were men like Dwight Foster who evoked older notions of service. He debated the merits of the ministry over the advantages of the legal profession. Finally, he decided on the bar. "I thought I might Serve my God with more Advantage to Myself and my Generation and then to more Acceptance."[35] Foster, however, hid his individual desires behind the shield of Godly service. Continued residence in Providence, Rhode Island, would allow him to serve his generation more effectively, he argued, than returning home to Brookfield, Massachusetts, to begin his law practice: "I have a Fondness for a rural Life but can chearfully forego its Pleasures if I can

Serve my Generation to better Advantage in a Seaport—In this Town there is a Door open for some Gentlemen of Knowlege & Ability—Within a few Years the Number of Attornies has greatly diminished—Colo. Hitchcock & Mr. Cole are dead—Mr. George Brown has removed to another Part of the State—Arnold has become a strict Quaker and entirely left the Practice of the Law and Dawner does Nothing in that Way—No one has come in to Supply the Places of these Gentlemen."[36] He could better serve himself in Providence because his competition had conveniently died, moved, or converted.

Usefulness in the seventeenth century was synonymous with serviceableness. Cotton Mather remarked, while trying to arrange a ministerial settlement for his relative William Williams in 1711, "The best Service I can do for him, is to procure him Opportunities of being serviceable." He thought to place him among the Natick tribe "where the Interests of Christianity are extremely languishing." This would provide him with "some Opportunities to be useful."[37] As the eighteenth century progressed, usefulness became a more practical description of keeping busy.[38] Industriousness rather than sloth defined a useful man. To be useful rather than useless was the goal.

John Adams, of Braintree, Massachusetts, noted, "~~The great secret therefore, the main~~ The primary Endeavour therefore, should be to distinguish between Useful and unuseful, to pursue the former with unwearied Industry, and to neglect with much Contempt all the Rest." A man should not just work hard, but work hard for significant goals. "Suppose you had chosen the study of Nature, for the Business of your Life, should you not inquire in the first Place, what is the End of that study? Is it to improve the Manufactures, the Husbandry, or the Commerce of Mankind, or is it to adorn a Library with Butterflies of various sizes, Colours and shapes?"

He applied this principle to history in the following way:

Or suppose you had chosen the study of History, should you not inquire is the End of this study the naked Knowledge of great Names and [. . . Actions?] or is it a personal Improvement in Virtue and Capacity, by imitating the Virtues and avoiding the Vices of great men, and by judging of the Effects of Causes now at Work, by those Causes which have appeared heretofore? Should a Student in History inquire chiefly of the Dress, Entertainments and Diversions, instead of the Arts, Characters, Virtues and Opinions of ancient Nations, and the Effects of these on their public and private Happiness would not you laugh?

Usefulness meant meaningful work. As Adams composed this draft, his editing reflected this clearly when in one sentence he rejected "importance" and "usefulness" for the word "utility." Likewise, while bemoaning the time he wasted on such musings, he lamented, "Why am I so silly to trifle away my Time in such useless unprofitable scribbling—waste Paper, Pen, Ink, Time, Wood, Candles, in this idle Amuzement."[39] To be useless meant to be unprofitable—a man's time and energy resulting in no obvious result. Unlike Cotton Mather, John Adams did not naturally equate usefulness with service to God. Usefulness was industry with a distinguishable outcome.

Usefulness, like service in both centuries, implied social obligation.[40] Cotton Mather had a "mighty Desire" that his children be "useful in the World."[41] In 1747, William Samuel Johnson proclaimed his desire to be "Useful to Mankind" in his chosen profession.[42] Isaac Sherman, son of the Connecticut patriot Roger Sherman, joined the army during the Revolution for employment and glory, but also to be a "useful Member of Society."[43] As with the concept of service, some men strove also to be useful to themselves. In 1779, Sheriff Ezekiel Williams, of Wethersfield, Connecticut, similarly hoped his son John would be useful "in the World," but he went on to say he should also be useful to himself.[44] Or as Williams put it in another advice-filled letter to his son, a profession that was "Useful to you in Life" would be most advantageous.[45]

Over the course of the colonial period, the Puritan notion of the calling evolved from a purely religious construct to one increasingly linked to industry and self-fulfillment. A man worked to provide service and be useful to his God, community, or family in the seventeenth century. By the end of the eighteenth century, the domestic world remained central as divine imperatives receded.

What were the financial goals of men as they attempted to be serviceable? Naturally, aspirations varied with social condition, but men from all walks of life throughout the colonial period spoke of broad notions of an adequate income. William Samuel Johnson described to his father in 1743 his need for "some kind of Business or Profession for a subsistence."[46] In an attempt in 1776 to solicit funds for the grandson of "ye late pious and venerable Dr. [Joseph] Sewall," to attend college, minister and historian Jeremy Belknap urged a potential patron to open his purse or "it is feared the discouragmt of Poverty may prevent his progress in his Studies & oblige him to turn to some other employment for his Subsistence."[47] A subsistence provided little more than a man's basic necessities.[48]

A maintenance, on the other hand, furnished the means of subsistence.[49] Isaac Sherman found himself in Revolutionary Massachusetts unable "to obtain any employment sufficient to procure a maintenance." His solution was to join the army.[50] Fitz-John Winthrop had used the word "maintenance" in a similar way in a letter to his father, John Winthrop, Jr., in 1661.

He was loath to return to New England and find himself short on cash and, therefore, social standing. He preferred to have a "small maintenance" in England "then a certaine income" in New England "or in any other place, exept such as would afford me a handsom and competent maintenance."[51]

Beyond subsistence and maintenance was competency. A man with a competency was comfortable if not wealthy.[52] John Davenport, founder of New Haven colony, found himself as a young man in 1624 bereft of friends willing to foot the bill for the completion of his university education. He hoped to return to his studies after he had attained a "certayne competencye of meanes," a goal he accomplished the following spring.[53] Joel Stone, reviewing his childhood in Litchfield, Connecticut, in the mid-eighteenth century, reminisced about his father's "indefatigable labor and industry" culminating in a "competency in Land."[54] Mather Byles, newly married and comfortably settled in his New London pulpit, claimed in 1763 to be "in full Possession" of the "three grand Essentials of humane Happiness, 'Health, Peace & Competence.'"[55] Men needed their work to provide at least a subsistence, perhaps a maintenance, and ideally a competency, or as John Hull of Boston put it in his diary, his skill as a goldsmith allowed him "to get my living."[56]

Men also wanted job security. The idea of getting a settlement or settling into a profession highlighted this need. Ministers in New England spoke of their settlement in a church.[57] Ebenezer Parkman of Westborough, Massachusetts, noted in his diary in 1744, "It is this Day 20 Years Since I gave my Answer to Settle in this Town."[58] In describing his father's life in the 1650s, Josiah Cotton noted that he was "a Preacher At Weathersfield, and had some Calls to other places Viz. Haddam and Kellingsworth in the Colony of Connecticut—But the divine Providence Did not permit his Settlement tho, it provided him A wife in those Parts." He "Remained Unsettled

Several years" until he finally answered a call to Plymouth.[59] Men in more secular employments also yearned for this kind of certainty. In a 1645 letter to his father, Stephen Winthrop discussed his brother Samuel's desire to apprentice himself to a merchant to learn the trade. The young Samuel "resoluing not to trust to his study for his future maintainance, did thinke it his best cource to setle to some setled callinge."[60] Looking for a permanent and reliable career, the young Samuel took the present opportunity over an uncertain if educated future.

To settle could also suggest something about financial compensation. Josiah Cotton took a position as schoolmaster in Marblehead, Massachusetts, in 1698, "Where I settled at fifteen pounds pr. Annum Salary from the Town" plus extras from the students.[61] Peter Pratt of Colchester, Connecticut, received an early inheritance from his father in 1761 while still a college student. "My Part of it which if I mack a good improvement of will Be Enough to Settel me well in the world."[62] After struggling, financially, to graduate from Harvard in 1695, Joseph Green found himself with few opportunities after graduation. Instead of going to sea like his brothers before him he took up school teaching because he was "desirous of setling because of want."[63]

The worst thing to befall a man seeking his way in the world was to remain unsettled. Samuel Sewall struggled in 1695/96 to place his young son, Samuel in a likely apprenticeship. Arrangements fell through repeatedly and worried Sewall as he struggled to find a solution. "I am very sorrowfull by reason of the unsettledness of my Samuel."[64] A settlement assured a productive and secure manhood.

Men needed a living and a settled career, but some had visions of more. Silas Deane of Wethersfield, Connecticut, as a West Indian trader himself, advised his stepson, embarking on a merchant's career in 1772, that business information and useful contacts led to financial success. Keeping a close eye on currency values and prices and making connections with "Men of Judgment" could "lay the Foundation of Your ease & affluence in Life."[65] In 1778, Dwight Foster wished his friend Joseph Clarke "an Abundance both of Pleasure and Profit in the pursuit of" in his new career in "Business and Commerce."[66] Making more than a competency pushed some men to pursue their careers with vigor. As William Smith, a lawyer in New York, advised his friend about the practice of the law in Revolutionary Connecticut, "The practice in this province will keep you from Poverty, *that great evil*, and enable you to spend the latter days of life * Bishop-like in an easy abundance." He added as explanation, "* Don't be angry—some lawyers have not their Religion."[67]

Although material wealth motivated some men to work hard, the pursuit of wealth in one's calling in the late eighteenth century was still suspect. John Adams felt that the pursuit of fortune alone without fame was "low." A lawyer ideally pursued his calling with an eye to knowledge not lucre. John Adams was urged by his mentor Mr. Gridley in 1758, to "pursue the Study of the Law rather than the Gain of it. Pursue the Gain of it enough to keep out of the Briars, but give your main Attention to the study of it."[68] Samuel Sewall made a similar observation in a letter to John Woodbridge, a disheartened schoolmaster in 1720. He had suffered a reduction in his salary but carefully "avoided taking any thing of the Children lest" this "should discourage the Parents from sending them to School." Sewall sent him £5 and commended him with the injunction to "be more concernd for Work, than for Wages!"[69]

Ministers in particular were thought to work for loftier motives in both the seventeenth and eighteenth centuries. Increase Mather struggled with the deacons of his church for an adequate salary in the early 1670s. His pleas went unheard and caused him great "grief." He later mused about this common convention of reluctant and tightfisted laity: "Little do people think how much they wrong themselves, when they have ministers amongst them whose Hearts are sett upon nothing but their studyes and spiritual Employments, that nevertheless shall not be sutably provided for as to their outward subsistence, and that food and raiment which whilest they are on the earth they need as well as other men."[70] Samuel Chandler in 1751 confronted similar reluctance in his negotiations with a Gloucester, Massachusetts, congregation. He received a financial offer that included a house, barn, and garden plus £80 a year. There was obviously disagreement in the church about the choice of Chandler, but the primary concern was money not professional ability. Some church members worried that when their other minister (there were two in this congregation) died Chandler would ask for either a replacement for this colleague or a larger salary. Chandler chided the church committee saying their questions "bore very hard on me & was a very Great reflection and Seemed to look with this face as though I were of a mercinary Spirit." He made clear that the ministry provided few financial rewards. "The difficulties I had formerly met with in the work of the ministry and the Prospect of a Better Support in Some other calling wd have made me — decline. but I delighted in the work."[71] A minister pursued his calling, properly out of an altruistic not "mercinary" spirit.

Men looked for work that would provide at the least an adequate subsistence. Competency, however, was the goal. To pursue more was risky. The overt quest for wealth remained suspect throughout the colonial period. Each man instead should settle for a comfortable subsistence.

Perhaps most important, young men made their career decisions within the context of family imperatives. Parental advice, networks, and financial backing were essential. The family offered aid that benefited not only an individual child, but the family in general. Who would go to college, who would farm, and who would be apprenticed reflected, in part, family priorities. The desires of a son converged with what the family could facilitate.[72] Parents throughout the colonial period wanted their sons to find careers that pleased them *and* fitted the family's notion of an appropriate profession.

Collective distribution of resources sometimes meant individual sacrifices for the benefit of the family. Arrangements could vary from child to child, but parents provided for each with the welfare of the entire family in mind. In a thankful letter written in 1780 to his son's tutor, Ezekiel Williams spelled out his hopes for his boy. He had a "high Sense" of the "importance of well Educating Children." Unfortunately, his financial circumstances had become precarious due to the declining value of money during the Revolution. He nonetheless continued his "Endeavours to Educate my Eldest Son" to be a "Learned & virtuous Man." He hoped that with the help of his college-educated son he would "be enabled to do Justice to my other Children."[73] For Eliphalet Pearson, later a prominent Massachusetts educator, this hope was made explicit when he made a "Promis to his father" in exchange for his tuition.

> I, Eliphalet Pearson, being in my minority incapable of making a Lawful Obligation and having a great Desire of a liberal Education and being sensible that my Father is not able to be at the whole Cost of the same without wronging himself & the other Branches of the Family, Do therefore in the Fear of God and upon the Principles of Honesty and Uprightness Solemnly Promise to my Father, that I will do my best Endeavours to pay him all

the money for all the Charge he shall be all for my
Education from my Admission the twenty second
Day of July 1769 to my Dismission from the College, (except for my Clothing and Chamber Furni-
ture) the one half of said Money to be paid in two
Years after I leave College & the other half in four;
in Confirmation of What is above written I here
unto set my Hand this thirtieth Day of October
1769.[74]

This arrangement insured that the family would not suffer because of Eliphalet's "Desire of a liberal Education."

Joseph Green became the scholar in his family because "God
blessed me with a good memory" and his older brother, Per-
cival, destined for the ministry, had succumbed to "consumption." The family wanted to train at least one son for the work
of God. John Green, Joseph's father, had a large family and a
simple trade. The Greens had fourteen children, ten of them
boys. All, but the two scholars, were apprenticed as tailors,
blacksmiths, carpenters, and sailors. While financing a second
college education, John ran short of funds "& began to think yt
he shd not be able to make" Joseph "a sch:." The elder Green
died shortly after his son's admission to Harvard. Joseph recalled that the family was "about to take me away and to put
me to something else."[75] Instead, charitable friends and tutors
agreed to pay the tuition of the needy student. He graduated
from Harvard in 1695. Joseph fulfilled his parents' expectations
and became a minister. He began his career in the infamous
village of Salem, Massachusetts, in 1697.[76]

When young men acknowledged family assistance they referred to their parents, not just their fathers. In 1763, Ebenezer
Baldwin, as he came to the conclusion of his career at Yale,
wrote, "I was born of ~~Persons~~ Parents capable of bestowing on

me a liberal Education; & again confirming yt it was with Difficulty they go thro' with ye Costs, I must Esteem it a great Favour yt God Inclined their Hearts to it."⁷⁷ Benjamin Trumbull composed several drafts of an essay on the reverse pages of his diary of 1765. As a student at Yale he struggled to express his gratitude to his parents for their "Tender Care and inspection over me from my Infancy even untill now." He drafted, "I who have allways enjoy,d your wise and Seasonable Counsels, and from whom you have withholden nothing in your power to bestow that might Serve for my Advantage and whose welbeing you have always regarded even as your own."⁷⁸

Sarah Lloyd of Stamford, Connecticut, began a letter to her son in 1749 with, "I want to set Down and have a Long Dish of Chat with you." She then confessed that she "accidentally saw a letter you wrote your father some time ago requesting his advice what business you best follow." She claimed not to know her husband's response to the inquiry. "But as you are intitled to my best advice I shall give it though unasked."⁷⁹ She proceeded to reassure him that his path would become clear; he simply needed to continue to work hard and finish college. Whether or not consultation in truth occurred between the concerned parents of Henry Lloyd, Sarah clearly had an opinion and felt no compunction about advising her son accordingly.

A mother's input could carry more weight than a father's. Increase Mather's mother, Katherine Holt Mather, prejudiced her son to pursue the ministry. Mather felt unsure of his path and overwhelmed by comparisons to his father and brothers. "I was the youngest and least amongst all my brethren." His mother prayed often for "2 things on my behalfe, first that God would give me grace, secondly that Hee would give me learning." Katherine pushed her son toward the ministry even on her deathbed in 1654/55: "Moreover, when my mother lay on her death bed, she d[id with] much affection exhort me to resolve (if the [Lord] should see meet to continue my life) to serve [God] in the work of the ministry; and desired me to [consider the] Scripture Dan. 12. 3. *They that turn many to Righte[ousness] shall shine as the stars forever and ever.* And these were the last words which my dear and precious mother spake to me, the remembrance whereof has had no small impression upon my spirit. I was then allmost 16 years old."[80] A mother could also act as a powerful advocate in the family. When the son of Captain Edward Goddard of Framingham, Massachusetts, did not get the support he wanted from his father in 1727 to follow a scholarly career he "gave another hint to his mother" emphasizing his desire to go into the ministry. His mother apparently convinced his reluctant father, because Goddard soon found himself at Harvard College.[81]

An older brother likewise could suggest options and facilitate choices. Ebenezer Parkman waited for a permanent settlement as a minister boarding in his brother Elias's home for almost two years in the 1720s. "I went [to Elias's house] as to my home when I was at Boston and kept my Library, etc. there, and had a Chamber Study and entertainment occasionally there."[82] Without his brother's help it would have been difficult to manage on occasional preaching for his income. James Cogswell wrote to their father about his brother Mason's career options in 1781. James was a surgeon and settled in Stamford, Connecticut, after his years as an army doctor. Mason, newly graduated from Yale, wanted to pursue a medical career.

> His education since he came here, or his instruction, has been rather miscellaneous. Sometimes he has studied physic, sometimes practiced Surgery. He has officiated as Clerk for the Whale boats in collecting their accounts, has been some in a Shop, & has assisted the Majr. in writing. On the whole,

I have come to this determination, with regard to him, which I shall do my endeavour to carry into execution, if you approve of it, that is, to prepare him for Trade, and put him into it as soon as I can. I do not think, he will make a distinguished figure as a Physician, tho I believe he would as a Surgeon, if his forefinger had not been injured. He is very carefull in keeping accounts, and appears to have a genius for & liking to the business.[83]

After trying his hand at various professions, Mason seemed destined, because of physical disability, for the merchant's life. In fact, his finger improved enough that he became a quite successful surgeon, pioneering work in cataract removal. Brothers took on a parental role if age and experience made their counsel or financial help appropriate.

A brother could act as a buffer between parent and child. Eliphalet Williams, pastor in East Hartford, Connecticut, tried to arrange an appointment as a schoolmaster for his brother Thomas in 1765. Like many college graduates, Thomas was forced to find a living while waiting for his real career to start.[84] School teaching was hard, poorly paid work. The position his brother procured for him was particularly so. Thomas angrily listed the many friends he had in the same line of work with much larger stipends. In addition he implored, "Is it reasonable to trudge & sweat a whole day at a, b, cs for 18 or 20 pence, when a Farmer won't at ye Scythe (a much better Employment) under half a Crown at least." In a postscript he acknowledged that his "Father has a mind I should keep School." Eliphalet's response to Thomas, who was left to break the news of his refusal to his father, was to tell him he wanted more money than a "shitten Farmer."[85] Thomas probably rephrased his brother's opinion before passing it on to his father.

Other kin also became involved in a young man's job search. Eliphalet Pearson struggled to find a suitable place for his nephew Johnny in 1782. A lifelong educator, Pearson was the first principal of Phillips Academy and founder of Andover Theological Seminary. His business was forming young adults into men. He confided to his sister that Johnny, a frail lad, might make a poor showing as a farmer because of the strenuous nature of the work.

> I have made further inquiry for Johnny, but meet with no encouragement as yet; & still think, that almost any trade, he is capable of would be preferable to a farmer's business, several parts of which, such as mowing, reaping &c, he would ~~not~~ be as unable to perform, as to go up to the mast head. However, if a suitable place can be found with a farmer, I should not be against making trial of him in that way. Experience would determine best.— I am told. that a painter's business is very profitable; has John no taste for *painting*. Mr. Holyoke is going to put his oldest son to a painter in Boston.— With due submission to Doct. Holyoke I should think a trade the most eligible, & next to that the sea, especially if peace should soon commence, of which desirable event we seem to hve some prospect.[86]

Whereas Johnny's mother wanted him to take up farming, his uncle felt painting might prove more lucrative and less physically demanding. Least desirable would be a life at sea, but tolerable if peace provided his nephew some safety.

The eighteenth century saw more open conflict between young men and their families over career objectives. Josiah Cotton had "very disagreeable" thoughts in 1737 about his son,

Theophilas's career choice. He chose the "roving unsettled life" of the sea. His father feared for his safety and worried about the company he would keep. "Sailors, one would think, should be the best of men, there being, as we say, but a Step between them & death; & yet experience shows, that they are commonly the worst."[87] His disapproval and concern had little effect.

Ezekiel Williams in the 1780s thought a clerking career might suit his son John. His son, however, wanted to study the law. John requested permission to live and study with Judge Charles Chauncey. "Am very willing you should Study Law or any other Studies that may be Useful to you in Life, and if Mr. Chauncey will bord you as Cheap as another shall like well your Living there but as I suppose you do not mean to pracice Law for a livelihood, trust he will not demand a fee for his Instruction, but if he will advise you what Books may be most profitable for a Civilian, to Read, shall be much obliged to him." He saw nothing wrong with John studying a new field among "other Studies" as long as the cost was low. Nonetheless, Ezekiel encouraged his son to "Learn to write well" and with luck he might "be able to get a Birth for you for awhile as a Clerk."[88] A few months later, Ezekiel advised his son again about his career choice. "If you Chuse to Practice the Law I shall not hinder you as I believe it not a dishonest Calling, & as there are many worthy Men of that Profession, tho' I should not have wish'd that for you, if your Genius & Inclination had Led you otherwise."[89] John became a lawyer, and his father settled for his son's concession to move home to Wethersfield, Connecticut, to practice his new profession.

Nathan Niles wanted his son to follow in his footsteps and become a Congregational minister. Nathan had a pulpit in Colchester, Connecticut. He had fourteen children by his first wife, Mary Sexton, who died of consumption in 1773. He quickly remarried Dorcas Bechwith of Lyme. His son Elisha had some difficulty with his stepmother and, his "mind being more & more wean'd from Heavenly Entertainments," he yearned to join the army. He convinced his reluctant father to send him in his place when drafted for a month's military service in 1779. What followed was a military career that lasted the rest of the war. On returning home he went to farming and teaching school. Not only did Elisha not enter the ministry, he actually became, from his father's perspective, a godless Baptist rather than a proper Congregationalist later in life.[90]

Isaac Sherman also joined the military, but without even a reluctant father's permission. Sherman wrote his father after the fact, claiming his desire for income, glory, and usefulness led him to join the cause against England. He apologized for not consulting his parents: "The distance being so great, the necessity of being expeditious in recruiting, rendered it almost impossible to have consulted with you on the affair—I am so far from thinking the advice of the experienced disadvantageous to Youth, that I apprehend it to be the incumbent duty of Young Men to consult and advise with those who are acquainted with the various manoevres of Mankind; and especially with a kind indulgent Parent, who always consults the good of his Children."[91] The sincerity of his contrition is unclear.

Parents were not powerless, but their authority over career decisions was increasingly challenged as colonial society evolved. A parent's perspective was no longer the only perspective, even by the middle of the eighteenth century. In part this challenge to parental authority reflected the decreasing opportunities that family resources could provide. For the average man, parental assistance came through a gift or inheritance of land. Land provided the foundations of male adulthood. As families struggled to divide their meager resources in the long settled areas in New England, their sons were forced to look elsewhere for opportunity.[92]

Ebenezer Parkman, minister and farmer, mourned his inability to provide for his son in 1748. Unable to give his namesake a farm, he struggled to find him an apprenticeship. After many unsuccessful placements he began to despair. The only alternative—carving a farm out on the frontier—he felt was more than his son could handle: "My Thoughts have been of late greatly discompos'd, and I don't know that I have ever felt so inwardly sunk and disheartened and unable to sustain my Infirmity. What has brought me into this has been my inability to do for my Children, when they come to be of age. My son Ebenezer in particular. All my schemes and Designs respecting him fall to the Ground. He has chose to be a Farmer, but I have not a Farm to give him that is handy or desirable. . . . Nor has he strength of Body to drudge and bring to a place."[93] A viable farm, large enough to support a family, became a costly gift beyond the resources of many.

Family members joined together to promote their collective well-being. For a young man coming of age, this meant turning to parents and other kin to help find and facilitate a career path. This aid came in the form of land, advice, business contacts, money, and a college education. As New England matured, young men found new and perhaps dubious freedom to pursue their own inclinations. Although weakened, family concerns were still at the center of decision-making.

Work was the essence of adult manhood in early New England. The day a son inherited a farm, a former apprentice opened his own shop, a young lawyer argued his first case marked a beginning. On the 28 August 1725, the day he was ordained, Ebenezer Parkman wrote in his diary, "This was truely the Greatest Day I ever Yet Saw—The Day of my Solemn Separation to the Work of the Gospel Ministry and my Ordination to the Pastorate in Westborough."[94] For ministers this date often became an anniversary and a special time for reflection. In 1749, Joseph Emerson from his pulpit in Groton, Massachusetts, remarked, "This Day being the Annoversary of my Ordination I devoted to Fasting and For Prayer."[95] This pivotal day deserved notice and careful recording. Armed with shifting notions of service, competency, and family obligation men in colonial New England weighed their options and made their choices. A man's economic independence from his childhood family began with the choice of a "business for life."

The pursuit of a career involved more than piety or financial gain. Men pursued their work and chose the form it would take within the family context. Even when a man knew that farming was his only option, domestic concerns were central. A working man proved his worth through service to his God, his community, and most centrally his family. The relative weight of these imperatives changed over time. Increasingly New England looked at a man's purse as well as his soul for evidence of his usefulness.

2

"It Will Not Injure You": Men and Courtship

During the Revolution, General Nathanael Greene wrote to his friend Colonel Webb about the progress of the war, the maddening politicking of Congress, and Webb's fear of marriage. Greene cajoled, "Be not afraid of Matrimony, trust me it will not injure you." He assured his friend that his liberty would not be compromised, and in fact marriage could assure it. "They who engage in this connection, live for themselves, those who avoid it live for others." He concluded, "Strange as it may appear, I firmly believe, that Matrimony generally speaking, lessens our expenses as well as enlarges our felicity." Not only would he be grateful for his wife as a financial resource, but "I am sure a mind possessed of your Sensibility must enjoy the most refined pleasures from so tender a connection."[1] Greene talked of a man's hopes for a good economic match, but also his yearnings for companionship and "felicity." What did men want in a wife in colonial New England? Why was Webb afraid?

In that time and place, most men chose to marry. As soon as economically able, they surveyed the possibilities. They pursued feminine perfection but eventually settled for a flesh-and-blood woman. As the pursuer they began and continued the courtship. This role exposed them, unlike women, to a higher level of public humiliation if their efforts proved unsuccessful.[2] The stage on which the courtship drama was performed changed as the eighteenth century progressed. As the population grew and land became more and more scarce, new opportunities for courting men emerged; particularly for those with the wealth or status to take advantage of such developments. Thanks to these changes men found themselves valuable commodities in a lopsided marriage market. They increasingly made decisions about courtship in an atmosphere of increased sexual freedom with less parental control.

The late colonial period also brought a new emphasis on romantic love which, unlike these other developments, presented new risks as well as new opportunities. As pursuer, a man faced the danger of rejection. Public shaming could be devastating in a small community where reputation determined economic as well as personal success. In small communities with informal credit networks a good name was priceless.³ New sentimental norms of the late eighteenth century made the humiliation of rejection even more threatening. If turned down, a man now had to face the possibility that he—not his estate— had been inadequate. In this emotionally charged atmosphere a man's concern over being rebuffed took on a new urgency.

Without marriage, sexual expression in colonial New England was, by definition, illicit. Legal as well as religious authority prohibited sodomy, onanism, and fornication—terms loosely equivalent to modern notions of homosexuality, masturbation, and premarital sex.⁴ Only heterosexuality took on the mantel of acceptability, and only after marriage. Unlike other forms of sexual expression, heterosexual intercourse had the sobering potential of unintended parenthood. Pregnancy, because of intense cultural pressure, usually led to marriage.⁵ If a man, therefore, wanted to enjoy social approval as well as sex, marriage provided the only avenue. A man was supposed to chose between marriage and celibacy.⁶ In 1685, Cotton Mather, a newly ordained minister, characterized the single life as "embrac[ing] *Celibacy*."⁷ Ebenezer Baldwin, comfortably situated in his pulpit in Danbury, Connecticut, almost one hundred years later, thought of bachelorhood as "a life of Celebacy."⁸ This ideal was hard to maintain, however, in both centuries. Simeon Baldwin, brother of Ebenezer, in 1782 carefully considered the tongue-in-cheek advice of a male friend. "Perhaps you are fond of Celebacy—But I rather think it is only in Theory—Some fair Damsel or Nymph or Dulcinea will undermine your Theoretical foundation and the Fabric will tumble into Matrimony."⁹ For Daniel Allen, writing to his sister in New England from his trading business in Jamaica at the beginning of the eighteenth century, just the idea of "dying in an unmarryd State . . . knocks me down. . . . I am forc'd to be at the expence of 7 1/2 d. for a glass of wine to set me to rights."¹⁰

John Dane, an immigrant to the colonies in the 1630s, carefully navigated these treacherous seas of sexual enticements as a young man in England. He was propositioned by a maid who "put huself in sutch a poster, as that I made as If I had sum speshall ocashon abrod and went out: for I fared, If I had not, I should haue cumitted foley with hur." His next encounter was with his hostess at an inn where he lodged. He came home late to find her "in a chare by the fyer, in hur naked shift, houlding hur brests open." She wanted him to "drink a pot" with her. He claimed he "was so slepey that I could not stay with her now, but I would drink a cup with hur in the morning; and so I hastend awaie to my Chamber." Finally, the Lord saved him from a woman who stole into his bed. He retired and "puld of[f] all my Clothes and went in, and thare was this fine lase in the bead." He quickly dressed and went downstairs to berate the landlady. She assured him "thars nobody would hurt you." He replied "if I hired a Rome, I would haue it to myself; and shoud my self mutch angrey." When he woke in the morning he realized he left some "lettell bundell of things" in his first bedchamber. He apologized for disturbing his former bedmate but she replied, "you are welcum to me." Again he did not succumb. Dane remarked in his journal, "For all theas, and manie other of the lyke, I thank god I neuer yet knew any but thos two wifes that god gaue me."[11]

James Cogswell, a young physician in Preston, Connecticut, described his exquisite torture in a letter to his sister in 1772: "I find it absolutely necessary for me to find out some agreeable Fair to fix my heart upon: for since I have begun to think of it; there is an inexpressible softness insensibility grown upon me, & I perceive in myself such a proneness & aptitude to love, that I am allmost affraid of every pretty face I meet."[12] This lovesick twenty-five-year-old suffered for four more years until he finally married. Similarly afflicted, Samuel Crosby in 1775 wrote from Harvard College to a friend: "It appears to me that I never shall be perfectly Happy—till I can with propriety call some beautiful & accomplished Female, by that endearing Term, *Mine*—But that such a Time will ever be with respect to me—I know not. It seems to look far distant.—But this I am certain of—That I am happiest either when I am permitted to enjoy the Company of some lovely Fair, or when I am with Vigour pursuing my agreeable Studies."[13] Marriage was the proper outlet for sexuality. Other avenues of course were well traveled, but only marriage provided social respectability.

The eighteenth century may have provided more opportunities for men to go, "Girling of it."[14] Penalties for illicit sex, particularly for men, abated as the eighteenth century progressed. At the same time, opportunities for socializing multiplied.[15] The result was heightened sexual temptation coupled with less daunting consequences. The increased production of religious tracts concerning the sin of masturbation and the rise in premarital pregnancy as the colonial period came to a close suggest some of the consequences of these changes.[16] On occasion, even the character of the rake himself emerged from the pages of fiction to roam the courting landscape of eighteenth-century New England.[17]

Some men became highly skilled at wooing women. Ebenezer Baldwin described the "triflings" of such a man in a 1767 letter to Betsey Partridge, the sister of his love interest, Sophia.

He that can trifle most politely, is the most accomplished Character—the most refined Gent[lema]n the Best Company according to the modish Taste & Usage of almost all Companies—he is applauded by all—But what is this polite Trifling—why Nonsence gilded with a little Humour & Show of good Nature—to make the compleat Character accompanied [by] an over Officiousness in y[ou]r Service (we observe shows itself only in Trifles)—with a Dose of . . . Poisoning flattery whenever it can be thrown in . . . & how often do we hear the Conversation Carried on by Innuendo's double Entenres wh[ich] stript of their Disguise are right down Obscenity—how many think they cant talk with a lady but in such Language as this—tho' to the honor of y[ou]r Sex I dont think the better Part are pleased with it . . . I Cant but severly reflect on the Inconsistance of our Sex, that they entertain them whom t[he]y design for their nearest Companions, the Partners in Every Scene of Life, w[it]h Nothing but Nonsense, Trifles & what is worse Blow t[he]m up with a vain Conceit of their Angelic Excellencies.

He concluded that the better sort of woman (no doubt the recipient of this letter for one) would never be taken in by such a rake. It was clear that Baldwin both envied and was disgusted by such men. "I know tis Easier to find fault t[he]n to Mend it—the Proverb, 'heal thyself before you presume to mend the [world]' may Justly perhaps (you may think) be retorted upon me—I wont deny the Charge—But only assert that the folly appears Glaring in Private Meditation." Shifting the blame from himself and his sex, Baldwin instead condemned women who encouraged such men. If women would simply scorn such fatuous flirtation, men would reform their ways.[18]

William Smith wrote to a Yale classmate in the mid-eighteenth century contrasting his virtue with rakish vice. Their "highest Ambition is to Saunter through a Coffee-house—to spend their Days in Idleness, and their nights in frothy and fullsome Complimts among falsely so called Ladies." Again, both the gallants and the gullible women were blameworthy. He acknowledged, "some time spent in Company with the Ladies I allow myself." His purpose in seeking out female company was, according to Smith, educational: "There are many prettynesses of Behaviour and Conversation which are required in a Gentleman and which are peculiar to the fair and cannot be learnt by precept in the Confinement of a Study." Female company "Scowered" or "polished" a man's soul.[19] Both men blamed women for their shallowness rather than acknowledging their own insecurities.

"Cards, Fiddles and Girls. Kissing, fidling and gaming. A flute, a Girl, and a Pack of Cards"—these were the joys and distractions of a young man according to John Adams, a budding lawyer in 1759.[20] Samuel B. Webb, a future military leader of the Revolution, knew only one foolproof cure for melancholy. In 1772, after spending the night in "Middletown, where I pass'd the evening in Dancing,—the pleasure of the Lady's Company and Madeira made me again Sam. B. Webb."[21] George Hough, away during the war, declared to his Norwich, Connecticut, friend Simeon Baldwin in 1780: "the thought of having a plenty of Wine and Ladies, makes my mouth water. *Who could live better,* says you?—Ah! sure enough!—Let those who can, despise such living as that, I say—For my part I desire no better."[22] Women, wine, and song provided entertainment and diversion.

Sexually laced sociability, dubbed "frolicks," tugged at even the straight laces of John Adams in 1760.[23] "Every Room, kitchen, Chamber was crowed with People. Negroes with a fiddle. Young Fellows and Girls dancing in the Chamber as if they would kick the floor thro. . . . Fiddling and dancing, in a Chamber full of young fellows and Girls, a wild Rable of both sexes, and all Ages, in the lower Room, singing dancing, fiddling, drinking flip and Toddy, and drams.—This is the Riot and Revelling of Taverns And of Thayers [the name of the tavern owner] frolicks."[24] Although judgmental in tone, he seemed content to stay and observe the debauchery. In 1775, Samuel Crosby, while a student at Harvard College, bragged of his social escapades to his friend: "We were favour'd with a Company of very agreeable Ladies, (nine Exceptions). What think you? My Friend, concerning our Frolick?—We met with good Treatment from all except at Punch-Bowls."[25]

Bawdy conversation naturally accompanied flirtation. The subject of such talk often revolved around the size, name, or use of sexual organs. Breasts received particular mention and praise. A college friend wrote to Simeon Baldwin in 1778: "Well, how do you spend the vaction? where are you? what are you about? and how many pretty Girls have you felt of since you left college? Where are they? and how big are they? but hold! I don't mean to communicate any thing that is bad by the word, Big."[26] "Let vulgar Bards &c," a tune to the liking of the future minister, Mather Byles, praised the beauty, power, softness, and taste of the "Nipple-Shell." "Let sons of Bacchus cease to rore, And praise a Nip of Punch no more, Forsake all meaner Nips and dwell, On Pleasures of the Nipple-Shell."²⁷ A man's penis also deserved humorous attention. William Smith's 1746 response to a letter from his former Yale classmate William Samuel Johnson quoted his friend as saying in his last, women *"hang upon us and we ought to Contribute to their happiness in spite of all their scorn."* He queries Johnson, "What do you mean by a woman's *Hanging* on us? I have heard of Men's having an Instrument called a *Hanger* I suppose they sometimes get upon that."²⁸

These men also recorded their sexual pranks and adventures. John Adams described in 1759 the unfolding of a practical joke designed to scare a certain Nat Hurd into thinking he had gonorrhea: "Some fellows in Boston, who found out that he had such a Girl at his shop, at such a time. One went to him and pretended to make a confidant of him. Oh god, what shall I do? That Girl, [. . .] her, has given me the Clap. That scared him and made him cry, Oh damn her, what shall I do? I saw her such a Night. I am [peppered?]. He went to the Dr. [. . .] and was salivated for the Clap. Then they sent him before Justice Phillips, then before Justice Tyler, in short they played upon him till they provoked him so that he swore, he would beat the Brains out of the first man that came into his shop."²⁹ Joseph Hull, later collector of customs for New London, Connecticut, during a trip to New York in 1724, recorded the comic events surrounding the amorousness of his traveling companion. After stopping at an inn and being "pleasantly Merry over a Cup of ye. Creature" his friend spied a "Pretty Damsel." He took a fancy to her and asked a servant to carry her an invitation to his bed. As the two friends slept a dog climbed into Hull's bed. His companion "believing it was her and thought She had Mistaken his bed & Got to mine." The dog and the woman's disdain were quickly revealed. The two men laughed and joked about the adventure on their travels "which highly Diverted us both."³⁰

Sexual expression could accompany courtship and go on outside the well-traveled road to marriage. In the eighteenth century, parental authority lost its punch as young couples found more room for experimentation. For some men this resulted in a new, bold, and at times rakish approach to women. By the end of the eighteenth century, some elites tried to reimpose sexual boundaries to protect their women but perhaps more important, to distinguish themselves from the lower sort. Bundling, the practice of spending the night with a suitor, specifically came under fire and finally went out of fashion as the century turned.[31] Not everyone, even among the elite, thought the new restrictions were for the better. In 1761, John Adams found the new custom of "concealing" a young woman from "all Males, till a formal Courtship is opended" foolish and wrongheaded. He assured his daughters that "no Man that is free and can think, will rush blindfold, into the Arms of any such Ladies, who, tho it is possible they may prove Angells of Light, may yet more probably turn out Haggs of Hell." He felt it preferable to "associate yourselves in some Degree, and under certain Guards and Restraints, even privately with young fellows." He concluded "I cannot wholly disapprove of Bundling."[32]

Throughout the colonial period the qualities in a wife that these men seemed to universally desire were a good temper and a virtuous demeanor.[33] In the seventeenth and early eighteenth century, men searched for a pious helpmeet as well. By the end of the eighteenth century, however, men began to search boldly for more than virtue and piety; they wanted beauty, wealth, and intelligence. All were desirable qualities in a spouse before this period, what changed was their relative weight in a man's decision-making.[34]

Such a shift in language was at least temporally linked to a new demographic environment for courting men in established areas of New England. Marriageable women for the first time outnumbered men at the end of the eighteenth century. New Englanders had, through their extraordinary good health, reproduced a stable, gender-balanced population. Movement away from crowded older towns along with successful population growth provided a favorable marriage market for those men who stayed behind.[35] At the same time, the shortage of land available to divide among children sabotaged the foundations of parental power.[36] No longer constrained by the need to wait for an inheritance, young men increasingly married whom they wanted and when they wanted. In addition, for men now less likely to receive a generous inheritance, the pursuit of a comfortably situated wife carried a new urgency by the end of the eighteenth century.[37] This changing demographic and economic environment gave men the confidence to brazenly state their preferences in a partner with some expectation they might find such a one.

This shift in courtship patterns can be seen in the changing age of marriage for men and women. First marriages for men in New England usually took place when they were in their late twenties, but as the eighteenth century progressed men began to marry earlier. Women, in contrast, married in their early twenties in the seventeenth and early eighteenth centuries but by the late eighteenth century began to marry later.[38] As the sex ratio began to even out and eventually in some areas became lopsided, young women stayed unmarried longer; whereas men married younger because of their expanded choices and freedom from parental control.[39] They were no longer dependent on the timing of an inheritance. They could seek their own fortune and marry whenever their efforts made supporting a family possible.

"And the Lord God said, *It is* not good that the man should be alone; I will make him an help meet for him."[40] A helpmeet eased her husband's burdens. This ideal of wifely duty often appeared in formulaic language such as this closing phrase to a seventeenth-century letter, "Comend my deare love to yo[u]r good wife y[ou]r companion of y[ou]r labors & Traveyles and Sorrowes."[41] In a condolence letter, written in 1635, John Davenport, soon to begin his life in New England, assured a grieving widow that she had been "an helper meet for him, yea a quickner, and encourager of him in that way, wherein you walked together as heyres of the Grace of life."[42] In 1699, John Cotton of New Hampshire, in his often-cited sermon "Meet Help," concluded a wife could provide "comfortable Living for man."[43]

In addition, a helpmeet was a religious partner for many seventeenth-century men. Cotton Mather in 1685/86 wanted someone who could assist him "in the Service of my Master, and whose company I might also at length have in the Heaven of Heavens forever."[44] Thomas Shepard, Puritan pastor in Cambridge, Massachusetts, described his wife (they married in 1632) as "full of Christ & a very discerning Xtian; a wife who was most incomparably louing to me & euery way amiable & holy & endued with a very sweet spirit of Prayer."[45]

The importance of religious companionship was more pressing for a minister to be sure, but the need, even among this select group, lost articulation as the colonial period progressed and other qualifications received more intense scrutiny and open consideration. By the early eighteenth century, both the seventeenth-century helpmeet and the late-eighteenth-century beautiful and wealthy companion combined in the marital desires of Thomas Clap, a young minister in Windham, Connecticut, in the late 1720s: "I thot I wanted one near Friend & Acquaintance, that should be another Self & Help-Meet for me. And among all the Qualifications of a Good Wife an Agreable Consort. I seemed more especially to have in my View these Two viz A steady Serene & Pleasant Natural Temper, and True Piety: For these Two Qualifications seemed most directly to Conduce to my Real Comfort. Contentment & Happiness both in this World and that which is to come." He wanted both "another Self" or companion and a "Help-Meet." He wanted both a "Good Wife" and "an Agreable Consort." He wanted comfort in "this World and that which is to come." When describing the woman who became his wife he claimed, "her Natural Temper to be the most Agreable Pleasant & Attracting (and Indeed discovered it self in a very Beautiful & Pleasant Countenance)." Physical beauty, although desired, was still secondary to more lofty qualifications.[46] In addition, he chose his wife despite her "Small Portion (as is usual with Ministers Daughters)" because he "Considered that a portion was the Smallest Ingredient of a mans real Happiness."[47] Although he seemed ultimately to discount her limited dowry, the choice did need careful explaining. As Nathaniel Saltonstall, longtime public servant in Haverhill, Massachusetts, wrote in 1697, during his son's unsuccessful marriage negotiations, "I would not have any marry for money, neither would I have them so fondly and foolishly marry without money, or at least a convenient Quid or Modicum Bonum."[48]

By the end of the eighteenth century such ambivalent and qualified statements were rare. Ebenezer Baldwin unreservedly declared his preferences. In a letter to a friend in 1774, he trumpeted, "I want Virtue & Beauty & Money & all centering in the same person."[49] James Cogswell outlined in a letter to his sister in 1772 the character of his ideal woman: "She must be, or at least I must think her to be, uncommonly handsome." He embellished: she must "be at the fartherest remove from any thing that is rough or Masculine." She must have a "quick sensibility" and "strictest modesty." Finally, to make her the perfect companion, "She must have such a taste for Books." He implored his sister to tell him "Where I shall find A blooming Virgin with an Angels mind."[50]

Courting men in the late eighteenth century openly declared their desire for a handsome wife. Laurel Ulrich has even found this pattern in portraiture. The stoic helpmeet gave way to the eternally youthful and sexually tempting consort.[51] Henry Livingston, writing to a friend from Boston, rhapsodized over his love interest in 1777: "she far exceeds my description— Venus De Medicis—is a fool."[52] Ebenezer Baldwin wrote often about the physical characteristics of the women he pursued. Some descriptions were short, as with Miss Elizabeth who "Looks Tolerably well."[53] Some were more elaborate, as with Polly Hazard who "is midling Handsome—tall, & gracefully shaped in Body—but not very handsome in the face & rather too dull an eye."[54] He told Sophia Partridge she had "Beauty that might attract the Heart of the most obdurant Stoic."[55]

John Adams advised his daughters that cleanliness, dress, and comportment were as important as natural beauty in attracting a suitor. "Now the finest face, and shape, that ever Nature formed, would be insufficient to attract and fix the Eye of a Gentleman without some Assistance and Decoration of Dress. And I believe an handsome shoe, well judged Variety of Colours, in Linnen, Laces &c., and even the Rustling of silks has determined as many Matches as any natural features, or Proportions or Motions. Hes a fool that is determined wholly by either or by both, but even a wise man will take all these, as well as others less, into Consideration."[56]

Modesty was also a necessary accompaniment to beauty. John Jenks of Salem, Massachusetts, in a military diary he kept in the 1770s described the power of this combination: "Bare-fac'd lewdness stricks horror, bold brutish impudence raises our indignation; but modest beauty is much more dangerous & ensnaring." Such a suitor may in fact fancy himself "in love with virtue only." Such insidious beauty, however, made a vulnerable young man "yield to the deceitfull allurements of a passions which we can scarce perceive, before it is almost too fierce to be extinguished."[57]

The power of modest beauty was formidable. Such allure could overwhelm a man's resolve and tumble him headlong into matrimony. Lieutenant Samuel Benjamin of Waltham, Massachusetts, in a notebook full of unusual occurrences and accounts from his service in the Revolutionary War, lampooned the shameless beauty as she sung her own praises: "I'm the Prettiest, littlest, softest, soundest Plumpest, properest, gracefullest creature that I Ever Set my Eyes on. have the most Virtue, bauty, Wit and Reputation the finest Eyes, the best Presance, the Prettiest Ways, the loveliest haire, the Eveinst teeth, the most Ensnarring Fingers, the most Surprizing foot, the best Shaped:—the most Charming Elbow tip of an Ear, of any in Christendom."[58] Beauty needed refinement to have power. As William Smith noted in a 1748 letter to a love-stricken friend, "Modesty polishes every other beauty and without it a thousand excellencies are but palliated deformities."[59]

Men pursued women with wealth as well as beauty in the late eighteenth century, openly evaluating each woman's financial potential. Ebenezer Baldwin compared two women in a letter to his sister Bethiah in 1773. Polly Hazard's "Fortune I believe is near or quite as good as H.H. [a previous love interest]." A Mrs. Houghton, in contrast, has "Poverty & her Child" as "Considerable Objections."[60]

Pursuit of a wealthy woman, however, could leave a man with uncomfortable feelings of inadequacy and uncertainty. Baldwin pursued women who could remedy his small minister's salary while simultaneously protesting that money was unimportant. Miss Elizabeth was "Rich, but I think I set but Little by ye Last—I doubt not but I can get a comfortable Maintenance in ye World." Even when successful in attracting a wealthy woman he harbored doubts: "I wonder She Likes me so well as She Does, her Fortune may certainly Invite muc[h] Richer Suitors t[ha]n I."[61] William Williams of Lebanon, Connecticut, pursued an unidentified woman of means in 1761. In a four-page letter he outlined his thoughts on matrimony and his love interest's potential. Although she had a very wealthy and generous father, he insisted he had no "sanguine Expectations of, nor desires after great affluence or worldy Prosperity, riches may be improved to valuable & excellent Purposes, & I pretend not to a stoical Contempt of e'm, tho I suppose Happiness even in this Life is far from being confined to or necessarily connected with them." He declared his sincerity although he acknowledged she might "think it Hypocracy & Grimace." Noting "My Fortune is indeed small & possibly may be allways so," he hoped he would "never want a competency." He finally married ten years later to Mary Trumbull, daughter of Governor Jonathan Trumbull. For Williams, this shrewd marriage brought political and economic power. As for the woman discussed in this intimate letter he simply noted after his postscript, "never Sent to any Body."[62] Perhaps the venting of feeling on paper was enough. A man wanted his marriage to augment his pocketbook; yet open acknowledgment of this goal made some men uneasy. As William Smith carefully phrased it to a newly married friend in 1746, "I heartily Congratulate you, upon your Marriage with a Lady, whose Fortune, tho' it has made a considerable Accession to yours, did not so much recommend her to your Choice, as those Virtues and Graces, which made you esteem her the Ornament of her Sex."[63]

As men embarked on their own overt if ambivalent quest for a wealthy spouse they accused women of being guilty of avarice. The late eighteenth century saw little change in this jaundiced, male view of female motivation. Men continued, as they had a century earlier, to ridicule women for their shallowness while minimizing their own. As one man explained to his sister, "The takeing a partner for life is a trifling consideration with most ladies, if the man hits their fancy & has a gentell subsistance."[64] The choice of a spouse was, in fact, a deadly serious business for a woman, determining her financial future. Some men did at least acknowledge the logic of a woman's pursuit of a good provider. Advising his sister about her suitor, Daniel Allen in 1714 remarked, "I must confess the Man is very far from being dispicable on any acct. what his—temper may be you may know better than I." He did, however, have "the main article money wch. in these parts of the world—attracts wonderfully." Even as he chided women for such behavior he understood their thought process. Daniel Allen continued, "I could be very well Satisfied to hear you had a good husband wth a competency to maintain you as you deserve."[65] Wait Winthrop, the son of John Winthrop, Jr., in 1688/89 explained the importance of a potential suitor's estate for the future security of his "cousin," Mary Winthrop. "Unlesse somthing considerable be proposed to be settled on her in case he should dye before her, or other accident hapen, I cannot advise you to dispose of her. She is well now; but if a woman be left with nobody knows how many smale children, she had need haue somthing to trust too."[66] This advice was particularly compelling because of the bride's young age. Mary, the illegitimate and only daughter of his brother Fitz-John, eventually did marry a New York Livingston, but not until 1701.[67]

Intellectual charm at times took precedence over more corporeal beauty. William Williams bestowed on an unknown love interest in 1761 the dubious compliment that she was "not disagreable or unlovely, an accomplishment sufficiently attractive of Esteem, tho not an essential or prime Consideration, the inward Beauties of the mind incomparably surpass those of the external Features."[68] Eliza Watson received thoughtful advice from her brother, "Let your endeavors be rather to excel them ['your inferiors'] in the ornaments of the mind than the more glittering gaudy splendor of dress."[69] As William Smith fully acknowledged to his friend William Samuel Johnson in the 1740s, an attractive appearance did not always indicate a beautiful spirit: "I agree with you that young Gentlemen are often dazeled with a fine Equipage—and apt to fancy the mentall Qualifications as good as the Externall—and the soul regulated in a Harmonious Oconomy equall to the glittering Outside of a Gay Lady. I am pleased with your Advice of making a *Closer inspection* and as an instance of my Gratitude I shall make this day a more *Accuarate observation* and agreable to your request shall Endeavour *Not to be decieved.*"[70] A man had to make certain that a beautiful face did not lead him to choose unwisely.

Men spoke openly about wanting a woman who could provide intellectual companionship. The late eighteenth century saw men frequently looking for a mate with sensibility or often, interchangeably, a good mind.[71] As Mr. Perkins wrote to Simeon Baldwin in 1782 about his intended: "Mrs. _____ is agreable as to her person, but the beauty of her person is far surpased by the amiable and truly estimable qualities of her mind. Understanding & memory are hers in an eminent degree."[72] Ebenezer Baldwin wanted an intelligent wife, someone "Sensible, Virtuous & agreeable." A friend suggested a potential candidate as "one of the most sensible & withall serious Young Ladies that he was ever acquainted with."[73] One of Polly Hazard's failings, from Baldwin's perspective, was her weak intellect: "Her Genius is not the first Rate—I should like a Wife rather more sensible—Or that would make rather more of a scholar than I suspect she will."[74] Sophia Partridge lacked some of this sharpness of intellect, but he was hopeful that she would improve.

& now my D[ea]r will you be offended If I say I wish to have these improved & heightned, with more reading & a larger Acquaintance with Books. By this y[ou]r Charmes will every Day Increase — & in this if any thing y[ou]r Education has been defective — I was going to Say this is the only accomplishment I could wish you to improve in (But this is too much to say to any Creature) — This thing I should not mention; had I not the Warmest affection — & the sincerest Desire to have Minds knit together — & as it were moulded into one — since I trust we shall soon sustain that relation t[ha]t requires the strictest Intimacy.

This man approved of female education because it served his needs for companionship. "I know tis apt to be ~~said~~ thought & said Books & Learning are out of a Womans Sphere — But why should the fair Sex be deprived of that wh[ich] tends to heighten the Joys of Life & to render them vastly more agreeable Companions to their Partners in Life."[75] Sophia's reaction was also revealing. She agreed that the advice he gave her was "good, but I ant born to spend my time to improve my self as I might wish."[76] She concurred that education was "a fine thing In a Woman as well as in a Man but I have no time at Present the Circomstancses of the Famely are such and when they will be better i cant say."[77]

Many men spoke of conversation style when making a distinction between wanting women to be bright for their own sake and wanting them to have the qualities of an entertaining companion. One man warned his sister "to distinguish between polite conversation & pedantry." He described pedantic women as "disagreeable" and "ridiculous." She should not, however, "be over solicitous to persuade the company she has read nothing but her primmer." She could, if she so chose, quote from and discuss various authors in a way that would enhance "polite conversation."[78] John Adams made the same point to his daughters in 1761.

> I would not have you Pedants in Greek and Latin nor the Depths of science, nor yet over fond to talk upon any Thing. When your opinion is asked, give it. When you know any Thing, that the Company are at a loss for, disclose it. But what I mean is this. Attend to the Conversation of Gentlemen even when News, Politicks, Morals, OEconomy, nay even when Literature and science but beyond the fathom of your Line make the subject: do not attempt to turn the Conversation to Billy's Prattle — To the Doggs, or Negroes or Cats, or to any little contemptible Tittle tattle of your own.[79]

By the late eighteenth century, an educated woman who could entertain her husband or male company was highly valued.[80] As a courting man wrote to his "Dear Lady" in 1781, "O what a beautiful lustre shines forth in the character of those whose minds instead of being wholly immers'd in the cares and amusements of life, are . . . often engaged in contemplation on matters which have no concern with the trifles of sense." A woman who had such a mind, "should she possess every embellishment which both nature & art could lavish on her, none of them could by any means be set in competition with this inestimable qualification this excellent endowment."[81]

In summary, what changed as the eighteenth century progressed was the open and obvious search for an attractive, financially desirable, well-read companion as well as, or as a substitute for, a pious helpmeet. Certainly there was overlap. Men throughout the colonial period coveted all of these qualities in a wife to some extent. Thomas Shepard, in the 1640s, remarked that his future mate was "the best & fittest woman in the woorld vnto me" not only because of her Christian demeanor but because her relatives had kindly "enlarged her portion."[82] John Page, a recent graduate of Harvard in the 1760s, copied this injunction into his diary even as his peers let their heads be turned: "Love not for Riches or for Beauties Sake Most fail who Wealth instead of Virtue take."[83] But as the colonial period came to an end there was a new priority put on particular traits as more desirable in a mate. Finally, it is important to acknowledge that some choices defy analysis. Ashley Bowen, a mariner from Marblehead, Massachusetts, after a prophetic dream at sea in 1757, determined he could marry only a woman with five moles on her right cheek.[84] As John Adams put it, "A Man may prefer a Woman, or a Woman a Man, for some Property or Qualification, that he or she may be unable to name."[85]

Tied to this new open search for beauty, wealth, and charm was a yearning for romantic love.[86] It must be said at the outset that difference in emphasis does not presuppose a difference in feeling. Men looked for loving marriages in both the seventeenth and the eighteenth centuries. The new romantic ideal of the late eighteenth century, however, pressured a courting youth to measure up to new standards of sentiment.[87] A man was now expected to engage a woman's heart. If rejection occurred in this new cultural context, the blow could be severe. A young man knew it was *he* rather than his status or estate that was found lacking.

Ideally, in the courting process, men pursued, women accepted or rejected potential lovers.[88] Women could and did manipulate circumstances to their advantage, but men were more publicly exposed. If after repeated visits a woman broke off a courtship, the blow to one's ego and standing in the community were significant. William Williams in 1761 called it the "Danger of Disappointment."[89] This danger included emotional upset as well as damage to one's name and public character. Getting "bagged," as it was called, was bad enough without the additional burden of patching up a sullied reputation. A broken heart could, therefore, be emotionally, socially, and economically devastating. The combination of active pursuit and severe consequences led to unique patterns of courtship among young men. They learned how to attract women, how to deal with competition, and how to minimize their defeats. The object was to find a mate, but also to avoid being bagged.

George Hough assured his friend Simeon Baldwin in 1780, "if courting is continued with spirit" success would follow.[90] The opposite, however, was also true. A man unwilling to take the initiative in courtship failed and accordingly deserved derision and mockery. As Henry Livingston remarked to his friend in 1777, "a faint heart never wins a fair Lady."[91] John Adams noted in his diary in 1759 the "dronish effeminacy" of P[arson] Wib[irds]: "He says he has not Resolution enough to court a Woman. He wants to find one that will charm, conquer him and rouse his spirit." The parson reminded Adams of a female turkey: "She is difficult, looks a[t] several Places, to roost on, before she fixes on any, and when she has fixed on one she stretches her Neck, squats, and changes her Posture several Times before she flies up."[92] This unflattering portrait of the hapless parson clearly displayed Adams's contempt for such a man. Oliver Ellsworth, a young Connecticut attorney, similarly outlined to his wife Nabby in 1781 the efforts of two "old Batchelors." They both visited a church in Springfield to "take a look at" a likely woman of that congregation. Ellsworth predicted neither would "proceede farther, being allways at a loss how & where to take hold." Ellsworth speculated, "Tho' courting is said to be no very difficult matter after one has learned the secret yet it generally requires art & management in the first place to bring an old Batchelor on."[93] The diffident man remained a bachelor unless a persistent woman managed the courtship and reversed the natural order of things.

Courtship meant an investment of time and travel for a male suitor and a public pronouncement of his intentions. He made clear his preference for a particular lady and if subsequently rejected, he faced humiliation. Regular visits to his intended's home meant family and friends were sure to notice if these visits stopped. As Asahel Heart reminded his former Yale classmate Ebenezer Baldwin in 1767, "you know or must if you get a Wife that a Lady must be taken Notice of . . . they estimate the Quantity of Affection much by the Quantity of Time you do or they find you are inclined Agreably to Spend in their Company."[94]

Before too much visiting went on it was expected that a man ask permission to court a woman. He asked her parents as well as his own. Friends also were consulted.[95] But this is not to say parents and others dictated his choice. The relative power of parent and child varied according to financial circumstances and temperament. Parental power in marriage decisions usually took the form of economic control, but love had its place. The question was simply one of balance.[96]

Whether essential or symbolic, a young man could not dispense with the formality of parental permission. Such flouting of custom might land him in court or expose him to church censure. In fact, this first important step could actually help a man gauge his potential for success. If the parents of a woman allowed a courtship to commence, this signaled that his company was welcome. If parents and friends were discouraging, he might expect failure. This provided a method of measuring one's risk for rejection before public courting commenced. A young man could protect his reputation and his ego before his desires became generally known.

In 1649, Mathew Stanley received a fine from Salem court officials of £5, "for drawing away the affections of the Daughter of John Tarboxx his wife without libertie first obtayned of her parents." Similarly, John Gilman in 1651 was accused of "unlawful enticing of Hanna Cross, daughter of the widow Cross, using means to draw her affections contrary to the minds of her mother and governors made known to said Gilman." The Ipswich court found him innocent of the charges against him. In both cases the men in question were thieves of a daughter's "affection." For Stanley, the fact that he married his conquest meant nothing to the court. He had taken her heart without her mother's permission and that was his crime. The court even fined Theophilus Salter £5 in 1653 because he professed love to Mary Smith and tried to "marry her without consent of her friends."[97] Parents, friends or "governors" needed to be consulted before a young man could speak of marriage.[98] The church also felt that a man had to ask permission to court a woman. Joshua Fletcher of Chelmsford, Massachusetts, was excommunicated in 1668 for his stubborn refusal to admit that his conduct toward his wife before marriage had been inappropriate. The church accused him of "making love to her and consequently entangling her affections toward him without consent." His defense was that her parents had approved of their liaison. The church found his reasoning difficult to accept. If her parents had approved why did he climb the wall of the house to enter her bedchamber? Why did he come in the dead of night? They were in her room for hours in bitter cold, "And thus rationally conceived it hardly can be how it should be tolerable to have sat and abode with her without fire or other help of warmth, in a modest way." Finally, they met on a number of occasions on the sabbath and sometimes "the evening after the Lord's day exercises," making their conduct even more reprehensible. His crime was likely sexual, but the proof of an early birth was apparently lacking. Instead, the congregation focused on his enticement of his future wife in the dark and in private and, therefore, clearly without parental consent.[99]

Caleb Hitchcock did not climb the walls of his sweetheart's home, but the disgruntled father of his love interest found the young man's conduct sufficiently vile to keep him from church membership. The unknown father wrote to Reverend Benjamin Trumbull of North Haven, Connecticut, in 1771 to record his outrage at the possibility of Hitchcock joining the congregation. "First, that said Hitchcock without my Consent or Liberty, or ever so Much as asking it frequented my House, and was frequently in the Company of One of my Dauters; and afterwards entirely without any Consent or ever so much as asking it, or giving either to me, or my Wife the Least intimation of any Such Thing, was publickly Cried off, and published intentions of Marriage between himself & my said Daughter." This conduct to the mind of this frustrated father violated the fifth commandment, "Honour thy father and thy mother," and Christ's admonition in the Sermon on the Mount, "Therefore all Things whatsoever ye would that Men should do to you do ye even the same to them."[100] His sin was not fornication, but disrespect for his future father-in-law and his privileges as a parent. This father simply wanted to be asked.

How did a young man approach this delicate task? Samuel Sewall, Boston merchant and jurist, was gatekeeper for his daughters and a granddaughter as potential beaux came to his home. Samuel Gerrish, bookseller and town clerk of Boston, began his courtship of Mary Sewall in 1709. With the help of his cousin, who served as intermediary, Gerrish asked "if he might have admittance." Sewall fretted over a rumor that Gerrish still pursued a courtship with Sarah Coney. After some careful investigation Sewall discovered that the visits to the Coney home had ended. "Mr. Coney thought his daughter young."[101] Sewall wrote to Gerrish's father and eventually met with him. The young lovers began their courtship. Gerrish told his intended that "except Satterday and Lord's-day nights [he] intends to wait on her every night; unless some extraordinary thing happen." Gerrish married Mary Sewall in August 1709 about seven months after the courtship began. She died in childbirth in November of the following year. In 1712, Samuel Gerrish married for the second time. His second wife was his first love, Sarah Coney.[102]

When his daughter Judith's time came, Sewall first negotiated directly with the hopeful, William Dudley. Sewall accused him of asking Judith before seeking her parents' approval. In addition, Sewall noted in his diary, "His waiting on her might give some Umbrage: I would Speak with her first." Soon William's father, the ex-governor, arrived in his "Chariot" on behalf of his son. He asked Sewall to "give him leave that he might visit my daughter Judith." Sewall evaded the question saying "'twas a weighty matter" and he would "consider of it." Either Judith had some hesitancy or Sewall was loath to give a second child in marriage to this family. The earlier match between Rebecca Dudley and Sewall's son Samuel, Jr., was tumultuous to say the least.[103] Whatever the case, Sewall presided at the marriage of his daughter Judith to another suitor, Rev. William Cooper, a year later in 1701/02.[104]

Sewall also found himself, in 1729, arranging for the marriage of his granddaughter, Jane Hirst, who lived with him. Judge Davenport came to visit Sewall to receive his consent for his son Addington to "have Liberty to Wait upon Jane Hirst now at my House in way of Courtship." The father thoroughly outlined his son's economic future: "He told me he would deal by him as his eldest Son, and more so. Inten'd to build a House where his uncle Addington dwelt for him; and that he should have his Pue in the Old Meetinghouse." Sewall shook his hand and "granted his desire." Two month later, Jane Hirst married Addington Davenport.[105]

Even after permission to court was given, parents expected to be regularly consulted and fully informed. Benjamin Douglas, a lawyer in New Haven thinking he had parental consent to announce his engagement to Rebecca Fish, promptly published banns in 1762.[106] Joseph Fish, his future father-in-law, erupted in indignation. Douglas responded with some heat as well: "If I have mistaken meer Civility & Complaisance for an explicit Consent in the affair, impute it to Ignorance of Mankind, a Blunder, Forgetfulness, Heedlessness—or any thing but *casting off* all *"Duty"* & *Respect* to your self & Madam,—a Presuming 'such an Alteration is your Family when you were not even privy to it.'" Douglas had concluded that since Fish had let the time of marriage be assigned by "the Decision of the Parties" he "imagin'd) the *Time of Pub,g* wh. was *less* Important might with equal Propriety be left so too." Joseph Fish understood differently and worried that Douglas's high-handedness might be a "Foreboding of future Sovereignty."[107] The two men eventually reconciled and the marriage proceeded. Once courtship had commenced the continuing goodwill of parents, and an appropriate respect for their authority, was essential. Even when, as in this case, a parent seemed to defer to the two lovers.

Permission to court was the necessary first step to marriage. The formality of asking a parent or guardian was crucial. Parents protected their children's interests. A young man had to convince these gatekeepers that he was worthy. In return, he received a clear indication of his potential for success in the endeavor. William Dudley surely suspected his chances were slim, whereas Addington Davenport had every reason to look forward to his wedding day.

Once permission had been obtained, a man embarked on the visiting rituals of courting. This exposed him to public scrutiny. People noted the comings and goings and talked among themselves about the progress of the couple.[108] Lucy Clarke of Boston gossiped to her relative Sally Bromfield in 1772 about a new love match, warning her "you must keep this a secret and dont carry this Letter in your Pocket." Admonishing Sally to "Attend to my tale," Lucy told of "A certain young Laidy" who met a Mr. Kneeland with his two friends at "Neighbour Greens." He "was very much smittin with the young Ladiy; and when he went away, express'd himself, very raptureously to the other gentlemen." He went back to the Greens' and enquired where he might find his new love interest. He was directed to see a Mrs. Copley, where "after half and hours conversation in private he went off what the determination was we must leave to time to discover."[109] Lucy knew all the details except what had conspired during the private conversation.

After a certain number of visits, if a couple did not announce their intention to marry, the community looked for a cause. John Adams became the subject of rumor when he frequented the home of Hannah Quincy. His father warned him of the town's watchfulness: "He says I have waited on H. Q. two Journeys, and have called and made Visits there so often, that her Relations among others have said I am courting of her. And the Story has spread so wide now, that, if I dont marry her, she will be said to have Jockied me, or I to have Jockied her, and he says the Girl shall not suffer. A story shall be spread, that she repelled me."[110] In fact, Adams had an interest in Hannah, but never formally declared his feelings. He ultimately married her second cousin Abigail Smith.

John Adams described in his diary in 1759 the adventures of the unfortunate "Dr. S." who found his personal life the subject of gossip and merriment. He went to church one day to find himself in the same pew as a former girlfriend, "L. R." She apparently had ended the relationship or as Adams termed it, "turned him off." "She smiled, and almost giggled at him. That stung him. He cryed a nasty, stinking Jade, he did not think she was such a nasty yellow Jade, before. Thus the Dr. diverted him self with her Colour. He laughed at her yellow Colour, in Revenge of her Ridicule of him." Adams remarked, "Thus human Nature, when despized and laughed at, is vexed, naturally vexed, and looks about for some Imperfection, Deformity, folly or Vice to laugh at in turn."[111] A very public display, indeed. If anybody at the church had not known before, they knew then that these two had courted and she had rejected him.

A failed courtship produced depression in some men, for others fury.[112] When Joseph Emerson, minister of a new congregation in Groton (later Pepperell), Massachusetts, received a rebuff in the late 1740s, he struggled with his sadness: "I was considerable melancholly under my Disappointment at Northampton." He found his dark thoughts so numerous "I could not study, I could not have tho't what I have lately met with would have had this Effect." A month after his one meeting with Esther Edwards he continued in his low state: "I was this Day so pressed down under the weight of some peculiar Burdens both of a temporal and spiritual Nature that I could not fix my mind to do any thing at all in the forenoon." The next day he noted, "Melancholly all Day, it seems to be growing upon me." He finally tried again by enlisting the help of Esther's sister Sarah. She "entirely discourages me from taking a journey again there to visit her sister, who is so near my heart." Finally, he turned to the Lord, "may I be resigned."[113]

For the unknown author of a letter penned in 1774, anger accompanied frustrated desires. After sending an opening letter to a likely young lady, he found out she already kept "company with a gentleman." He wrote a second letter to withdraw his proposal "to cultivate a nearer & more intimate Acquaintment with you." He asked her "the truth of affairs respecting you." Since he was "quite averse to works of Darkness but rather choose to Dwell in the Light," he would quietly retire rather than see her secretly. Although the content of the letter contained little in the way of emotion the back of this draft correspondence was covered with the words "Command your temper" written in a bold hand, over and over again.[114]

Matthew Rockwell refused to admit defeat when Hannah Edwards, sister of the famous Jonathan Edwards, wanted to end their courtship in 1735/36. She solicited advice from her brother-in-law on how to proceed. Rockwell had threatened to kill himself if deprived of her company.

> I will allow t[ha]t you know more of Mr R. than I do. but you must allow t[ha]t I am better acquainted with our Sex than you be and I will give you this one direction, to help you in your Conduct for ye future. when you see a man about to die for love. you must attribute one half of his mallady to Conceit . . . one quarter (if he be a pretty honest man) you must attribute to dissimulation; and the quarter that is left will never kill him. tho I am jocular in this passage, yet there is a great deal

of truth in it. and I am Sensible, by my own Ex-
periance, t[ha]t men Can't die by ye bagg half so
Easely as they think.

Rockwell's behavior showed him to be conceited and dishonest, and as Hannah's helpful relative pointed out, "the person
t[ha]t is so unmanly, as to Compel a woman to have him, by
such a plea, has not enough of ye man in him to make a good
husband." [115] The "manly" thing then would have been to retreat quietly. Getting the bag was humiliating and painful, but
a gentleman took it well.

A year later, the tenacious Mr. Rockwell was still trying to
force Hannah to the altar. He even wrote to her new beau, John
Sergeant, staking his claim to her. Sergeant wrote Hannah
about receiving this letter remarking "it [is] very unreasonable,
ungenerous & unmanly in him to bring the private transactions
of lovers upon the public Stage." Rockwell, therefore, showed
his true character both by pursuing Hannah too long and then
by making his disgrace public. The issue of privacy in these
transactions was particularly poignant for men. After aggres-
sive pursuit, a discreet refusal and gracious defeat were essential
in maintaining a trustworthy reputation—a commodity inte-
gral to a man's personal and public success.

John Sergeant, in contrast to his rival, pursued Hannah in
a more appropriate fashion. He asked permission to visit her
saying: "I Seek no man's wrong in it; but my own pleasure.
If that gives any body uneasiness, I am Sorry." [116] A year after
their courtship commenced, exhausted by Rockwell's hound-
ing, Hannah broke off with Sergeant. He took the news gracefully: "I lay no blame on you, but rather accuse my own fondness. I still think of you with all the tenderness, that is due to
the most intimate friend." He went on to wish her "a match,
whenever you shall choose to make one, a thousand times more

deserving."[117] Certainly, Sergeant's gracious retreat in the face of disappointment helped her to see clearly who was the better man.

The ill-fated relationship of Sophia Partridge and Ebenezer Baldwin lavishly details the bagging process. Baldwin, a tutor at Yale College, had a lengthy and intimate correspondence with Partridge in the late 1760s. Ebenezer clearly thought Sophia would be his future wife, but he felt unable to propose until he had the means to support her. "My all you know depends upon the little flock of Leamings I am master of [students at Yale]—To this I must be Indebted for my Support in Life—For a Maintenance for my dearest Sophia when we shall be so happy as to live together If providence should ever allow the happy Moment to Arrive. & not to have a Comfortable Main-tenance for so Charming & agreeable a Companion & Partner; how unhappy will it make my Life." He was uncertain about Sophia's ability to settle for the small competence that he would eventually be able to provide. "Im pretty Certain [it]'will never be my lot to make a Splendid & Illustrious Figure," and yet his fond hope was that she would agree "to live a life of Virtue with the Friend she Love tho' In moderate Circumstances, be-fore the highest Grandeur wh[ich] the O[world?] Affords."[118]

By the spring of the following year he was still mulling over this issue of his economic readiness for marriage. He began to fear that Sophia would leave him for someone with more wealth. Although he spoke of his confidence in her unerring love, it was clear that the time required for him to become financially secure concerned him. He addressed her as Philo-mela as he did in many of his letters; she named him Philan-der.[119] "But will my Phil be constant year after Year, if Provi-dence so orders that we must postpone till then the happy Day that makes us one. Yes she is too unlike those Giddy rattles of the Female Sex (pardon my Freedom of y[ou]r Sex) to change her true, her constant P: for Linsey Jacket or a gold bound Hat these Trifles want weigh[t] in a Mind so form'd as hers to Virtue—I rest assured from P steadiness, her to & honesty; from her Intimate Acquaintance & warm affection for ~~her~~ Philander, None can supplant him in her Heart."[120] For Ebenezer Baldwin, his lack of financial resources blocked a proposal of marriage to his beloved Sophia. Without an engagement the relationship became strained and ultimately ended.

Their breakup began in the spring of 1767. Sophia was disappointed by a too brief visit. She took the opportunity to press Ebenezer to a firmer commitment. She wrote in a complaining letter that she had other men pursuing her: "You see how I am exposed to every ones Company if I dont speake that grate word (Ingaged)."[121] He responded with practicality rather than emotion: "You must Expect but Little from yr Phil[ande]r—either by Letters or otherwise; untill he changes his Situation in Life—However he never can forget his P[hilomela] to Visit her as oft as possible—at other Time to write by every Conveyance."[122]

Still unsettled, their troubles continued at a later visit. Sophia became "cold & Indifferent" in response to Ebenezer's mistreatment of a common friend. He found the offense trivial but endeavored to reform. She then compared his behavior to "a certain Person" of her acquaintance giving "a great Preference to the Latter." This prompted Ebenezer to remark, "but I must confess it shock'd me a little, to find her whom I designed for my Partner in Life, to be not a Whit prejudiced in my Favor." He lamented "how can we be happy together." Faced with such demanding truculence, Baldwin fell back on his own insecurities for explanation: "How frequent Madm were your Observations on the Impropriety of unequal Families matching together, twas easy to see where twas aimed."[123]

Although it was already a fait accompli, they quarreled over the appropriate forum for their official breakup. Sophia argued that breaking up in person was their agreement: "I find by yrs of March 18 that you think I Disdain to write an answar I freely own I had much rather answar it by Word of mouth than any other way you may remember when we first agreed to be ingaged to each other we agreed never to brake up unless face to face & I cannt see how it can be done other ways."[124] Ebenezer lamented, "Is not latent meaning plain—she chuses to do it by mouth—yt she may have a fairer opportunity to Disgrace Philander."[125] This was the crux of the matter for him. She focused on the promise they made, he on the disgrace of a confrontation. She wrote, "if its a Disgrace to part why not one way as well as other."[126] She failed to see his concern, but for him the distinction was vivid.

Sophia was not, however, immune to the issue of reputation. She heard a rumor reported by one of Ebenezer's students that disturbed her.

> the Question is when you was at Boston larst Spring
> (whether you told one of your Former Pupels (that
> saw you their) that you was not a Comeing to
> Hatfield any more, especaly on my Account. for
> you had done with me; he told you he thot you
> was playing the Farce with him, no you said you
> was not; you said H[at]f[iel]d Popple Drank in a
> Strange Notion that you had a grate regard for
> me. but you Could tell them you had no more re-
> gard for me than any body els & if you ever come
> to Ha[t]f[iel]d again it would not be to see me
> more than any body) & what was more you would
> let H[at]f[iel]d Popple know that you could Live
> without me.

What upset Sophia the most was not the sentiments presented because "Doubtless you might think as much." She was concerned rather that "you could be so Familiar with him" and that this conversation apparently went on "in company." She claimed to have kept their breakup a secret although Ebenezer had accused her of being "fond of leting it be known."[127] Ebenezer Baldwin, like Matthew Rockwell, made his case public, but for Baldwin the purpose was not to regain his sweetheart. Baldwin tried to prevent further disgrace by minimizing his feelings for Sophia and leaving the initiator of the breakup obscure.

Asahel Heart and Betsey Partridge, Sophia's sister, ended their fledgling affair about the same time. A Doctor Sergeant entered the picture and displaced Asahel. Their "agreement was if either of us found another more agreable in Person Situation or Occupation we should let the other know it." Like Sophia, Betsey showed a preference for a face-to-face discussion. Asahel, like Ebenezer, chose instead to write: "I sent a sheet & a half wrote fine—the product of a warm feeling unintimidated Heart & Brain—& left her to do as she pleased." She ended the affair face-to-face after Asahel finally relented and agreed to call on her. "She said she meant not to bagg me but to part Friends & by Agreement—& she never should own that she turned me of[f]." Getting bagged meant bad feelings and a unilateral decision by one member of a couple. Secrecy was essential in such circumstances because the reputation of the party "turned off" needed confidentiality. Similarly, in a discussion with his ill-fated lover over the breakup of Sophia and Ebenezer, Heart made clear the risk men faced in this process. "His Character must suffer if she turns him of[f]—for their Connections are known as far as their Names."[128]

A man ran the risk of a damaged reputation as well as a damaged heart when he courted a woman seriously. Women also ran a risk both emotionally and in terms of their social standing. As the romantic aggressor, however, a man's humiliation was more public and more damaging. Without a good name a man risked his livelihood as well as his feelings. If bagged or turned off they either fretted and fumed or reluctantly accepted "no" for an answer. Either way, a man's heart and reputation both received a public battering.

Elite men wanted both a helpmeet and a consort. As the marriage market became more favorable, they became more vocal about the latter. For the common man, the sources are less forthcoming and, therefore, the picture less clear. Nonetheless, all men in late colonial New England, regardless of status, benefited from a flush marriage market. Rakish men pursued sexual pleasures as opportunities expanded and social and parental sanctions declined. Some men reveled in the fair field. They openly pursued the beautiful, the wealthy, and the stimulating. At the same time, however, the emotional risks of courtship increased. Failure still meant disgrace and a damaged reputation, but now disappointment also carried the heavy toll of personal defeat. This was particularly true as romantic love became an important part of the language of courtship. This auspicious time for a courting man in New England was also ironically full of peril. A poor choice could, as women knew only too well, ruin all. As one New England man put it in 1782: "This choice, my Friend, is the most important—the all-important step in a mans life. Without domestic happiness, farewell to all hopes of happiness."[129]

USEFULNESS

3

A Husband "Well-Ordered"

In his 1712 sermon *The Well-Ordered Family*, Benjamin Wadsworth concluded "the Husband is ever to be esteem'd the Superior, the Head, and to be reverenc'd and obey'd as such." So powerful are such declarations to modern sensibilities that other, equally common, colonial New England representations of marriage as a partnership seem impossibly hypocritical. Men who recorded their feelings, however, felt female subordination and affection were essential and complementary parts of a successful marriage.[1] A husband was part of an interdependent family in both the seventeenth and eighteenth centuries, a family system that required mutual support to function successfully. Cooperation, not simply coercion, kept a family well ordered. Although the words came more freely by the end of the colonial period, the tender language of love marked the writings of men in both centuries.[2] Maintaining the delicate balance between household head and loving husband assured domestic bliss as well as social acceptance.

Partnership in marriage was both an ideal and a reality in colonial New England.[3] This is not to suggest that men and women were equal. Rather, both had a stake in their household and their children. Often their daily routines and duties were different, but both worked toward common goals. Men counted on their wives not only to handle their own responsibilities but to assist them in their husbandly duties if needed.[4] In a happy union, the mutual support of marriage and the well-being of the family were central.

G. Selleck Silliman, a lawyer from Fairfield, Connecticut,

and a general during the American Revolution, referred to his wife Mary and she to him as "dear partner."[5] John Winthrop, founder of Massachusetts Bay Colony, like many seventeenth-century husbands, described his wife as his "yokefellowe."[6] When marrying in colonial New England a man entered a partnership that provided support for both husband and wife. In describing his vision of marital bliss to his betrothed, Silliman pictured them passing "through all the Scenes of this Life mutually supporting, blessing & assisting Each other in the Ways of Duty."[7] Reverend John Walley of Ipswich and later Bolton, Massachusetts, hoped, on the eve of his marriage in 1748, that he and his wife "might be Helpers to each other."[8] Together, husband and wife shared the joys and sorrows of life. William Dawes, in defending his new wife to his doubting friend, Worcester merchant Stephen Salisbury, in 1773, declared that with her he could "Share Equily in trouble & Afliction As Well As in Joy & prosperty both is Equall."[9]

Tapping Reeve, the famous Connecticut jurist, wrote to his "lovely Sally" about his "Pleasure of reflecting that I have one friend in you that will be ever an unshaken friend."[10] A man could gain a rare kind of friend in a successful marriage, one whose faithfulness and loyalty surpassed all others. John Walley spoke of his approaching marriage to his "dear Friend" in 1748.[11] Boston minister Cotton Mather lamented the loss of his wife in 1713, "My dear, dear, dear Friend."[12] The mother of Mary Silliman stayed with her daughter while Mary's "best Friend" remained in the army during the Revolution.[13] Like friendly companions, a husband and wife chatted with one another, supported each other, asked each other's advice.

The newly married Eliphalet Pearson, a Massachusetts educator, wrote to his "friend" in 1785 as he struggled to get his home ready for her arrival: "You will excuse my just hinting at, the happiness your friend would enjoy in the company &

converse of his other *Self*. However, if you should, upon a full view of all reasons & circumstances, think it expedient to come next week, I shall readily acquiesce in your opinion. I never wished so much to see my friend. Shall have many matters to communicate, on which I shall wish for your advice."[14] Selleck Silliman consulted his best friend often about decisions great and small. Silliman, because of economic difficulties brought on by his imprisonment during the Revolution, contemplated leaving public life.

> What shall I do my Love? — My late expensive Ab-
> sence has cost me a great Deal of Mony, — should
> I again fall into the Enemy's Hands it would hurt
> me irreparably almost, — To reduce myself to a pri-
> vate Character would be my best Means of Safety,
> as the Enemy would make no Efforts after a Pri-
> vate, — [section deleted], were it not for the Advice
> of some great Characters, and for Fear that the
> People of my own County would be disgusted at it,
> I should most certainly do this, — What shall I do
> My Dearest? I wish I had Your Advice, — I am at a
> great Loss how to conduct.[15]

Lasting friendship characterized such marriages.

Some men loved their partners deeply. John Winthrop wrote to his wife while waiting for the *Arabella* to set sail for New England in 1630. He began, "My Love, My Joy, My Faithful One." He also labeled her "dear heart," "my Most Sweet Heart," and "My Sweet Wife."[16] Tapping Reeve in 1773 called his wife "lovely Sally," "my Sweet girl," and "innocent chicken."[17] Likewise, William Williams, a Lebanon, Connecticut, states-man, addressed his wife Mary as "my Dear Love" and "my dear Child" a few months after signing the Declaration of In-dependence, assuring her that he loved her as his "own soul."[18]

Similarly, John Winthrop addressed one of his loving letters to "Mine Own Sweet Self." He read and reread his wife's letters during his crossing to the New World: "I am never satisfied with reading, nor can read them without tears; but whether they proceed from joy, sorrow, or desire, or from that consent of affection, which I always hold with thee, I cannot conceive."[19] John Walley thanked God before his wedding in 1748 "that I have such abundant Reason to think that we have a sincere & fervent Love to each other."[20] Soon after his marriage, Mather Byles confided to his father, "I enjoy all that full Satisfaction, which results from the tendrest Connexion of humane Life." He claimed to have "no romantic Ideas of visionary, unattainable Bliss: I really possess much more than I thought possible."[21]

The concept of love was often paired with the notion of "tenderness" or affectionate concern.[22] Selleck Silliman, in a letter to his father-in-law, related his homecoming from the army in 1776 "to that Dear, Beloved Woman, whose uniformly endearing & Vertuous Conduct, deserves all the Tenderness that can possess a human Heart."[23] In a church investigation of the unhappy Mr. and Mrs. Tilden in eighteenth-century Connecticut, a witness was asked to characterize the behavior of Stephen Tilden toward his wife Mary. The witness and former boarder reported that "his Love & Tender Regard toward Her, which he so variously Manifested & so often Repeated . . . I Did Esteem him (and have Since that Time often Thought him) a Real Patern of Conjucal Love."[24] A good husband was tender as well as loving. A witness on the wife's side, Mary Nicols, had quite a different perspective. According to Nicols, Tilden arrived home once when she was there "in a gratte passion," frustrated at the slowness of his children in performing their farm chores. A young son of the Tildens had died two or three days earlier, and Nicols chided Tilden for his violent temper with the house still in mourning. His response was "I have laid two Children In the Grave and he threatens to Knock another in ye head." Mary Nicols concluded "I See him Act so toward his wife and children, yt I thought he had ye Least Tenderness yt I Ever see in any man in my Life."[25] Both witnesses agreed, if not about Stephen Tilden's character, on the essential ingredient of tenderness in a loving marriage.

Husbands also wrote of their passion for their wives. The bed was a private place where a couple shared warmth, quiet conversation, and love-making. William Henshaw, a farmer from Leicester, Massachusetts, wrote to his wife Phebe during his sojourn in the Continental army, "these Cold Nights I am Sensible of the want of a Bed fellow, I know not how long it will be before I enjoy the satisfaction of having you by my side."[26] Benjamin Bangs, a Harwich, Massachusetts, coastal trader, noted in his diary in winter 1764 that his wife tended her sick mother all night with the notation, "I sleep alone."[27] Tapping Reeve cautioned his beloved Sally in 1773 to "not abuse my sweet Lips with your savage little teeth."[28] John Winthrop often ended his letters to Margaret with phrases like "I kisse my sweet wife," "kiss me my sweet wife," or "with many kisses and embraces."[29] Finally, Selleck Silliman assured his lonesome wife in 1776 that her letters did not make her "a fond Hussey." He thanked her for "being so particular in your Letters the more prolix the better; are You not a married Woman my Dearest, may You not delight your Husband with saying to him just what you please?"[30]

Such worldly passion, for some, paled in comparison to the heavenly love of God.[31] In the seventeenth and early eighteenth centuries more than in later years, men carefully included a caveat in their declarations of affection. John Winthrop often referred to his wife, Margaret as "more dear to me than all earthly things." He was careful to follow his loving words with a reminder to himself as well as to his wife to value salvation more than earthly delights.

> I pray God that these earthly blessings of mariage, healthe, friendship, etc, may increase our estimation of our better & onely ever duringe happinesse in heaven, & may quicken up our appetite thereunto accordinge to the worth thereof: O my sweet wife, let us rather hearken to the advise of our lovinge Lord who calles upon us first to seeke the kingdom of God, & tell us that one thinge is needfull, & so as without it the gaine of the whole world is nothinge: rather then to looke at the frothye wisdome of this worlde & the foolishnesse of such examples as propounde outwarde prosperitye for true felicitye.—God keepe us that we never swallowe this baite of Sathan: but let us looke unto the worde of God & cleave fast unto it, & so shall we be safe.³²

Love for a spouse should not distract a pious man from his primary task of glorifying God and seeking his favor. Thomas Shepard, later a Cambridge, Massachusetts, divine, almost lost his wife in childbirth due to "an vnskilfull midwife." The pious Shepard thought his wife's affliction in 1633 was the Lord's response to his sinfulness. "I began to grow secretly proud & full of sensuallity delighting my soule in my deare wife more then in my god." The Lord "learnt me to desire to feare him more, & to keepe his dread in my heart."³³

Men spoke most eloquently and passionately about their love for their wives on their wedding anniversaries, at the birth of a child, and when separated by the exigencies of war. These events made a man take pause and describe his feelings. An anniversary prompted a tender husband to thank God for his good fortune. When the fear and joy of childbirth loomed, a man again examined his heart. When war threatened his life, he recorded his most intimate thoughts about husbandly love and duty.

Ezra Stiles, minister, educator, and future president of Yale, remarked in his diary in 1775, "This day 1757 I and my Wife were married. She has been a great Blessing to me; may the blessed God continue her a Blessing." The next entry in Stiles's diary explained the timing of the first. He acknowledged, "My wife very ill."[34] A husband marked an anniversary when the happiness of their wedding day contrasted with the less happy present. Boston merchant John Tudor observed in 1748, "This day we have been Marred 16 Years, and by the goodness of God to our Famaly and Us, we have not had one Death in it til Yesterday Died our Negro Man Named Town."[35] Although focusing on God's mercy, Tudor clearly feared that his wife or other family members might be next. Samuel Sewall recorded in 1711, "This being my Marriage-day, and having now liv'd in a married Estate Five and Thirty years." He celebrated the event by retreating into his "Closet" for "Meditation and Prayer" and later attending a friend's funeral. The previous week he had lamented the recent deaths of "ancient friends."[36] His own continued life and marriage made his anniversary a time of solemn thankfulness. Cotton Mather was less fortunate, as his anniversary in 1702 marked his impending widowhood. "When I had been married unto her just sixteen Years, (and as near as I can recollect, on that very Week, sixteen Years, that I was married unto her) God began to take her from me."[37] His wife languished and finally died due to complications from a miscarriage.

When husband and wife were apart on an anniversary, written expressions of love replaced private commemoration. Ebenezer Parkman, minister and farmer in Westborough, Massachusetts, in September 1746, lamented the "Foul Weather" and the absence of his wife. Visiting her parents she left him "dull without my Dear Consort." He reminisced: "But how Ardent and United were we this Day Nine Year ago! when our Nuptials were Celebrated at Mr. Pierpoints at Boston. The Lord has pleas'd to overlook the many miscarriages and Defects which we have been chargeable with since, especially my own! and make us Mutually Blessings, and Helps to the Kin of God! O how soon the Time will come when there will be neither marrying nor giving in Marriage, but the Saints shall be as the Angels of God!"[38] Selleck Silliman found himself away from home on his wedding anniversary in 1780. He wrote to his disappointed wife: "I am sorry to inform You, that I have no Prospect of keeping our happy Anniversary with You,—I hope You will have a Pleasure in observing it, in the Company of our Dear Sons, & Friends that I expect will be with You Each of whom I hope will think it an Anniversary that deserves Commemoration. My Love & Compliments to them respectively,—I regret the Occasion that keeps me from my Dearest at such a Time,— A Time ever to be observed by me with Delight & Pleasure."[39] An anniversary was properly shared and celebrated together.

John Tudor was among the fortunate to be married to "the beloved Wife of my Youth" for fifty years. On his anniversary in 1782 he recorded in his diary, "we have lived the whole time very comfortably and at this Day are so." He marked the dear legacies of their long life together. "In our Youthfull Days had Six Children, 3 Sons and 3 Daughters, but our two Eldest Sons died at Sea." His surviving children provided him with "12 Grandsons and 4 Granddaughters, but we have lost by Death 6 Grandsons" and one granddaughter. This loving couple in fifty years had "never, in all that Time, been absent from each other more than 5 Weeks at one time." They marked the day with "an Entertainment for our Children, and their Children, and a lovely Sight and Day we had of it."[40]

A husband was poignantly reminded of his love for his wife as the dangers of childbirth approached.[41] Even though the risk of loss was great most men remained strangely removed from this stage of the human drama. Childbirth was a female-centered effort and celebration. A woman had her female relatives, friends, and a midwife by her side.[42] Her husband waited anxiously, often close by, listening to his wife's groans and awaiting the outcome. Still, men were knowledgeable about pregnancy, childbirth, and their complications.[43] Left on the periphery, however, a husband felt fragile.

A man prayed his wife would be a "Living mother of a Living Child."[44] Michael Wigglesworth, minister in Malden, Massachusetts, received the news of his daughter's birth after his wife's thirty hours of hard labor in 1655. "After about midnight he [the Lord] sent me the glad tidings of a daughter that an[d] the mother both living."[45] Ebenezer Parkman recorded in his diary in 1747 that "About 7 o'Clock a.m. a Fourth living Son was born, and my wife liv'd through it and becomes Comfortable through the tender Mercy and Goodness of God."[46] Women were acutely aware that childbirth meant potential death, but husbands also trembled at the thought of their own widowhood. One night in spring 1760 both Benjamin Bangs and his wife had trouble sleeping: "My Dearest friend is much Concern'd being in and near a time of Dificulty & Dreamd a Dream that troubl'd Her much I put it off Slightly for fear of Disheartning Her but Directly upon it Dream'd much ye Same my Self of Being Bereft of Her & Seeing my Little motherless Children about me which when I awoke was Cutting to think of."[47] He had the same anxiety-ridden dreams as she.

A husband was involved in assembling the birth assistants. When Ebenezer Parkman's wife went into labor in 1740 he went to get the midwife and the women who would attend her. Confronted with a snowstorm as he went to "fetch Granny Forbush," the midwife, he found the snow so deep that it was "extraordinary difficult passing." When he found himself floundering in front of a neighbor's house he enlisted the aid of two men of the house who "rode before me, by which means I succeeded." Local men brought their wives and a load of wood to help with the snowbound birth.[48] In 1738 at another birth, Parkman summoned the midwife and other women when his wife "call'd Me up by her extreme pains prevailing upon her and changing into signs of Travail." The women came and stayed "all Day and Night." The following morning "the Women Scattered away to their several Homes" except the midwife who stayed behind. Late that night he was again "call'd . . . with great earnestness to gather some women together." The weather was bitter, but he "ran on foot" to assemble the women.[49] Peter Thatcher, minister in Milton, Massachusetts, realized his wife "was very ill" and sent a neighbor for the midwife in winter 1682/83. It took two hours for her to arrive because she was attending another birth. When "shee came shee sent for ye women."[50] The young Samuel Sewall awoke in early April 1677, at two in the morning, and "perceived my wife ill." He lit a candle and raked the fire. At five, when his in-laws woke, he informed his mother-in-law of his wife's condition. She "bad me call the Midwife."[51]

With the women assembled, the husband waited and prayed. As Parkman put it, "I resign my Dear Spouse to the infinite Compassions, allsufficiency and soverign pleasure of God and under God to the good Women that are with her, waiting Humbly the Event."[52] Although peripheral, he was still aware of the progress of the delivery. The overly sympathetic Michael

Wigglesworth probably would have preferred ignorance: "The nearnes of my bed to hers made me hear all the nois. her pangs pained my heart, broke my sleep the most off that night, I lay sighing, sweating, praying, almost fainting through wearines before morning. The next day. the spleen much enfeebled me, and setting in with grief took away my strength, my heart was smitten within me, and as sleep departed from myne eyes so my stomack abhorred meat. I was brought very low and knew not how to pass away another night; For so long as my love lay crying I lay sweating, and groaning." This was his first child. He pondered that if childbirth were so painful "then how dreadful are the pangs of eternal death."[53]

Samuel Sewall stayed with his mother-in-law in the kitchen during a birth in 1694. She had joined his male vigil because "my wife was in great and more than ordinary Extremity, so that she was not able to endure the [bed]Chamber."[54] At a previous birth, Samuel Sewall and his father-in-law waited in the "great Hall" where they "heard the child cry."[55] Cotton Mather tried to sleep through his wife's labor in 1699 so that he could attend to his sabbath business the next day. He awoke "with a Concern upon my Spirit" and felt compelled to pray in his study. "While my Faith was pleading, that the Saviour *who was born of a Woman,* would send His good Angel to releeve my Consort, the People ran to my Study-door with Tidings, *that a Son was born unto mee.*"[56]

With the child born, the women settled down to a repast organized by the grateful husband. Samuel Sewall feasted his wife's attendants with "rost Beef and minc'd Pyes, good Cheese and Tarts."[57] The women assisting Ebenezer Parkman's wife finished eating before dark "tho some of them tarry'd in the Evening."[58] Slowly the women went home either by foot or by horse. Samuel Sewall "Went home with the Midwife about 2 o'clock, carrying her Stool, whoes parts were included in a

Bagg. Met with the Watch at Mr. Rocks Brew house, who bad[e] us stand, enquired what we were. I told the Woman's occupation, so they bad[e] God bless our labours, and let us pass."[59]

War, like childbirth, was life threatening and galvanized a man's feelings. With visits rare, some couples were separated for years with letters as their only link. Wartime letters, therefore, provide a rare glimpse of private expressions of love in colonial New England.

Selleck and Mary Silliman waited anxiously for correspondence from one another during the Revolution. Mary described her vigil: "Last night about sunset the horses I saw come up to the door, I went swiftly to meet the lads that brought them, hopeing for a letter from my Beloved, but was told they had not any; still I hop'd I had one on the road, or in Town, and should receive it at meeting; and this morning my expectations were rais'd on seeing an Officer ride up to the Gate he immediately presented me with a letter, which I made no doubt was yours, but after he was gone found it was from our dear Son only."[60] Selleck also waited anxiously for news from home.

> I have heard nothing from You my Love since your Dear Favour by Brother Deodate, I trust there are more on the Road, and that they will by & by find their Way to your expecting Husband, who with longing Expectation looks out for every Man that comes into Camp from the Eastward; with (as soon as they get within Reach) how do you do Sir?, did You come through Fairfield? Have You any Letters for me? and the Answer is a great Part of the Time No. and on Inquiry I find that even our Neighbours are many times so thoughtless that they come away

to our Camp and never say a Word to You that they are comeing; I tell them sometimes I wish them to be for a while absent from their Dearest Connections that they might learn how important it is in those Circumstances for a Man to hear—frequently from a Beloved Wife & Dear Children, it is the greatest Pleasure I know in this World.[61]

Mary and Selleck both yearned for news of one another's safety and the accompanying relief from their loneliness. The threat of loss made wartime correspondence poignant, and the emotional expressions uniquely revealing.

When called to war, a husband performed his duty to his country but also to his family. Selleck Silliman explained to his wife in 1777, "the Safety of our Country requires this Sacrifice of our domestick Delights." He assured her he would return home "as soon as the Duty we all at this Time owe, to our Country, for its Defence and for the Defence of the Dear Wives of our Bosoms, and our Dear Children will allow of it."[62] Love of wife and country seemed obviously linked to Selleck. Mary, who gave birth to their two children while he was away, was less sure. She wanted him to "run home" before his "Time is out."[63]

David Waterbury, Stamford, Connecticut, farmer and major in the Continental army, also spoke of war as a duty owed his family. When he and his wife parted in 1775, Mary Waterbury was convinced it was "our Last farewell." He responded that "I hope I shall Do my Duty Stand or fall I put my trust in God to Defend me in the Day of Battle." If it was his "Lot Never to se you more" he hoped she would do her "Duty to Wards your Self & the Children."[64] This was little consolation to Mary. "I dont think I [k]new any body Lived a more Lonesome Life than I do in Your absence." William Henshaw explained his responsibilities to his wife Phebe in 1776: "I am as Happy here as

I can expect to be whilst absent from my Family & which any thing would tempt me to consent to, but the G[lorious] Cause we are engag'd in, but who my Dear could [remain] at home in peace & enjoy himself when every[thing] that renders life dear is at stake."[65] Without fulfilling his duty to his country a man could not hope to do his duty as husband.

Not all marriages were happy and not all husbands were loving. Even for a couple blessed with a strong union conflicts arose. The worst that a disgruntled wife could do, even in a marriage characterized by loving partnership, was to challenge a man's authority as family head. If he was further humiliated as a cuckold or even beaten, the damage was severe. In such cases, a woman took aim at her husband's most valued commodity—his reputation. The loss of his good name could lead to social humiliation. His livelihood, so dependent on personal networks, suffered if familial conflict became public.[66] When men were challenged they turned to the familiar rhetoric of male authority.

An ideal wife did not disturb the peace of a household. Mather Byles, from his pulpit in New London, Connecticut, wrote to his spinstered sister, Mary, about his new wife in 1762. He described the "Peace & Tranquility" of his home. If only Mary could be so happy in her marriage. "That your Husband may say of you, as I can of your Sister *Byles,* that he never saw your Brows wrinkled into a disagreeable Frown, or your Lips polluted by a peevish Syllable."[67] Selleck Silliman listed the wonderful qualities of his first wife to the father of his second in 1775. He wanted to assure his new father-in-law that he had been happily married and that his new wife miraculously compensated him for his loss.[68] Among her gifts was "a most happy, mild & calm Temper." With such a disposition "she never gave her Husband any Uneasiness by any Excess of her own Temper." Recalling the many merits of his recently deceased wife in 1736, Thomas Clap, minister and later president of Yale college, remembered that not "so much as Short Word ever pass between us upon any Occasion whatsoever." If they disagreed "about any lesser matters, we used to Discourse upon it with a Perfect Calmness & Pleasancy."[69]

Any expression of temper in a woman was a sign of trouble. An angry wife by definition challenged a husband's right to rule. John Adams recorded a "conjugal Spat" between his father and mother in 1758 that caused such a ruckus that he was forced to leave the room and take "up Tully to compose myself." At the center of the conflict was a young girl, Judah, slated to board in the Adams household. The real issue was that the elder John Adams had made a commitment that increased Susanna Adams's workload but brought little to the family coffers. After heated discussion "My P[apa]. continued cool and pleasant a good while, but had his Temper roused at last, tho he uttered not a rash Word, but resolutely asserted his Right to govern." Mrs. Adams's response was less than deferential: "My Mamma was determined to know what my P. charged a Week for the Girls Board. P. said he had not determined what to charge but would have her say what it was worth. She absolutely refused to say. But 'I will know if I live and breath. I can read yet. Why dont you tell me, what you charge? You do it on purpose to teaze me. You are mighty arch this morning. I wont have all the Towns Poor brought here, stark naked, for me to clothe for nothing. I wont be a slave to other folks folk for nothing.'— And after the 2 Girls cryed.—'I must not speak a Word [to] your Girls, Wenches, Drabbs. I'le kick both their fathers, presently. [You] want to put your Girls over me, to make me a slave to your Wenches.'" Asserting his right to rule did little to defuse the situation. According to the younger John Adams this was the normal course of their disagreements—she raged and he remained cool. "Cool Reasoning upon the Point with my Father, would soon bring her to his mind or him to hers."[70] When a man was backed into the corner he declared himself ruler.

Richard Prey appeared in a Salem court in 1647/48 to answer charges that he had beaten his wife. Among the witnesses was Jabisch Hackett who had seen him try to hit her with a large stick, kick her across a room and throw a "porridge dish" at her. Prey's wife had contradicted him in front of neighbors saying that he had profaned the Lord's Day with his swearing and cursing. This enraged Prey. One brave soul tried to intervene. "Some one present told Prey that the court would not allow him to abuse his wife so, and he answered that he did not care for the court and if the court hanged him for it he would do it. It was said to him that the court would make him care, for they had tamed as stout hearts as his, and Prey answered that if ever he had trouble about abusing his wife, he would cripple her and make her sit on a stool, and there he would keep her." His justification for his behavior was "that he would beat her twenty times a day before she would be his master." The court fined him "10s. for swearing, 10s. for cursing, 20s. for beating his wife, and 40s. for contempt of court, or to be whipped at the Iron works."[71] Obviously, contempt of court was the most serious charge. A husband had the legal authority to physically correct his wife; the issue here as in all such cases, was simply one of degree.[72]

The center of the maelstrom that surrounded the marriage of Edward and Betteris Berry was financial control. Married previously, Betteris negotiated a prenuptial agreement with her new husband to protect her property from being claimed by him as the law allowed. Edward assured her at the time that he "desired nothing of my estate he desired nothing but my person." After the ceremony, Edward apparently changed his mind and wanted to void the agreement. She refused and so he began his campaign to force her into compliance. He told a friend "that if I would not give up ye writings that were made between us he would make me weary of my life & so indeed I found it." She left the house with his consent in 1676 because she was "not able to liue with such a Tyrant." The court ordered them to "live together according to God's ordinance" or face a fine of £5. She complied, but appeared in court a year later to obtain relief from his drunken rages. She had tried to persuade him to "live in Love & unity as other Folks doe." He responded by calling her an "old cheating Rogue" and hoped "The Divell take thee." Berry enlisted the help of his son who threatened to throw her down the stairs and destroyed a chest of drawers she had brought to the marriage. In Berry's view his treatment of his wife was justified, "she should have nothing of him because he had nothing of hers."[73] He could not abide his wife having the power to decide his financial future; this was a husband's prerogative. He felt foolish for relinquishing his financial prerogatives before marriage and wanted his masculine privileges returned.

The difficult third marriage of Cotton Mather to Lydia Lee George in 1715 floundered in part because of Mather's compulsive devotion to work. He often spent his entire day in his study, emerging only to pray with the family and eat. His wife finally left him in the midst of an argument.[74] Her rage seemed like a "Satanical Possession" to Mather. "After a thousand unrepeatable Invectives, compelling me to rise at Midnight, and retire to my Study that I might there pour out my Soul unto the Lord; she also gott up in a horrid Rage, protesting that she would never live or stay with me; and calling up her wicked Niece and Maid, she went over to a Neighbour's House for Lodging." His children joined him in a "Vigil" of songs and prayers until the house finally went to bed as the sun rose.

When his wife's frustrations reached their zenith she took aim at her enemy's weak point. She exposed their differences to public scrutiny thereby attacking his "Esteem in the World" and threatening the "Success of my Ministry."[75]

Jacob Eliot found himself in a similarly contentious marriage when he approached the altar in 1760 at age sixty with his young bride, Ann Blackleach. This Lebanon, Connecticut, minister discovered his wife had little patience for his devotion to spiritual work. Her anger flared when he refused to allow her to enter his study because he was "Engaged deeply in Devotion." She aimed to wound. "You are no more fit to go into a Pulpit than the Devil Himself." After one battle he got angry and threatened to "Complain to her Friends & expose Her." Her equivalent threat was to "expose me to all the Parish."[76]

The elder John Adams knew he could not take in boarders unless his wife willingly provided the domestic service necessary for their support. Richard Prey knew that nothing short of crippling his wife could assure her dependence and his control. Edward Berry knew he could not overturn a prenuptial contract without his wife's approval, and this reduced him to coercion and cruelty. Domestic disputes tested the limits of a man's power, leaving him frustrated and angrily insisting upon his right to rule.

Women upset the balance of power in the household most vividly with sexual betrayal. A promiscuous wife not only publicly humiliated her husband, but threatened the legitimacy of his children. Cuckolded men were aberrant and despised.[77] In law, the penalties applied to an adulterous woman exceeded the punishment meted out to her male counterpart. In the early laws of Massachusetts, for example, a woman who had sex with a man other than her husband was considered an adulteress, a crime punishable by death. For a man, such sexual impropriety was labeled simply fornication and was penalized by a fine or whipping.[78] Women were told that philandering husbands should be ignored or at least tolerated.[79] A cuckold, however, received scolding from his community rather than sympathy. He was a fallen man unable to control his wife's behavior. Among the European elite, such a husband was unfit for public office. In European villages he was subject to public shaming rituals.[80] Men who suffered from their wife's adultery endured public ridicule as well as private pain.

Laurence Turner struggled to regain his honor in the face of his adulterous wife's flagrant behavior in 1650. He came to court to try and end the gossip, if not her sexual propensities. John Chackswell, a witness in his defamation suit and a boarder in the Turner home, recounted a sexual dalliance that occurred in Turner's absence. Sarah Turner "in a sporting way, throw water at one Tobias Saunders" also a boarder in the Turner household. "Sauders, who was looking in at the window, ran into the house and took said Sarah in his arms and assaulted her." A female neighbor came to the door and was also assaulted by Saunders and John Smith. Thomas Billings "came in from the forge" and was pushed into the sexual fray. Chackswell "being troubled, rebuked them saying, 'Heere is good doeings, take heed wt you doe' and went to an upper chamber, not countenancing their lascivious acts." Sarah Turner was also reported to have enticed Roger Tyler with her carnal language. She called to him as he left his house, "Tyler you have eaten Turnopps." He replied "Thou Lyest Turners Wife." She challenged him "Come hethr & let mee kisse thee & then I'le tell yee." Laurence Turner challenged his neighbors' testimony in court. He wanted to redeem his reputation if not his marriage.[81]

William Beale went to Ipswich court in 1670 to end the idle talk about his wife and their servant Benjamin Chandler. William Beale had "warned" Chandler out of his house. According to Goody Beale, "her husband was jealous of him.

Further, she said that her husband said all her children were bastards save one." William Beale went looking for his former servant. When he found him at the neighboring Chandler farm "he took an ax and beat down Benjamin Chandler's cabin to try to expel him." The court case, however, involved not adultery or assault, but slander and defamation. William Beale brought William Hollingworth to court "in behalf of his wife" because Mary Doninge heard from Alexander Giligan that Mrs. Hollingworth "said to Beale's wife that her husband would not join the church so long as such as she was in it." Beale's concern was scandal. He did not want the reputation of being a cuckold.[82] The damage of the town rumormongers threatened these men as much if not more than their wives' real or imagined infidelities.

Like the cuckold, a husband beaten by his wife suffered public ridicule. In early modern France and England it was common to make such a man, like his cuckolded counterpart, ride backward on a donkey holding the donkey's tail. Like his backward ride, the man who endured such treatment reversed the natural order of things and reinforced it for those who gathered. The woman who did the beating rarely received social censure. To go to court to stop such abuse or even to acknowledge publicly such treatment was not an option for most men.[83]

Jacob Eliot fought bitterly with his second wife, Ann, in the 1760s. He kept an extraordinarily detailed record of their confrontations. By recording their battles, Eliot not only carefully justified his behavior but provided evidence that he had acted justly in the face of great provocation. According to Eliot, Ann tormented and abused him. "She flew into the most Violent passion imaginable, & with her fist doubled, fell upon me & struck me with all her might, upon my Head & Breast, arm & shoulder, half a Dozen times or more." A similar outburst demanded his reaction when his wife "flew into the utmost Rage

& fury again, Calling me a Cursed Devil Kicked at Me, & struck me with her Fist again, & took up a Powder Horn, to strike me over the Head with, but defending my self, I warded off the blow."[84] At the height of a confrontation that ended with her attempted suicide, Ann "Strook me with her Fist as hard as She could in the face, & about my Head & Belly several times & hurt me very much (especially with one Stroke in my face which I felt very sore for several Days after)." She even tried to kill him when she "took me by the throat, got both her hands into the handkerchief about my Neck, & try'd, with all her might, to twist it round to Choak me." She threatened to tell the neighbors about "my abuse to Her, twitching & halling her about to kill her, when only to defend my self & prevent Her runing away to destroy her Self, I, as gently as I could Sometimes took hold of her Arms or Cloaths."[85] Eliot very carefully noted that he met her physical abuse with restraint.

Ann's anger relentlessly found fault in her husband. "I can't Speak loud to a Servant, or so much as mend the fire, but Snubbed and reproved Sharply."[86] To Jacob her railings were "all for nothing, or for the least trifle in the world."[87] Eliot described what he considered the ridiculous circumstances that roused his wife's ire: "My Singing to the Child to get him to sleep (being mad before) cry'd out with great Vehemence & Spight, o don't don't don't don't Mr. Eliot make that noise! I am almost killed with it already &c—Soon after She letting a rousing Fart, I pleasingly & Jocosely Said that was as bad a Noise I thought as my Singing, at which She flew into a prodigious Rage, & wished She had dy'd in her Cradle, before She had been bro't into so much Trouble &c."[88] Of course her real provocations even the long-suffering Jacob knew only too well. From her cutting remarks, she clearly resented his absorption in his studies and his pious condescension toward her. She often vented her anger by "trifling, Jesting & playing with

Sacred things" to provoke a response. He would quote scriptures during their confrontations "by way of Caution or advice, with a design to expound upon it—[she] not staying to hear me out, but turning quick & in great rage replying—Shitt of the Text."[89]

In addition, Ann was obsessed with the fear her elderly husband would die and leave her and her child with few resources. Eliot had two children from his first marriage who also needed part of their father's estate. Ann and Jacob married in 1760. They had two sons: Joseph, born in 1762, and John, born in 1764. She understandably urged Jacob to revise his will to include his second family. After her first son was born she became consumed with worry that "her & Jose [would be] . . . left destitute." Jacob dismissed her concerns saying, "I intended to take Care about [you] . . . as soon as I could Conveniently." Her long-standing request being again deferred threw Ann into a "most Violent & uncurbed passion."[90] In the midst of another confrontation she declared that his son Jacob, by his first wife, "might be content with what he had got, for he should have no more. . . . He had much more than his part already, & She would Say it to all the World."[91] These real worries and provocations produced great frustration in Ann causing her to lash out verbally as well as physically. Her urgency was well founded, her sixty-six-year-old husband died in 1766 only six years after their wedding day.

Jacob's anger was more than fury at his wife's violence; it was rage at his own weakness. He did get angry and thunder back at her, but he considered this a defeat. "I shew'd some heat & anger (God forgive me)."[92] Or when he answered her with "some Zeal" he justified himself with the aside, "it is marvellous I have born so much."[93] He also berated himself for giving in to her demands. When she refused to sleep with him, he "(like a Fool for Peace Sake) Consented & Submitted."[94] His passive responses may have fanned the fires, however. After ordering him not to touch her in bed saying he "Stank so Devilishly she could not bare me," he responded with cutting kindness: "I bore all with invincible patience & for the most part Silence—at last without the least Ruffle I faced my Dear—if by a few words you will say what will pacify you, & put an end to the Controversy, that we might go to Sleep in peace & love—otherwise, I was resolved by the Grace of Heaven, to Disappoint the Devil & Her, by not being Mad, let her say what She would."[95] He turned the other cheek because he, in his mind, was strong. The martyred Jacob at times, however, had the uneasy feeling that he was in fact "a page, or Servant" in his own home.[96] At the conclusion of one of their many quarrels in their bedchamber, Ann "with Sovereign Authority said, I command you to go & lie up Chamber." He "laugh'd, & reply'd, that she had expressly inverted the Sacred Text . . . Husbands obay your Wives." His laughter was soon replaced by a "profound silence" which he broke by begging her "to admit me to bed."[97] A furious wife could threatened the natural order. An abused man's shame led to silence and private humiliation.

When a man married he risked not only his heart, but his reputation. Marriages, particularly for the men examined here, were based on both a loving partnership and male dominance. The question of whether one or the other dictated marriage patterns in a given place and time overshadows the obvious; both were always present. For the men studied here these two imperatives did not seem contradictory. By the end of the eighteenth century more open expression of sentiment was certainly encouraged, but loving expressions characterized male writings throughout the colonial period. The less articulate men, emerging in court documents at least, also struggled with the proper balance of affection and control. Unless the scales were properly weighed, a man suffered social censure. An unhappy marriage threatened a man's power both in his own home and in the broader community. If a woman dared to challenge his authority through adultery or abuse he became an object of open ridicule. As an insufficient husband he became an inadequate member of society.

4

Provider

Men in colonial New England were providers but not absentee breadwinners. In the nineteenth century, the white, middle-class, American man left the farm for the public world of work.[1] In contrast, income-producing work was shared in the interdependent families of colonial New England. Within this reality of shared providing, however, a man felt a unique obligation to support his family. This was society's expectation as well: providing was a husband's legal responsibility, his sacred duty, and his unique burden. He provided what was "needful" according to his resources. When a family faced economic hardship the courts and the religious community turned to the husband for remedy. In the end, the husband was the responsible party.

In practice, to be a good provider a husband needed the cooperation and support of his wife. His new wife was an "excellent OEconomist," Rev. Mather Byles of New London assured his sister Mary in 1762.[2] Rev. Thomas Shepard of Cambridge, reflecting on his wife's death in 1646, extolled her "great prudence to take care for & order my family affayres being neither too lauish nor sordid in any thing so that I knew not what was vnder her hands."[3] Cotton Mather's wife Abigail ably handled their joint financial concerns. This well-known Boston divine listed his wife's charms in 1701 making note of "her *Discretion* in ordering my and her Affairs, and avoiding every thing that might be dishonourable to either of us."[4] Women monitored and managed family resources. If frugal, a wife could stretch a meager budget to cover a growing family's expenses.

In describing the circumstances of his brother Roland, minister of a poor parish in Sandwich, Massachusetts, from 1694 to his death more than twenty-five years later, Josiah Cotton remarked, "Notwithstanding the Smallness of his Salary & the largeness [of] his family, yet, by the blessing of God on his own prudence & his excellent wife's industry &c he lived very handsomely & brought up his children so."[5] Such a wife was indeed an asset and a necessity if a man's efforts as provider were to be successful.

Theodore Foster, a lawyer born in Brookfield, Massachusetts, dubbed his wife in 1773, "the Partner of My Fortune."[6] Josiah Cotton of Plymouth, Massachusetts summarized his mother's duties in his diary from the mid-eighteenth century. She "managed Secular affairs (most of which Past through her hands) with Singular Prudence And Industry." She took on her husband's duties "in my Fathers absence." Finally, she "by private advice and Discourse was a helper to my Father in the work of the Gospel."[7] In this kind of union, a husband had a companion who could ease his financial responsibilities and remove him from the cares of household management.

In most families, a wife had to provide an income, not just manage her husband's. Women helped support their families in occupations ranging from midwife to seamstress. Most women, however, made their financial contributions through marginal occupations with meager pay and received little in the way of steady income. They also exchanged their labor and goods with neighbors.[8] Families patched together monies generated by husband, wife, and children to provide a competency for the whole.

In Watertown, Massachusetts, in 1712/13, "Nicholes Wyeth & his Wife" were given "three Bushields of Indien Corn for their Relief in their Necessitous Condition." The town also assigned a kind of guardian "to inspect sd Nicholes Wyeth & his

Wife that they do not Idle away & mispend their time but that they follow some honest Imploy According to their Ability towards their Relief & Support."[9] A wife's work was essential and expected. Ashley Bowen of Marblehead struggled, along with his wife, in the 1760s, to support their family in the competitive marketplace of that bustling seaport. As a rigger he was undercut by the less skilled but cheaper "jobbers" who captured what business there was. This forced him to follow suit. "Between jobbing at rigging and my wife's making color[s] we touch and go. Poor times with us." When his wife died, his second wife continued the flag-making business.[10] Both incomes were essential.

John Tilison was sentenced to "the house of correction" by an Ipswich court in 1657, but the court proved merciful that day; his sentence was commuted and he instead ordered "to liue with his wife & pvyde for her according to his place as a husband ought to doe."[11] Despite the reality of shared providing, only the man was legally bound to support his family. A woman brought her dower to marriage and a man, in turn, promised to supply her needs.[12] Benjamin Woodrow petitioned the Salem court in 1661 for a respite from a 40s. fine. Paying off his obligation, even in installments, Woodrow found untenable. He told the court, "much difficulty payd the first 40s., cannot se any possible way how he could be able to pay the other in regard of his pouerty." He was impeded by "hauing a wife & 2 smal children & nothinge where with to relieue them but my daylie labour." The court acknowledged the priority of providing for his family and released him from his financial obligation.[13]

A husband had to provide even after a marriage ended. In cases of divorce or separation a man still had to support his family.[14] Most divorce cases actually sprang from a concern over adequate providing.[15] Women could and did sue for "neglect of duty" or nonsupport.[16] In addition, desertion, the most common cause for divorce in eighteenth-century Connecticut, also concerned issues of providing. A man who left his family for "parts of the world unknown" was unlikely to feel compelled to contribute.[17] The courts were more than attentive to a woman and her children in such circumstances. A wife claiming nonsupport or desertion received a divorce and the freedom to remarry. A family without a male provider could become a public charge. If a woman remarried she might remedy her precarious circumstances by choosing a better provider. In addition, a divorced woman could try to provide for herself and her children free of husbandly interference. Divorce allowed her to regain control over her own wages,[18] and she also got back her dowry as if the marriage had never occurred.[19] Her husband, however, as the guilty party, was barred from remarriage.[20] In this way, society could be spared the expense of shoring him up again.

A man also had to provide for his illegitimate family.[21] Colonial New England courts relentlessly pursued the identity of fathers of children born out of wedlock. A swelling belly proved a mother's guilt; a father's name had to be discovered.[22] As the eighteenth century progressed, failed providing—not morality—became increasingly important in such cases. Illegitimate births began to appear as bastardy, rather than fornication, cases in court dockets.[23] A woman's sin was still moral. A man's sin was economic. Once found guilty, a woman endured the lash for her promiscuity; a man, however, was forced to take up his role as provider.[24] His failure, in the eyes of the court, left society chargeable.

Even after death, a man was expected to provide for his family. Many colonies, including Massachusetts and Connecticut, demonstrated the importance of the provider's role through their inheritance laws. A man's obligation to his wife, in particular, superseded all other claims. The widow's "third" was set aside before other debts were paid.[25] Through life estates, men carefully constructed legacies that provided economic continuity for their families.[26] A widow and her children, according to these provisions, would share the house, the harvest and the work.[27] A woman could not sell her legacy and the children could not inherit it until her death, ensuring that the family would continue to be bound together financially. If, however, the widow remarried, a new man took over her former husband's role as provider, and his legacies now went to the children. A man's obligations ended only with his wife's death or remarriage, whichever came first.

A husband received his mandate as provider from God as well as man. According to Benjamin Wadsworth in his 1712 sermon *The Well-Ordered Family*, a man "should contrive prudently and work diligently, that his Family, and his Wife particularly, may be well provided for." The power of this divine mandate surfaced in the case of Isaak Woodbery. The town of Beverly, Massachusetts, elected him to the position of constable in 1675. Woodbery refused to take the requisite oath of fidelity because he did not want the position. As a seaman he could not be both constable and provide for his family. "My Caling Is at sea wch as I have done heretofore soe I must still atend It In a constant way the greatest part of the year Constantly for the providing for my famely as the word of god Requires." When brought to court he pleaded that "he would be worse than an infidel in not providing for his family, if he was forced to take the office." Woodbery successfully persuaded the court of his sincerity and that his God-given role as family provider took precedence. A new election was ordered.[28]

A man had to provide for his wife and children; the courts insisted on this imperative despite divorce, illegitimacy, and even death. A man had the legal duty to make sure the family enterprise was successful. In times of crisis the law compelled a man to fulfill this duty. Finally, a religious man felt his role of provider was a sacred trust.

What constituted adequate providing? Certainly a family's basic needs had to be met. Richard Wharton asked his friend Wait Winthrop, still in New England, to look after his wife while he was away in Old England in 1688. He was concerned that her loneliness would make her "melancholy." He was also concerned about her material well-being. "I hope shee wants nothing that is conven[ien]t." The money he had left her "may be sufft for her supply without something extraordinary have brought some unexpected charge." In any case, Wharton asked his friend to make sure "shee want nothing needfull."[29]

In the protracted dispute between Edmund Berry and his wife Beatrice, the issue of providing "needfull" items for his wife stood at the center of the drama.[30] Beatrice was unwilling to give up a prenuptial agreement guaranteeing her separate estate. Edmund, infuriated by her refusal, reneged on his responsibilities as provider. As he put it, "she should have nothing of him because he had nothing of hers." According to his distressed wife the food he provided was inedible. He had an "absurd manner in eating his victualls." He took "his meat out of ye pickle; & broyleing it upon ye coales, & this he would tell me I must eate or else I must fast." In response she squirreled away "a Little of myne owne" or "I must haue perisht." Daily provisions of all sorts were lacking. "Neither will he allow me any necessary about house for decencey or that wch is absolutely needfull but am compelled to borrow of my neighbors."[31] At the least, a man should provide his wife and family with "needfull" supplies if not the accoutrements of "decencey."

What was considered needful obviously varied. Samuel Cooke found his salary hard to collect from his reluctant Stratfield, Connecticut, parishioners in 1745. On his death, his estate had an uncollected debt of £3,000.³² Although disheartened, he tried to focus on his good fortune. "I have necessary Food & Raiment and as yet can pay every man his Dues, & my Bread & Water is Sweet." He also noted his inability to provide "large Portions for my Children: tho I have little I have enough, and can quietly leave my Children to the Care of a Covenant keeping God."³³ He had food and clothing, he could pay his debts and still have a small legacy for his children; these things to Cooke's mind were "needful."

In a letter to his father-in-law, Selleck Silliman, a lawyer in Fairfield, Connecticut, described his financial circumstances after the Revolution: "The total Stop put to all my Bussiness for so long a Time,—the very great Expences that have attended my own Situation abroad—the inevitable Expences of Family at Home,—but above all the amazing Depreciation of our Mony, which diminished What Cash I left behind faster than all the other Matters did has however reduced us in Point of Cash somewhat low; but it is not quite gone." In an aside to his wife he wrote reassuringly, "But those are Trifles, my Dear Mrs Silliman, our Dear Children & Family, our Habitation and the Residue of our Substance are all safe,—tis enough I complain not, but desire to rejoice & give Thanks to our great Preserver."³⁴ Silliman celebrated the safety of his family, his home and his few assets that remained. Resources were slim but not insufficient.

An adequate maintenance for one's family was measured in relative terms. A good provider, however, lived within his means regardless of financial circumstances. Josiah Cotton took up housekeeping with his bride after his marriage in 1707/08. In the first year they spent £100 "in House keeping which somewhat exceeded our income." He remarked that "it is the duty & interest of every one to cut his Coat according to his Cloth."³⁵

A good provider kept his wife in the way she was accustomed, be that low or high. A number of men were brought to Ipswich court in 1653 to answer to accusations that their wives were wearing silk hoods. They had to prove that they were of sufficient social and economic stature to make such attire suitable for their consorts. Dressing above one's station out of vanity or fashion was chargeable. Each man came forward to assert that they were worth at least £200 as the law required.[36] Alternatively, some responded that their wives had been "brought up above the ordinary rank." The ideal, not always realized, was for a husband to provide his wife with the same comforts she knew in her father's house. "Neither coushens nor loue doth yet teach me to maintaine her worss then i found her except god be pleased by his prouidens to call us to a lower condishion then yet he is pleased to doe."[37] A good provider stayed within his means regardless of the size of his coffers and kept his wife in her accustomed finery whether homespun or silk.

The community monitored and judged a husband's efforts. When John Blanoe lost his wife Hanna, probably in childbirth, he struggled to provide for his truncated family. He took over the farm left to his wife and children by her father. His in-laws soon brought him to court for spoiling the property known as Darlin's farm. They claimed that "the houses and fences were ruined and the wood and timber carried away." According to these disgruntled relatives, he "had spent the estate by drinking rum and strong drink." Blanoe responded in court in 1677 that he paid rent of £10 a year to his children's benefit and "I haue not nor will I dispose of it for RUM &c. as the plaintiff from his durty mouth with other filth cast at me." The question in this case was not simply the inheritance law or proper farming, but whether or not Blanoe was a good provider.

Much of the testimony involved the maintenance of his motherless children. He put one child to a wet nurse whom he struggled to pay, while the others were cared for by a number of women he hired for the purpose. A boarder at the Blanoe home testified that the children "wanted for nothing but were maintained as well as most children. He caused to be made up a piece of cloth to clothe his children." Other neighbors likewise claimed that "they never heard him or the children complain of not having food and raiment, and said Blano provided as well for them as any other man thereabouts. He had several times bought quarters of mutton, butter, cheese and milk for them." The court agreed with the neighbors' in their assessments. He fed and clothed his children like "any other man."[38] He provided for his family within his means, and his community, if not his former in-laws, acknowledged his efforts.

To provide adequately for his family a man had to look to future as well as present needs. He had to provide for his wife and children even after his death. John Adams, when he was a lawyer in Braintree, Massachusetts, in 1770, marveled at his cousin Samuel's disregard for the future: "He says he never looked forward in his Life, never planned, laid a scheme, or formed a design of laying up any Thing for himself or others after him." John, in contrast, had "to ponder in my Youth, to consider of Ways and Means or raising a Subsistence, food and Rayment, and Books and Money to pay for my Education to the Bar." If not for this careful planning "I must have sunk into total Contempt and Obscurity, if not perished for Want, if I had not planned for futurity." He noted all men should "learn the Art of Living, early."[39]

Josiah Cotton felt the power of this obligation when he left his farm to return to school teaching. Initially he had thought, "that if God should take me away, my Family must be obliged to remove, because the business, that had so long detained me at town [school teaching] would not fall to their share." His reasoning was "To lay up something for my Children, for altho'

I had a considerable income at town, yet the badness of the money, & our being under a necessity of buying so much, eat up (as it were) all our gains; And at the Farm I expected to raise much of our own provisions &c."[40] The family's relocation to the farm failed to assure either their present or their future needs. The family reluctantly returned to town. Cotton turned to the prudent management of his property rather than manual labor. He made a note to himself "To manage the Farm better." Cotton juggled his assets to assure both his immediate and long-term ability to provide for his family.

The burden of the role of provider increased as a man's family grew. He labored to expand his wealth as marriage and parenthood put increasing demands on his resources. Cotton Mather lamented in 1708/09 that the "Largeness of my Family" led to financial hardship.[41] Aaron Cleaveland of Malden, Massachusetts, found his ministerial income in 1750 absorbed by "the Necessary Support" of his family: "I have been Exposed to great difficulties for my Support, both as to the Sallery Granted me, & long delay of Payment, while my Family hath been Growing & demanded large Supplies."[42] The burden of a provider increased as marriage and parenthood stretched fixed resources.

Ministers, in their seemingly constant struggle to extract pay from reluctant and overly frugal congregations, wrote much about their struggle for adequate compensation in the face of growing needs.[43] Ebenezer Parkman of Westborough, Massachusetts, needed a considerable increase in salary during the inflation-riddled 1740s to continue to support his family adequately. His church pressed him for a figure. He negotiated carefully, not wanting to undercut himself and hoping to get some of his salary in-kind to guard against future currency fluctuations. Finally the church insisted he "say what would I have to support my Family?" To Parkman's mind the sum could vary according to the church's "manner of Maintaining the Gospel." His people could provide him with a sum that "would barely do it; there was also what would do it with some handsomeness and Decency; and there was a manner of doing it with a Generousness, when persons were in their Hearts enlarged unto Bountifullness."[44] His congregation chose to "barely do it."

Philemon Robbins, a minister in Branford, Connecticut, found himself in similar circumstances in 1754. He also suffered from the same rising prices and a static salary. When he initially agreed to his salary of £140 "wheat was then not above 8 Shill a Bushell now is above 5 times 8 — Pork a groat [four pence[45]] a pound — now above 5 groats." He wanted his salary to reflect this level of price inflation and asked for £800 a year. He realized he would never gain wealth as a minister. "They yt preach the Gospel should live of the Gospel." Robbins also did not expect the church to provide for his sons who were away at school. Nonetheless "£700 a year will not maintain my present family." For Robbins, an adequate salary had to support his family still at home at the very least.[46]

Men suspected, and to some extent rightly so, that women judged them by their ability to provide; but they likewise judged themselves and others harshly in this regard. Dwight Foster, schoolteacher and future lawyer, writing from Northampton, Massachusetts, warned his sister Nabby in 1777 to "Look well — weigh every Circumstance maturely" before making the decision to marry. Her suitor was certainly a "worthy, well meaning, honest *Clever Fellow* — and I doubt not will make a good Husband." Her brother did, however, see a bit too much of himself in her beau. "It appears to Me however that his Salary will not maintain Him, especially with a Family, these hard Times — I find I cannot support Myself by my School and indeed have not done it for some Months."[47] To Foster this was a serious consideration and perhaps delayed him in making a similar decision.

Ebenezer Baldwin, writing from Yale in 1766, also teasingly counseled his sister, Bethiah, to marry quickly or risk being an old maid. He poked, "I should esteem it one Excellent Qualification in a Wife, to be able to Spin my Shirts." Such a skill procured a quality husband. "Let me caution you in one Particular, & then you may do as you like about living an old Maid Viz—not to be anxious for a very great Farm, get an agreeable Companion, the rest 'ant much. The Homespun Shirts I make no Doubt will procure a Worthy Man, but I cant say they will a rich one, for ye Rich dont need Wives to Spin."[48] He penned this letter as he struggled with his own relationship with Sophia Partridge. He felt unable to propose marriage to his beloved Sophia because of his precarious financial circumstances as he waited for a pulpit as a tutor at Yale.[49] Perhaps he secretly yearned for Sophia to spin his shirts and be satisfied with his companionship.

Poor providers were ridiculed. Cotton Mather expressed his disgust in 1712/13 at a group of "wretched, idle, gaming Fellowes in this Town, whose Families are starving in great miseries, while they are following vain Persons."[50] Their behavior was contemptible particularly because of their neglect of their families. John Adams described a poor provider in 1770 as a "softly living Thing that creepeth upon the face of the Earth." Adams had only disdain for the man who owned the boarding house where he lodged. Although the landlord had been blessed with education and a fine family name he instead "attempted Trade but failed in that—now keeps School and takes Boarders, and his Wife longs to be genteel, to go to Dances, Assemblies, Dinners, suppers &c.—but cannot make it out for Want thereof."[51] This man had deprived his family of their rightful status. Whether rakish or slothful, failed providers received nothing but scorn.

Cotton Mather described his son-in-law Nathan Howell as "the worst Husband on Earth." His free use of money led to many debts that remained unpaid at his premature death in 1716. The settling of this estate fell to Mather who through marriage became the stepfather of Howell's widow. He scoffed, "Had he lived, he had soon brought a Noble to a Nine-pence."[52] Lucy Lechmere, concerned over her son's poor business sense, wrote to his father-in-law, Wait Winthrop, in 1716. Having arrived in England without the wherewithal to pay his debts, her son "blasted" his credit, and "twill be a difficult matter to revive it." She lay the blame at her son's feet. "I am sure Thom was sett out into ye world in as good circumstances as most younger bros., & plac'd in a house of as good busyness; therefor his parents are not to be blam'd, & I hope he dos not want capassity." She worried over his ability to provide for his family: "His famely now is not very few, & in all probability may increase, & tis his duty to take care to provide ym (wch I don't see how yt can be dun in ye way Tom has liv'd for some years)." She appealed to Winthrop to provide an early inheritance for his daughter to help the prodigal. "Fine horses quickly eat out their heads, & are only fitt for men of great estates; therfor not proper for Thom, I fear."[53]

Drink was often the handmaiden of the poor provider. Thomas Mirick and his wife having "differed to a great degree" divided their "stuff and children" as they prepared to live separately in 1762, now bereft of "all naturall affections and conjugall love" for one another. Benjamin Bangs painted the sad scene. "All in confusion and moving and parting we argued begged and coucild them: and stopt the carts etc for the present: a most unhappy sight to behold." The "first moving cause" for the couples' estrangement was "drink and poverty: I believe both to blame."[54]

John Sherman left a series of draft letters, written in the 1790s, concerning his troubled, alcohol-laced marriage on the back side of payroll lists for the Third Connecticut Regiment. To his father he admitted that he frequented the local tavern too much for his wife's liking. "It is true I have ~~been intemperate~~ given way to intemperance which is the worst of all medicines to restore a Sick mind." He claimed, however, that although "Insane not heated with Intemperance" the fault lay with his wife, Rebecca, because of her "Ill treatment" of him.[55] "I charge all my Misfortunes since leaving the Army to her. I return from there with honour & Riches."[56] Unable to take responsibility for his failure to stay sober and provide for his family, he instead blamed his wife. He claimed, even when drunk, "She & the Family have been supported by me down to the present time."[57] After their separation, Sherman arrived "to bring a Load of Wood for my family perfectly calm & cool." He had "not Intentions to Stay" and "was treated with Calumnies & reproach for even coming into town or my house." The verbal battle ended in a fist fight between Sherman and his father-in-law.[58] For Rebecca, at least, a drunken provider was worse than no provider at all.

A man could be frugal and sober, and still not successfully provide for his family. Even among ministers, members of the intellectual elite, the task of providing proved daunting. Unlike other providers, however, ministers received spiritual rewards if not adequate pay for their efforts. Although this compensated the minister for his poor income, it did little to help his family. When Thomas Mayhew, "preacher to the Indians at a place called Marthas Vinyard," was lost at sea in 1657, his widow and son were left to support themselves. John Winthrop the younger wrote on their behalf to Robert Boyle in 1663, "Governr of ye corporation for propagating ye gospell in New Engl." in hopes "for some continuance of allowance for hir selfe and educating of hir son." Her husband's service had prevented his accumulation of an adequate legacy for his family. "He might certainly have beene setled in a better place and condition for the more cofortable supply of his family, if he would [not] have beene taken of that employment."[59]

Abigail Graham also suffered materially as a result of her husband's religious calling. In a pleading letter written to her relative Nathaniel Chauncey in 1731, she outlined her deprivations. She began her married life in Stafford, Connecticut, as the wife of the town minister. His low and irregular pay did not provide adequately for his growing family. "There we lived some years under such pinching Straits as would make your heart bleed." Her husband, however, felt the "charge of that people lay so near his heart yt he could not entertain ye thoughts of leaveing them." He clung to the hope that "every year it would be better the next." Finally, their circumstances became so severe that "we could not get bread to eat, we have not had a morsel for 5 or 6 days at a time but when my children have cryed for Supper I have been obliged night after night to Sing them to Sleep having nothing to give them." The cries of the children moved him to confront his parishioners. Denied his rightful due, he left the church's employ. His congregation sued him in court. He refused to participate in the proceedings "as a minister he is sued & as such he know no Civil Judges." He would "Sacrifice Liberty, Estate nay & Life than submitt to their authority." His spiritual commitment and honor made him neglect his role as provider. His desperate wife hoped that Chauncey would try and convince him to be reasonable.[60] Heavenly compensation did little to fill the stomachs of hungry children, yet these men, because of their godly mantle, escaped public ridicule for their failed providing.

When men did ridicule their peers for poor providing their contempt came in part from the disturbing realization that any man could likewise fail in his duty. Thomas Shepard in 1641 contemplated the poverty around him and imagined "what would become of me and mine if we would want clothes and go naked and give away all to pay our debts." This frightful thought led to fervent prayers of thanksgiving for all his blessings.[61] The wolf was never too far from anyone's door. Men insulted one another's ability to provide in an attempt to deflect their own uneasiness. Richard Knott and Captain Joseph Gillam came to Ipswich court to settle a dispute about wages. Gillam had fired Knott, a ship's surgeon, and Knott wanted his wages. Gillam with heat replied "that he would pay him nothing but would pay it to his wife when he reached New England for she needed it more than he." Knott, insulted, flung back "that he had left his wife as well off as Gillam had left his." The verbal sparing continued until Gillam succeeded in imprisoning the surly Knott for a day and a half in the local jail.[62] Both men clearly demonstrated their own insecurities.

A "goodman," regardless of social status, provided for his family. This imperative applied during marriage, remained intact after divorce, and transcended death. In actuality, men shared this responsibility with wives and children. Few families could afford otherwise. This family focus, however, can obscure the fact that men received the righteous scorn of their community if their families went wanting. If a family found itself without what was "needful" a man—not his wife or children— received ridicule. The interdependent nature of family life did little to relieve a man of this burden. White men in colonial New England were expected to keep the wolf from the door.

5

"Ye Heart of a Father"

Little doe children think, wt affection is in ye Heart of a Father.
Increase Mather, *Diary*, 7 April 1675

Puritan patriarchs, according to many scholars, threatened their children with a delayed inheritance, divine retribution, and the rod.[1] From the late twentieth-century perspective, such religiously based child rearing often seems antiquated at the best and abusive at the worst.[2] To understand how such fathers could see themselves not as cruel, but actually loving, requires a fresh look at familiar sources. The men examined here were the educated, the monied, and often the churched of colonial New England. How did these familiar historical figures, those who are most often criticized for misguided parenting, interpret their own behavior?

Fathering, from their perspective, grew from a core concern over the fate of their children—body and soul.[3] They allayed their anxieties with scrupulous attention to the upbringing of their offspring. A careful monitoring of a child's growth, education, and religious training marked their love. These fathers, to borrow a classic phrase from feminist theory, expressed their affection using "a different voice."[4] Affectionate families were not a creation of the late eighteenth century as some scholars have argued; rather, familiar feelings simply came newly packaged in the language of sentimental love as the colonial period came to an end.[5] We might label the fathers of colonial New England controlling, harsh, and uncomfortably religious, but they would certainly find us equally inadequate and repugnant in our overindulgence, permissiveness, and godlessness.

Fathers asserted their authority in early New England within a context of mutual obligation and love. Cotton Mather, son of Increase, advised fathers to establish "sweet authority" over their children.[6] A father led his children to adulthood using affection as well as power. Men did have economic and political power, but in the home this power was always tempered by affection and mutual dependence. Paternal power was shared, checked, and occasionally rejected.

Clerical advice went out to both parents, not just fathers.[7] At the same time, however, the notion of family "head" made fathering seem a distinct endeavor. For example, Jonathan Edwards, at the start of the ferment of the Great Awakening in Northampton, Massachusetts, lectured his flock about the need to monitor children's behavior on the sabbath. He "urged parents to agree among themselves to govern their families." The next day he proposed a neighborhood meeting of "the heads of families, . . . that they might know each other's minds & agree every one to restrain his own family." As it turned out, the children changed their behavior without encouragement so "the parents found little or no occasion for the exercise of government in this case."[8] This kind of contradictory usage demonstrates the difficulty of determining what fell to parents and what devolved on fathers alone.

Certainly children felt both parents contributed to their upbringing. Benjamin Trumbull wrote his "Honoured Parents" from Yale in 1765, "if any youth has cause of Gratitude towards his parents surely I." Both father and mother provided "wise and Seasonable Counsels" and had "withholden nothing in your power to bestow that might Serve for my Advantage." This "Tender Care and inspection" continued "from my Infancy even untill now."[9] Samuel Chandler, at Harvard in the

1770s, likewise reveled over his good fortune to have "been brought up & instructed by indulgent Parents . . . who have taken us from our Infancy Cloathed us gave us Food for the nurishing of our Bodys protected us from all Evils & instructed us in every Branch of Learning which they themselves were capiable of have spaired no Cost for our Education nor through any Pains two great to be taken that was for our Advantage."[10] For Chandler, providing, protecting, and educating involved both parents.

In addition, parenting implied obligation for both the parent and the child. In *A Family Well-Ordered*, Cotton Mather listed not only a parent's responsibilities to his children, but also "The Duties of Children To their Parents."[11] When his father, Increase, published a sermon entitled *"The Duty of Parents to pray for their Children,"* Cotton attached his own sermon, *"The Duty of Children whose Parents have pray'd for them."*[12] This kind of reciprocity had its roots in the fifth commandment, "Honour thy father and thy mother: that thy days may be long upon the land which the LORD thy God giveth thee."[13] As Cotton Mather assured his young parishioners, *"Children,* If you break the *Fifth* Commandment there is not much Likelihood, that you will keep the rest."[14]

The image of God as the father of all believers presented a divine example of fatherhood in colonial New England. God disciplined his children with love.[15] "For whom the Lord loveth he chasteneth, and scourgeth every son whom he receiveth."[16] John Davenport, a Puritan divine, discussed the meaning of this passage with a bereaved widow in 1635, "As a father correcteth the child which he loveth; so doeth the Lord every sonne that he receiveth."[17] G. Selleck Silliman of Fairfield, Connecticut, found the idea of correction and submission equally compelling in the late eighteenth century after his return from

British capture in 1780. He rejoiced at his release and thanked "a most gracious God, who, tho he has corrected, has not destroyed, but hath corrected us as a tender Father does the Children whom he loveth."[18] Increase Mather and others also spoke of God's loving embrace: "Lord take vs into yi arms e keep vs by yi power through Faith vnto salvation. Wee cast or selvs into yi Armes, O o[u]r Father. If children cast yms. into ye Armes of yir Father, will not Hee take ym into his Armes."[19]

The Lord was also "A father to the fatherless, and a judge of the widow, is God in his holy habitation."[20] Michael Wigglesworth, who was at Harvard when he heard of his father's death in the 1650s, prayed that the Lord would "become a father to the fatherless" and care for his siblings.[21] Cotton Mather feared death in part because of his concern for his children. Through prayer he was "perswaded and satisfied, that God will bee a *Father* to my *fatherless* Offspring."[22] This concept had resonance beyond the clerical ranks. After a dispute with a neighbor over a hoe, Thomas Johnson found himself in a Salem, Massachusetts, Court accused of "breach of peace." During the confrontation Johnson had called his widowed neighbor "a preting oald foole." She responded righteously that "a curs pronounct against him for Ronging of ye widdow and ye fatherles and that god would plead tharr caus."[23] Even at the end of the eighteenth century, well-wishers still comforted "mourning Children" with the consolation that they had "God for their Father."[24]

Rev. John Williams found himself separated from his children by the Caughnawaga, or Macquas [Mohawk], as he styled them, after an attack on Deerfield, Massachusetts, in February 1703/04.[25] The Native Americans killed two of his children immediately. The rest of his family commenced the long march to Montreal. He began the journey with five of his children, ranging in age from four to fifteen. Ultimately the family was separated. Faced with the inability to watch over his own, Williams looked to God to care for his fatherless children: "That though my children had no father to take care of them, that word quieted me to a patient waiting to see the end the Lord would make, Jer. 49:11 'Leave thy fatherless children, I will preserve them alive.'" His prayers were answered, "God carried them wonderfully through great difficulties and dangers."[26]

Men were to follow the example of their maker as they parented their own offspring. Cotton Mather in *A Family Well-Ordered* (1699) and Benjamin Wadsworth in *The Well-Ordered Family* (1712) outlined the parental responsibilities of godly parents. Fathers, like their heavenly model, needed to show both firmness and love. Mather insisted that "Our *Authority* should be so Tempered with kindness, and Meekness, and Loving Tenderness, that our Children may *Fear* us with *Delight,* and see that we *Love* them, with as much *Delight.*" Correction with love instilled reverence not fear: "Let not your *Authority* be strained with such *Harshness,* and *Fierceness,* as may discourage your *Children.* To treat our *Children* like *Slaves,* and with such Rigour, that they shall always *Tremble* and *Abhor* to come into our presence, *This* will be very unlike to our *Heavenly Father.*"[27] Wadsworth, likewise asserted, "Parents should nourish in them selves, a very tender love and affection to their Children."[28] This love became manifest in the careful education of all children. A father should teach his children good manners and basic skills to make them "Useful in their place" or *"well settled in the world."*[29] Finally, and most importantly according to Mather, *"Instruct* your *Children,* in the Articles of *Religion."*[30] A father should teach his children their catechism, but also expose them to sermons. In religion and in all things *"Besure to set good Examples before your children."*[31] A good father, like the Lord, provided love, guidance, and a model of ideal behavior.

Fathers in colonial New England had a pattern of proper behavior gleaned from the Bible and reinforced from the pulpit. Like the Lord, a father had to be both harsh and gentle with his children. These seemingly contradictory imperatives fit comfortably together in colonial New England. A father guided his child with a loving but firm hand.

With godly imperatives in mind, fathering officially began with naming and baptizing a child. Baptism was both a formal ceremony welcoming a new child and a naming ritual.[32] Some, like Cotton Mather, had misgiving about this mix of religious and secular purpose. "Oh, Let it not be done, as an Empty *Formality; as if the Baptism* of your Children, were for nothing, but only a *Formal* and a *Pompous* putting of a Name upon them."[33] Still, whether for godliness or display, the father had a key role to play.[34] Often he held the baby as the minister sprinkled water on the newborn's head. Samuel Sewall, a wealthy Boston merchant, meticulously noted his children's demeanor during this ceremony. When he baptized his son Henry in 1685 he noted, "the Child was fine and quiet." Stephen, born in 1687/88, "shrunk at the water but cry'd not." Daughter Judith was particularly stoic when in 1690, "She cried not at all, though a pretty deal of water was poured on her by Mr. Willard when He baptized her."[35] He took pride in his offspring. Their behavior already reflected on his parenting ability. In this public place a man gave his child to God but also publicly announced his fatherhood.

The open announcement of a child's name fell to fathers, but the decision itself was often a more complex affair.[36] Thomas Shepard, safely settled in his pulpit in Cambridge, Massachusetts, in 1635, named his son, Thomas after a private exchange with his wife. "2d son Thomas; which name I gaue him; because, we thought the Lord gaue me the first Son I lost on sea, in this agayne, & hence gaue him his brothers name."[37] Both husband and wife clearly discussed their sadness over their earlier loss and an appropriate name for their new child.[38] James Cogswell announced the birth of his daughter in 1777 to his father from his ministerial post in Canterbury, Connecticut, saying, "My Wife proposes to call the Child after my Mother and Sister."[39] Selleck Silliman likewise left the decision of a name to his wife. "I had got an Opinion some how or other that *Polly* would be a pretty Name for it, but these last Letters have made that altogether improper [the child was a boy], and I am altogether at a loss what to say about it." In fact, his involvement was solicited by both his wife and his son once it was clear that Mary Silliman was "at a Loss."[40] A name was decided on in consultation with others.

Men honored a relative with a namesake.[41] Samuel Sewall named his daughter Judith "for the sake of her Grandmother and great Grandmother, who both wore that Name."[42] Cotton Mather named his son Increase in 1699, "in Honour to my Parent."[43] This practice was so common that Sewall felt the need to explain that he had named his son Joseph in 1688 for the biblical Joseph in Ezekiel "and not out of respect to any Relation, or other person."[44] Sometimes a child's name honored a dead sibling.[45] John Ballantine from his pulpit in Westfield, Massachusetts, in 1762 noted the baptism of his young son: "called his name Winthrop. My 5th child was called Winthrop and was suddenly taken away from us." He had also named a daughter Lydia after her dead sister: "We first lost a Lydia then a Winthrop The repairer of breaches granted us first a Lydia then a Winthrop."[46] William Cooper, town clerk of Boston, also in the 1760s named his son, John: "called after a fine Child of ours which lived but a short space of Time."[47]

Often a relative so honored had characteristics a father wanted the child to possess.[48] Cotton Mather named his daughter Jerusha in 1711 "to admonish her, if she lives, that she should walk in the Steps of Piety, which were taken by my deceased Sister of that Name."[49] Likewise, biblical names carried a hope for an infant's future disposition.[50] Mather named his young daughter Hannah in 1696/97, "that shee may bee a *gracious* Child, and imitate those of her Name, which are commemorated in the Oracles of God."[51]

More often than not a man wanted both to honor and instruct. Sewall toiled over the naming of his daughter Sarah in 1694: "I was struling whether to call her Sarah or Mehetabel; but when I saw Sarah's standing in the Scripture, viz: Peter, Galatians, Hebrews, Romans, I resolv'd on that side. Also Mother Sewall had a sister Sarah; and none of my sisters of that name."[52] Cotton Mather outlined his decision-making process when he named his new-born twins in 1713: "My Wife's vertuous Mother having worn the Name of *Martha*, the Relatives were fond of having the Daughter called so; which name also signifying, *Doctrix;* may the better suit (as my Father said) a *Doctor's* Daughter. I then thought, who was *Martha's* Brother; and that *Eleazar* was the same with *Lazarus;* and a priestly Name; and the Child must be led to look for the *Help of God,* which is in the Signification of the Name. I had also an excellent Uncle of that Name. So I called them, ELEAZAR and MARTHA."[53] Sadly, both children died shortly after their baptism. Fathers took the opportunity that naming a child presented to begin to instruct their children and shape their characters.

The child's development and growth absorbed the attention of both parents. Like the nursing fathers of the Bible,[54] even breastfeeding deserved a father's involvement.[55] Men describe their wives' pains as their milk came in. Rev. Peter Thatcher of Milton, Massachusetts, recorded in 1680, "my dear was but Ill & toward night was in much paine milk came into her breasts."[56] Ebenezer Parkman, farmer and minister in Westborough, fretted in 1738, "My wife in great Pain . . . thought to be the Coming of her milk."[57] Even once the milk was established a woman could struggle with breastfeeding. Parkman's wife was "distressed wth. her Nipples.—She got up, but she grows weaker by Reason of ye Childs suckg her wh her Nipples are so Sore."[58] Samuel Sewall watched his wife struggle to nurse their son in 1677. The nurse and other women that watched the new mother "first laboured to cause the child suck his mother, which he scarce did at all. In the afternoon my Wife set up, and he sucked the right Breast bravely, that had the best nipple."[59] If a wife's breast continued sore it threatened both mother and child. In Peter Thatcher's household a "plaster of bees was [wax] & butter & Nutmeg" was applied to his wife's breasts in 1680 as he sat and read to her.[60] The final solution was to lance an infected breast. James Cogswell described this procedure to his father in 1777. "It was opened, and discharged near a quart of purelant matter, it is now much easier than before it was opened, and seems to be in a good way."[61] Until breastfeeding was established a wife and child were not out of danger.

Men recorded the progress of their children's weaning. Peter Thatcher noted in his journal in 1679, "we began to wean ye Child."[62] Ebenezer Parkman recorded in his diary in 1744, "last night we began to Wean Sarah."[63] When "Nurse Randal" was "taken with an Ague in her Brest" Samuel Sewall lamented that his daughter Judith had to be weaned "though it be a few days before we intended."[64] Ebenezer Parkman found himself in a similar situation in 1726 when his wife's illness "put us upon Weaning the Child which this Night began."[65] For the widower Eliphalet Pearson, the first principal of Phillips Academy, in Andover, Massachusetts, weaning his child from her wetnurse in 1783 was his decision alone. "I have some tho'ts of weaning Marie before the vacation," he wrote his sister. He requested her wisdom on the subject. "Should you think of any objection to weaning the child . . . would thank you to inform me."[66] Fathers also carefully recorded the process itself. John Hull, mint-master and political leader in Boston, noted in 1659 that his daughter Hannah was "weaned without any trouble; only, about fifteen days after, she did not eat her meat well."[67] As pre-Revolutionary fervor shook the town of New London, Rev. Mather Byles assured his sister that his son Walter resented his weaning, "as an Infringement upon Liberty, Property, & the Rights of *Magna Charta.*"[68]

Fathers also carefully monitored their children's physical development. Mather Byles wrote to his father in 1763 about his "little *'Becca.*" He assured her grandfather that "She grows finely."[69] Eliphalet Pearson likewise informed a relative in 1782, "My *dear babe* is well, & grows finely—the day she was three months old, she weighed 15 lb."[70] Six months later Pearson informed his sister that "my dear babe is a little indisposed by cutting teeth, one is thro' & another is soon expected."[71] Ezra Stiles, minister and future president of Yale, marked the tenth birthday of his daughter Polly in 1767 with the careful measurement of each of his children after a family breakfast.

> Betsey—5 feet ¼ Inc
> Ezra—5—9
> Kezia T.—5—1 ½
> Emilia—5—1 ¾
> Isaac—4 feet 11 ⅓
> Ruth—4 10 ¼
> Polly—4 1 [72]

Regular growth and normal maturation reassured an anxious parent that his children had a hopeful future.

Similarly, fathers observed their children's play for evidence of proper mental development. His son Selleck "grows fast in Mind as Body," Selleck Silliman informed his in-laws in 1778:

"Our Dear little Selleck has got a Go:Cart (as they are called) in which he runs about the House out of one Room into another like a Spirit; and where I made the Pause [in his letter] he came runing out of the Kitchen to his Mamma; & lookeing and seeing Papa writeing at the Desk, nothing would do but that he must have his little high Great Chair (in which he commonly sits up at Table & Breakfasts with us, with as much Decency as most People do) and sit up at the Desk with Papa, and have some Papers to play with."[73] Silliman took particular pride in his son's imitation of adult behavior. The elder Selleck relished his son Benny's combativeness on his own return from military service. "In the Morning before it was light little Benny awaked,—heard a Man's Voice talking with his Mamma, he raised himself on one Elbow, and spatted one Hand full in my Face, and cried & quarrelled with me & fought." Finally, he recognized his father and calmed down. This episode pleased his father tremendously. "Ask Selleck who is Papa's Baby— Benny says he is Papa's Baby,—I is Papa's Man."[74] His young son playfully practiced his adult role.

A father's interest went beyond childhood accomplishments; fathers also simply took pleasure in their young children's company. Oliver Ellsworth, a young lawyer from Windsor, Connecticut, although absorbed in his country's business and far from his infant son in 1781, received regular reports from home on his progress. He missed his family but particularly its new addition. "I want much to see the little blue eyed fellow, & would have you give him one good hearth smack for me." He consoled his weary wife saying, "laughing & playing" of children "makes you some pay for tending."[75] On a family journey in 1778 from Stonington to Fairfield, Connecticut, Selleck and Mary Silliman were highly entertained by their young son's playfulness: "Our little Pratter contributed mightily to smoth the Way. He was through the whole of it constantly amusing us with his little innocent Prattle and Merriment." Once home "he gets busy at Play, often entertains us with singing Dol De Dol &c &c."[76] Mather Byles conversed with his infant daughter as he wrote to her grandfather in 1763. She "sends her Duty to her GrandPappa & thanks him for her gold Buttons: at least, when I asked her just now about the Matter, she did not deny it."[77] Selleck Silliman "had a long Chatt" with his son in 1777 "and if he had not began to grow hungry, I believe he would have kept me to a later Hour."[78] Such fathers reveled in their young offspring; they enjoyed their company for its own sake.

Once beyond infancy, a child needed careful guidance to assure proper character development. At this point a father began to parent in a way that distinguished him from his wife. Of course, women trained their daughters for their adult roles and fathers focused on their sons, but their parental techniques also diverged. Men concentrated their energies on teaching their children the secular and religious truths that would direct them toward adulthood. Such caretaking demonstrated their affection. They provided their children with the tools for a productive adulthood and for eternal life.

A father's instruction began with the proper rules of behavior. To some extent they were the same for boys as for girls. Benjamin Trumbull wrote to his six-year-old son from Harlem, New York, during the Revolution. He carefully outlined his parental expectations in easy-to-read block letters. "My Son, love God, learn to pray to him, to read his Word, and keep all his Commandments. Play not on the Sabbath, obey your Mama; help her all you can every day; Speak no ill Word, and always speak the Truth." Steal "not even a pin." Difficult indeed was his father's injunction to "love your sisters and do them good always." He was to be equally "kind and loving" to his "mates" and "treat everybody with kindness and good manners." The reward for such a good boy—"every One will love you."[79]

Josiah Cotton of Plymouth, politician and missionary to the Indians, made a careful list of "rules" for his children's "observation" in 1723/24. First on his list was the need for them to pray "as soon as they awake in the morning, & going to bed at night." They should likewise acknowledge their earthly "Superiours" by a "bow or Curtesy." To squelch childish chatter they were "Not to speak when others are Speaking, not talk too much or all at once, nor speak before they think." Equally inappropriate was the tendency among the young "to behave themselves awkwardly or untowardly by Gaping, Staring, &c." Hovering around the adults would not do. They were "Not to repeat what others say, or stand listening when they have other business to mind." Among themselves they were "Not to Contend or fight with one another." They must "keep themselves neat & Clean, & to be so in everything." To minimize chaos they were "Not to seat themselves first at the Table nor to stand between others & the fire, or put things out of their places." They must carry out their responsibilities to the household, "Not to stay to long when sent of an Errand or desert the business & Duty required of them." In addition, "Proper Titles & terms to men & Women" were to be used at all times, and children should "behave themselves decently in all other parts of divine Worship & at all other times &c."[80]

Once good behavior became well established, a child needed more formal instruction. A caring father took interest in the education of both his male and female children. William Samuel Johnson, a Stratford, Connecticut, lawyer and politician, advised his young daughter Nancy in 1769: "Apply yourself, my dear Child, with the utmost earnestness & assiduity, to make the best use of every advantage you enjoy. Early youth is the season in which to lay those excellent foundations of Virtue & Industry."[81] He hoped she would become a "wise & good" woman.[82] General Samuel McClellan, of Worcester, Massachusetts, and Woodstock, Connecticut, similarly warned his son in 1782, "Study now is your time & hope you Will improve all the opurtunity as it will Be Ever to your advantage."[83] A father wanted all his children to prepare for adulthood with care. Education was, nonetheless, gender appropriate. Josiah Cotton in 1723/24 expected civil behavior from both his sons and daughters, but educational goals were gender specific. "My Sons (provided they are not Educated at the Colledge [Harvard], may, when they are about Fourteen or Sixteen years old, spend about a Twelve Month at Boston to Study the Mathematicks, & any thing that may be usefull; And that my Daughters also spend some time there, not to render them prouder, but to better their behaviour, & by going to School to acquaint themselves with such knowledge, as there are not advantages for in the Countrey."[84] Timothy Edwards, father of Jonathan Edwards, in 1711 fretted over his son's education in his absence: "I desire to take care yt Jonathan dont Loose wt he hath Learned." For Jonathan this included careful attention to his Latin. Edwards also wanted "ye Girls keep what they have Learnt." Latin was not part of their regimen.[85]

Instruction was both secular and religious. To some extent the two were inseparable. William Samuel Johnson, in 1770 after a drubbing from his wife over his constant work-related absences, assured her that his family commitments came first. "I know how much Children need a father, & I *feel* how much I wish to be in every sense a Father to mine. No Man can feel it more, but I must do only what I can & as well as I can." With the next line he demonstrated his concern. "There is nothing I am so Solicitous about as that they should be Educated in Principles of Religion Virtue & Industry." He outlined his hopes for his children in detail. "My first Prayer for them is that they may be made wise unto eternal Salvation & have their Souls Sanctified thro the blood & sufferings of our adorable Redeemer." Only after such education should the children turn their attention to their more worldly callings. "The Son's be so Educated that by Gods blessg. upon their Industry they may in some lawful Profession get a decent Support in life." His daughters should receive instruction so "that they may make Virtuous amiable & useful wives." For Johnson, nothing mattered so much as a father's obligation to educate his children. For him it was "the most importt. Object we have to attend to in this world."[86]

Sheriff Ezekiel Williams of Wethersfield, Connecticut, in 1779 offered the same judgment to his son John. "Above all things a Religious Education is the most important." He urged him to study the Bible, "in that we are Taught the way of Life & Salvation by Jesus Christ, without the Knowledge of Which, all other Learning is but of little Consequences."[87] Williams spoke the same words to his son as his father had spoken to him. On his death bed in 1776, Rev. Solomon Williams of Lebanon, Connecticut, had told his children, "We must make Religion our Business, our Choice, our Delight, at all times, any thing Short of that would be nothing."[88]

A father ideally conducted family prayer and offered daily religious instruction. Some, like Cotton Mather, succeeded in making their homes "a School of Piety."[89] Most men, however, were hard pressed to keep up the regimen. The pressure of other concerns overcame the imperative for daily spiritual lessons. As early as 1639, farmers in Plymouth had difficulty fulfilling their family duties. Some farms, as the settlement grew, were "distant from the place of a mans habitacon and of the churches assembling three or foure miles or there abouts." Such distances meant "a mans famylie is Divided so that in busie tymes they cannot (except upon the Lords day) all of them joyne wth him in famylie duties."[90] Elisha Niles, a school teacher and farmer in Colchester, Connecticut, admitted after the death of his second child in 1786, "I had Never kept up family Prayer although I was fully Persuaded it was my Duty, Owing in most part to my living in a family with a Number of Children which with some other reasons I thought it not Expedient."[91] Some fathers felt family devotions were unnecessary. Describing a Baptist minister in Rhode Island, Ezra Stiles marveled in 1770, "He appears to be a solid substantial Man, yet don't believe that Christians are obliged to Family Worship; & seldom practises it; & that only on Lordsday morning, & this not every Ldsday; never pforms it on Sabbath Evening, nor any other day of the Week."[92] Pressed by business, numerous children, or lack of faith, many men failed to live up to Cotton Mather's ideal.

Benjamin Trumbull outlined the duties of a young Christian to his namesake in 1775: "My Son, love God, learn to pray to him, to read his Word, and keep all his Commandments. Play not on the Sabbath." His cooperation would please not only his parents but "These things the great God commands you to do; if you will do them he will have you for his Child."[93] Proper behavior, prayer, and study marked a young person's path to salvation. Once a child could read well and tolerate longer hours of study, a devout father could take the task of religious instruction quite seriously. Cotton Mather was such a father. His regimen for religious indoctrination was exhausting. He made long lists of his goals and methods. First, he prayed for each child before commencing any instruction. At the table he would tell them "delightful Stories, especially *scriptual* ones." Whenever he crossed the path of a child during the course of the day he "lett fall some *Sentence* or other, that may be monitory and profitable to them." He taught them to practice *"secret Prayer"* and set them to the task. He stressed the need for his children "to return good Offices for evil Ones" and be kind to one another. Mather also encouraged them to write *"excellent Things"* as soon as they were able. When old enough, he reinforced these lessons with private instruction and prayer in his study.[94] The family read various texts as well as the Bible. Each child should have a private place to "read, and write, and pray." They could write prayers and other things of value. What would be of "unspeakable Advantage," however, would be the careful contemplation by each child of the question *"what should I wish to have done if I were now adying!"*[95] Josiah Cotton made a list of Bible references for his children to refer to in time of trouble. He noted, "I hope my Children will search the places refered to &c, & lay up the divine precepts in their hearts, that they may not offend their Maker & Confound themselves."[96]

Secular and religious education formed the core of a father's display of affectionate regard for his offspring. Even if a father failed to express his inner feelings openly in words, he did so through such nurturing concern. Sitting down to a fine meal and surrounded by his children, one pious father remarked, "it would be a much more pleasing thing to See them all in Heaven."[97] Through religious instruction, a man demonstrated his deep love for his offspring. His efforts could provide them with a support that would not fail and, with God's blessing, eternal life.[98] Benjamin Trumbull, in 1775, gave his six-year-old son religious guidance with a full heart. "Dada sends you this Letter to teach you how to live, and to show you how he loves you."[99] What greater gift could a father give a child? Cotton Mather in 1711/12 described his religious teachings as "precious and pleasant Riches" deposited in the "Chambers" of his children's "Souls."[100]

As a captive in 1705/06, John Williams could care for his children only through prayer. He feared his children would die or worse, be converted to Catholicism. The Native Americans' allies, the Jesuits, often manipulated the religious sensibilities of their captives. Williams's son Samuel succumbed to this pressure. When Samuel took on the "Romish" faith he shattered his father who felt powerless to protect his child's soul. "I mourn over you day and night!" He pleaded with his son, "God knows that the catechism in which I instructed you is according to the word of God and so will be found in the Day of Judgment." He urged him to return to his Bible and secret prayer. "Accept of my love and don't forsake a father's advice, who, above all things, desires that your soul may be saved in the day of the Lord." [101] Eventually his son's soul was redeemed.

Love is easier to recognize in the affectionate language of the late eighteenth century. Eighteenth-century loving fathers were often dubbed "tender." William Williams, a merchant and a politician from Lebanon, Connecticut, comforted his dying father in 1776 saying, "that God had given us one of the best & Tenderest Fathers." A tender father like Williams loved his "Children greatly." [102] The young Peter Thatcher of Boston in his diary marked the passing of a "kind & tender Father" in 1765.[103] Benjamin Bangs of Eastham, Massachusetts, mourning the loss of his father-in-law in 1763, remarked, "A tender compassionate father he was." [104] Jonathan Edwards in 1721 thanked his father for a recent letter "and the Abundance of Fatherlike Tenderness therin expressed." [105] The lack of such endearments, however, cannot be interpreted intuitively as a lack of feeling. Without the familiar language of sentiment as a guide, we need to listen for a different voice.

When faced with the tragedy of losing a child how did these men demonstrate their feelings? A man nursed his offspring with peculiar attention to her spiritual health while women cared for the child's more corporeal needs. A man bargained with God for the blessing of health in his family. These Puritan men took out their religious arsenal to counter the assaults on their families. They risked even their souls to save their child. Some thought themselves to blame for a child's sufferings. If a father lost his battle, he struggled with his anger and grief, trying to wrestle meaning from tragedy.

Samuel Sewall had a disturbing dream in 1695: "Last night I dream'd that all my Children were dead except Sarah; which did distress me sorely with Reflexions on my Omission of Duty towards them, as well as Breaking oft the Hopes I had of them. The Lord help me thankfully and fruitfully to enjoy them, and let that be a means to awaken me."[106] His fears were justified. Of his fourteen children only six grew to adulthood. He outlived all but three.[107] A year after this fateful dream, Sewall received "the amazing news of my Wive's hard Time and my Son's being Still-born." He came immediately home "to find a sweet desirable Son dead." He recorded, "These Tears I weep over my abortive Son."[108] Sewall's tears would return often as he made trip after trip to the family tomb.

Samuel Bradstreet, physician and eldest child of the famous poet Anne Bradstreet, wrote to his father, Simon, in 1678 of the loss of his son with similar emotion. "Ye 26th of Decmr last the Lord took from me my Dear Son Simon whom I cannot remember wth out tears." He embellished, "he was a lovely child Exceeding forward, Every way desireable, most dearly beloved by me in this life and as much lamented since his death."[109] On the death of his first-born son in 1679/80, Wait Winthrop agonized to his brother Fitz-John, "I lost my hope, and the greatest part of my comfort."[110]

As a child weakened, both mother and father provided comfort. Women nursed their sick offspring with extraordinary stamina. Cotton Mather's pregnant wife in 1709 "watch'd last Night, (as she had done every other Night) with the languishing Child." Her vigil was interrupted when "she suddenly fell into her Travail." The baby came so quickly that only a few women had reached the house to attend her and she had not even reached "her own Chamber, and safely."[111] Children died in the arms of the women who nursed them. Samuel Sewall lost his son Henry in 1685. He listened intently to his breathing. "He makes no noise save by a kind of snoaring as it breathed." Eventually even this quiet breathing ceased. Henry "Died in Nurse Hill's Lap." Two years later he lost his son Stephen with "two Teeth cut" to convulsions. Stephen likewise died "in Nurse Hill's Arms."[112] Fathers were, nonetheless, a presence in the sickroom. Cotton Mather read to his beloved daughter Katy in 1716. "Much of my Time, of late, has been spent in sitting by her with Essayes to strengthen her in her Agonies."[113] But the chores of nursing fell to women.

"I wrestled with the *God of Jacob*, for my threatened Family, as once *Jacob* did for his." Cotton Mather, like other fathers, braved God's wrath to save a beloved child from death. He set aside a day of fasting and prayer in 1699. "I sett myself particularly to consider, what special Duties, the Condition of my Child should awaken me unto." He proposed to spend more time teaching all his children "charming Lessons, of Religion." He also promised to "promote *Schools* for *Children*, in my Neighbourhood." He would increase the number of *"pastoral Visits"* to his neighbors and give them copies of his book *"Family well-ordered."* He would even write a similar book to be translated into the *"Indian Tongue."* Despite his efforts to bargain with the Lord for his daughter's life she continued to decline. Mather felt he had assurance from the Lord that the child would live, but her condition did not reflect his confidence. He determined to fast and pray again. "Wherefore, being in Distress, lest my *Particular Faith*, should prove but a Fancy, and a Folly, and End in Confusion." He feared not only his daughter's death, but losing his own faith. He was rewarded for his piety. "Now, behold the Effect of *Prayer* and *Faith!* On this very day, the Child began to recover."[114]

Mather made similar efforts for his son in 1699/1700 who "was taken with *Convulsion-Fits.*" He again prayed and fasted, but this time he took a different approach in his petition to the Lord: "I then heartily and cheerfully gave away my Son, unto the Lord Jesus Christ, professing, that if the Child may not be a *Servant* to His, I was far from desiring the Life of it; but, if the Child might serve Him exceedingsly, I cry'd unto him, to speak for it, the Word, by which it might live." The child continued to be racked by convulsions forcing his father "*thrice* to repair unto the Prayer-hearing Lord.*" Mather became more desperate *"Father, if it may be, lett the Cup* (the funeral Cup for this my Son) *pass from mee; Yett not my Will, but thine be done."* Again, Mather and his child were granted a reprieve.[115] Although clearly more contrite, he also offered the possibility of his son's service in exchange for his recovery.

Thomas Shepard made "many arguments to presse the Lord" for the life of his infant son in 1635. His son had a "sore mouth" that interfered with his nursing. As his wife began to recover from her delivery his son grew worse. Shepard reasoned with the Lord. He, like Mather, offered up the child to the Lord's service. He would take the saving of this child as a "kindnes" like "a fruit in season." He even scolded that when things were most bleak "was the Lords time to remember to helpe." If denied his request, "my soule would be discouraged from seeking to him because I sought for the first & could not preuayle for his life, & this was sore if the Lord should not heare me for this." Shepard scolded God for his lack of mercy and threatened him with the loss of his love. He ended his supplications with reference to Jesus' healing of the sick and his hope that God would see fit to heal his infant son.[116] Shepard, like Mather, wrestled with the Lord and his own religious doubts when confronted by the tragedy of childhood illness. Both men stood on the cusp of hubris as they negotiated with God for the life of their children. They cajoled, wheedled, and even threatened their maker. They risked their souls to save their children.

If his appeals went unheard, such a father was forced to examine his own religious condition. Had God visited such a calamity on his child because of his sinfulness? Thomas Shepard believed that "the Lord doth strike his people in that child they take too much affection in."[117] He received such a blow in 1635 while struggling to sail to the safety of New England. While in transit "my first borne child very precious to my soule & dearly beloued of me was smitten with sicknes." He begged the Lord to save his son. "The Lord now shewd me my weake fayth want of feare pride carnall content immoderate loue of creatures, & of my child especially."[118] This difficult lesson ended in the death of his sick child. His father's love led to his demise. Nicholas Wyeth, one of Shepard's parishioners, likewise felt himself the cause of his child's death in the 1640s. His lack of faith had forced a just God to take his heart's joy. "He gave me a child after my own heart and God hath taken it from me and 'tis so just for I have gone on so formally and coldly since I came here. Though I have enjoyed much in public yet I have been very unfruitful and unchristianlike."[119] As Samuel Sewall followed the funeral procession to bury his "Little Henry" in 1685, he also considered the righteousness of God in this most recent dispensation. "The Lord humble me kindly in respect of all my Enmity against Him, and let his breaking my Image in my Son be a means of it."[120] A sinful father could not successfully petition a benevolent God for his child's life.

Forced to acknowledge helplessness in the face of divine power, a defeated father struggled to find comfort. For some, their faith provided them the hope of meeting their children again in heaven. Cotton Mather watched his young son Samuel suffer for two days in 1700/01 "more than an hundred very terrible Fitts." When the pitiful infant finally died, his father spoke of his remarkable "Composure of Mind."[121] He preached on the trials of Job. Although buffeted by the power of the Lord he still proclaimed, "I know *that* my redeemer liveth, and *that* he shall stand at the latter *day* upon the earth."[122] Cotton Mather made this expectation explicit on the grave stone of his newborn son, "RESERVED FOR A GLORIOUS RESURRECTION."[123] Mather looked forward to the time when his whole family would be reunited *"in the Kingdome of God, World without End."*[124]

Less hopeful, but equally necessary, was a pious father's ability to acknowledge his weakness and resign himself to the will of God. Acceptance meant admitting the limited power of man compared to the strength of heaven. Even the most loving father could not save his child if the Lord decreed otherwise. Wait Winthrop urged his son John in 1714 to accept that the death of his five-month-old daughter Elizabeth was God's will. The child died while visiting his wife's father. Wait Winthrop broke the news to his son: "And now let us with humble submition be silent under the soverain good pleasure of that God who does every thing for the best. Let us not say, if this had been avoyed, or that been don, it might haue been otherwise. No; God's holy will is reveled; therfore let us say with him, The Lord giues and the Lord takes away, and blessed be his name." There was no point in wondering what could have been done to save her because God had determined to take her. Rather than mourning, Winthrop urged his son to be thankful: "And let us be thankfull that he has spared any of us when in any danger. He has yet left you fower sweet babes, and I pray and hope for his blessing on them."[125] The elder Winthrop had lived through similar hardships. When his son Joseph was born "wanting his right hand" he counted it a "sore affliction." He reminded himself, nonetheless, that the Lord was "Rituous in all his wayes, and it is less then we haue deserued."[126] When Cotton Mather lost his daughter Mehetabel in 1695/96 he revealed his struggle. "The Spirit of the Lord Jesus Christ, helped mee, I hope, to a patient and cheerful Submission, under this Calamity: tho' I sensibly found, an Assault of Temptation from Satan, accompanying of it."[127]

The illness or death of a child could be used to strengthen religious conviction. The recovery of his daughter Nanny from "a Pain of an unknown Original in her lower Bowels" moved Cotton Mather in 1700 to praise the "prayer-hearing Lord." The physicians had given the child up for dead. Mather trusted in the power of God and received his reward: "Behold, the *Trial* of my *Faith!*"[128] Mather saw the unfortunate illnesses of his children as opportunities for pious instruction. *"What use ought Parents to make of Disasters befalling their Children."*[129] He hoped his children would turn to God in the face of this awesome power. "Oh! What Endeavours must I use, that my living Children may improve the Death of their lovely Sister, to their best Advantage!"[130] He reminded his children of the fragileness of life and the necessity of preparation for death. When a child recovered from an illness he lectured all of his children on the need for thankfulness, "and make him know, what the glorious Lord, that makes him well, does expect from him."[131]

Thomas Shepard left a record "of gods great kindnes" to his son that he "may learne to know & loue the great & most high god: the god of his father." God had saved his son Thomas from a sore mouth at birth, a sudden fall in his mother's arms, another sore mouth that prevented him from eating, and finally an eye infection that threatened his sight. He urged his son to give "thy hart & whole soule & body to him that hath bin so carefull of thee when thou couldst not care for thy selfe."[132] These adversities had strengthened Shepard's faith and he hoped they would be equally instructive to his son. A father could love and nurture his children even in the face of his own helplessness. He could tend to the recovered child's soul or redouble his efforts with the siblings left behind. A father also ideally reaped a rich spiritual harvest for himself. Increase Mather spoke of this potential in a letter to his sister: "There is a memorable Passage, in yt Booke caled ye fulfilling of Scriptures (p. 49i) of a good man who wn his son was dead He went alone to pour out his soul unto, & afterwards was cheerful (as Hannah you know was no more sad after she had prayed) some wondered at him for it but he told ym yt if he might but enjoy such another manifestation of God as in yt private prayer Hee had met wth He could be Content to bury a son every day."[133] With death came loss and opportunity. A father's focus shifted from hopeful prayer to resignation and pious instruction.

A Puritan father expressed his feelings for his offspring freely when death loomed. Careful stewardship of their souls revealed his deep emotions. Such a father even braved hell itself to insure his child's recovery. The challenge, as always for these religious men, was to love their maker more than their children.

With God as their model, fathers in colonial New England struggled to parent with both firmness and affection. Fathers loved their children in both centuries and worried over their futures. They monitored their growth and educated their minds. Some lavished their little ones with attention; others showed their concern through careful heed to their education and spiritual well-being. Sentiment came to a father's lips easier in the eighteenth century, but seventeenth-century Puritan men also loved their children. Forms of expression—not feelings—changed. When a child teetered on the edge of eternity, a father wept.

THE SPECTER OF
USELESSNESS

6

Widower

Benjamin Bangs of Harwich, Massachusetts, feared for his wife's life in April 1760. Desire Bangs was pregnant. Husbands, like their wives, feared the mortality associated with childbirth. "My dearest friend is much concernd being in and near a time of difficulty." Her dreams were full of frightening images. Benjamin tried to reassure her, but he failed to comfort even himself. "I put it off slightly for fear of disheartning her but directly upon it dreamd much the same my self of being bereft of her and seeing my little motherless children about me which when I awoke was cutting to think of." Their anxiety heightened as the event neared: "my wife looks every day and is much concernd and I likewise." His "Coasting Business" required that he leave his fearful wife "in tears and under great concern looking every moment for a time of trouble and distress." While out on his schooner word came "that my dearest wife has been delivered of child supposd a daughter since my absence: which creates in me the greatest joy considering how I left her in fear and tears." Thankfully, disaster had been averted. "My dearest friend goes about house and child well: O: Let us praise thy great and glorious name."[1]

Men anticipated the birth of a child while fearing the death of their wife. Clearly, women's concerns were more immediate as they risked their health time and time again in numerous pregnancies. Nonetheless, men had their own burden to bear. They feared the loss of a partner. A man faced widowhood each time his wife became pregnant.[2] A husband worried for himself, but also for his children. After Abigail Mather's miscarriage, Cotton recorded in his diary in 1702, "I could not but fear, lest the Death of my Consort, and all the unhappy Effects of it upon a broken Family, must overtake me."[3] His fears were realized seven months later when his wife died of the combined effects of the miscarriage and what was probably breast cancer.[4]

Most men, however, though they feared the death of a spouse, never had to face its reality. There were more widows than widowers in colonial New England.[5] If women survived their child-bearing years, which most did, they often outlived their husbands. In fact, women and men died at about the same rate during the child-bearing part of the life cycle in many colonial New England towns. The fear of maternal death, however, could loom quite large.[6] If unlucky enough to lose a wife, widowers tended to remarry and quickly.[7] They did so because life without a partner was unmanageable. Emotionally their need was palpable. Practically, an interdependent family functioned poorly in the absence of a woman. Dependency on children was not as acceptable an option for a widower as it was for a widow. Therefore, this stage in a man's life, if it came at all, was short-lived.

"This was to me at first a disagreable task. To be the first to bear you these tidings. Now I know not where to leave off."[8] Thus penned Benjamin Douglas, a lawyer in New Haven, in a nine-page letter to his father-in-law, Joseph Fish about his wife's hopeless struggle against smallpox.[9] On an early winter evening in 1766, Rebecca Douglas complained of a headache. After dinner she retreated to her bedchamber. She had "a full persuasion that she should be hard sick." Rebecca motioned for her husband to come sit by her side because "she was not long to have the pleasure." He tried to lift her spirits "supposing her to be a little melancholy and vaporous." Kind words and a "sweat for a cold" did little to "ease her pain." The following evening a doctor was called. Benjamin administered the "powders" the physician ordered and the couple went to bed. He was awakened "by one of her old dreadfull fits." Once sensible, they discovered "the fatal Pock" on her face. She was removed to the "pest house."

Benjamin and Mrs. Punderson, "a kind carefull skillful woman," attended to Becca. "She was never easy when I was out of her sight saying where is my dear Husband? Will he leave me?" Over and over she pleaded, "don't leave me my dear." Douglas struggled with his wife to attend to her spiritual condition. She refused to acknowledge, when lucid, that death was close at hand. Finally, as she was "on the very verge of Eternity" he resorted to "shaking her" to bring her to her senses. Somewhat revived she prayed fervently and well for herself and for her aggrieved husband. "She asked me if she was dying, I told her she was." Her last moments were filled with the "most shocking pain" until at last she fell "into a gentle sleep." Benjamin Douglas had become a widower. He was "overwhelmed [with] Grif!"[10]

Eli Forbes and his wife Mary went to Boston from North Brookfield, Massachusetts, in April 1775 seeking a cure for breast cancer. Arriving at the same times as the Revolution, the hapless couple quickly moved in with their daughter in Gloucester.[11] The cancer, like a soldier, did its deadly work. The distraught Eli outlined the details of "the Darkest hour I ever saw" to his father-in-law, Ebenezer Parkman. Mary Forbes progressed from having a bad cough to a stomach disorder and finally the symptoms of what appeared to be "ye Cancer." "Her Strength failed, her flesh wasted but at times She was very comfortable enjoyed her Self and Friends." The doctors tried to discourage "a defluxion of humours of ye cancerous kind upon the Polmonary Glands." They applied "Plasters &c &c But all in vain." The grieving Forbes "held her by the hand My two children hung upon each arm." As she lay dying she begged her husband to thank her father for her religious upbringing. "I have great comfort in her Death she was calm resigned and Joyful having obtained after some struggle a full assurance of Faith and hope." Forbes ended his letter, "I am overwhelmed and can add no more."[12]

The only duty left for a grieving husband was to commit the "dear Remains to the Tomb."[13] When Ezra Stiles, future president of Yale, lost his beloved and "noble" Elizabeth in 1775 he remarked, "This day the Remains of my dear Wife were committed to the silent Grave."[14] Rev. Cotton Mather of Boston "interr'd the earthly part of my dear Consort."[15] Each man grieved for the loss of his companion body and soul. One unknown man in 1777 exposed the visceral nature of his loss to his in-laws: "The cruel grave, to me in a particular Sense Cruel, now holds within its narrow house her lovely form. (to you lovely, to me intirely so, and had in respect by all who knew it,) a meat ripening for worms, which as Shakespear words it. 'Like the baseless fabrick of a Vision. Leaves not the wreck behind.'"[16] To consign the body of an intimate to the corruption and silence of the grave worsened a man's grief. Sensuality became twisted into repugnance. As Timothy Woodbridge reminded the grieving Samuel Sewall in 1720, "all flesh is grass."[17]

Without even the comfort of his wife's "dear Remains" a man found himself wrestling with his grief in earnest. Eli Forbes called out his dead wife's name, "Molly!—Ah!—my dear Molly!!!"[18] Eliphalet Pearson lamented in 1782, "Oh Loss beyond Repair!"[19] When Hannah Sewall died in October 1717 her whole family grieved. "The Chamber was fill'd with a

Flood of Tears."[20] Samuel Sewall, facing the loss of his beloved wife of forty-two years, often dissolved into tears. When writing to Gurdon Saltonstall, the governor of Connecticut, in January of the following year he could "hardly write for tears."[21]

Eliphalet Pearson found himself dwelling on the memory of his wife in 1782 with "mixed sensations, which no language can express."[22] For some men, the intensity of their pain went beyond words. One man lamented to his dead wife's grieving parents in winter 1777, "your loss now is great" but he reminded them he had "Lost every thing. . . . My feelings upon this Occasion must be conceiv'd, they are too great to be express'd."[23] Benjamin Douglas in 1766 insisted on the necessity of describing his wife's last illness to his father-in-law. "My full heart must *out*, or I must hold my peace, which to do would be highly impious, as the particulars of this melancholy story must come from me alone." Yet when the long tale came to its sad conclusion he remarked: "the feelings of my rending heart you will not expect me to describe. The desolution of it only can be greater."[24]

The pain associated with the loss of a spouse came as somewhat of a surprise to a man who had never endured such an affliction. Cotton Mather, shortly after his wife's death in 1702, wondered at the depth of his sorrow. "I had rarely known any Tears, except those that were for the Joy of the Salvation of God. But now, scarce a Day passes me without a Flood of Tears, and my Eyes even decay with weeping."[25] For Ezra Stiles the death of his "Dear Wife Elizabeth" in 1775 caused him "great Grief & Distress, such I never before knew."[26] Shocked by the intensity of his grief, Eli Forbes chided his father-in-law for neglecting to prepare him for the blow. "I have been in former Tribulations, and I thot my heart could not be more tenderly touched then it has been in formr. Tryals But Oh Sir! Why did you not tell me ye pain of this parting Stroke, you had felt it?" Forbes's sadness found peculiar force because "Molly had my first affection, . . . She was my early, my old Friend."[27]

For some widowers their sufferings were extreme enough to lead to deep depression. For Samuel Sewall the death of his dear wife and son-in-law in quick succession in 1717/18 felt as if "BREAKERS were passing over me, Wave after Wave, Wave after Wave." He struggled merely to keep his "Weary head above Water."[28] Like the water threatening to pull Sewall under, men spoke of the heaviness of their affliction. John Winthrop, the younger, described in 1674 his grief over the death of his wife of thirty-seven years as "very heavy vpon me."[29] When Cambridge minister, Thomas Shepard lost his second wife, Joanna, in childbirth in 1646 he felt "this affliction was very heauy to me."[30] Writing only months before his own death in 1712, Nehemiah Hobart, longtime minister of Cambridge Village, Massachusetts, described "the heaviness I am in, by the late removal of my dear wife."[31]

Benjamin Lord, minister of Norwich, Connecticut, for more than thirty years, struggled under such a weight after the death of his second wife, Elizabeth, in 1751, only a year after their wedding. "My Stroke is heavier than I dare let my groaning Discover." He found it a great mercy, however, that he was "Still enabled to keep on In ye Business of my Calling: which were not Some pleasure In ye Admidst of Infirmitys & discouragmts, My Sorrow, would Soon Drink up my Spirits & depress me beyond Saving."[32] Ezra Stiles in 1775 found even this comfort denied him in his "Grief and Sorrow." He could not preach because "Affliction & mournful Sorrow have unfitted me." He wandered through his house overwhelmed by its "great Emptiness." His spirits exceeding low, he remarked "Every Thing reminds me of my dear departed absent Wife."[33] For Samuel B. Webb, a military man from Wethersfield, Connecticut, the loss of his beloved Eliza gave him "pleasing Idea's of Death" in 1782. To this widower the "World truly appears a mighty void, nor have I the least relish for its greatest enjoyments, time no doubt will soften my affliction otherwise nature could not support this shock."[34] Eli Forbes in 1776 longed "to exclude" himself "from the world" which now had become "a Blank" to him. He managed pretty well during the day "But the night Oh! how gloomy."[35]

For some men the thought of seeing their beloved in heaven proved consolation. Eli Forbes assured Ebenezer Parkman in 1776, "My affection is not lost, it is immortal, I love her *Name*, her *Dust*. her immortal *part*."[36] Some widowers felt that their partnership would continue in heaven in a more perfect form. James Draper of Dedham after losing his wife of "forty Eight years and abought four hours," reminded his daughter in 1776, "allthough my Dear wife hath Left me for the Present yet I shall Injoy her In a better maner in the havenly world."[37] Samuel B. Webb in 1782 waited patiently for "that happy, happy period when we shall have a happ pleasing reunion with our Dear Departed friend in the Heavenly Mansions of Bliss, never again to be seperated."[38] Heavenly love was more perfect and more lasting that its earthly counterpart. Spiritual doubt for some created uncertainty about such a heavenly reunion. Eliphalet Pearson worried in 1782 that he would be denied the comfort of his wife's companionship in the afterlife. "God grant, that I may so improve this dispensation, as to be qualified for *her Society & friendship* in heaven, of which I was so unworthy on earth!"[39] Life and love eternal reassured the pious widower that his loss was temporary.

A man resolved his grief with the support of friends and family. This support network included people who had suffered a similar blow, other men and women, who knew the pain of losing a partner. As one man put it in 1777, "You that have known Two happy Souls made intimately one And felt a parting Stroke—tis you can tell The Smarts, the twinges & the Racks I Feel."[40] Some were family members who could sympathize in the particular. Benjamin Douglas lamented to his father-in-law, Joseph Fish, in 1766, "Becca so near to each of our hearts, *is no more.*"[41] Samuel Sewall advertised his neediness when his second wife, Abigail, died a mere seven months after their wedding day in 1720. He wrote a note and made three copies to post in churches around town. "Samuel Sewall, depriv'd of his dear Wife by a very sudden and awfull Stroke, desires Prayers that GOD would sanctify the same to himself, and Children, and family."[42] Widowers openly acknowledged their need for support and were grateful for those moved to give it.

Expressions of condolence proved powerful sources of strength for the newly widowed. Receiving a sympathetic letter in 1717, after the death of his first wife, Hannah, Samuel Sewall "soked it in Tears at reading."[43] In November 1749, a month after the death of his wife of thirty years, Thomas Foxcroft, a Boston minister, received a similar letter from his friend and colleague Ebenezer Williams. Williams was reticent to list the "Excellent Endowments & Shining Graces & virtues of the Deceasd." because "it would serve, rather to Arise, than assuage your Grief." Instead, he simply sent "the Sympathy & Pitty of a Friend." Williams hoped to soothe Foxcroft's suffering, in part, because he knew "what affliction is." He reminded him that suffering had a purpose: "I have found by Experience we must not indulge it any farther then we can turn it into a right Channel & Improve it to our Spiritual Good." The key was to yearn for the "Enjoyments" of the grave. He could be an "Example to others, in Suffering" and thereby "comfort others with the Comforts wherewith you are Comforted." Williams realized that Foxcroft knew all of this well, having consoled many a parishioner in his long career. He did not "pretend to direct you or yours" rather his thoughts arose "from the abundance, of my heart I could not forbear, thus much, when writing to an old & Intimate Friend."[44] Such friends wrote, visited, and prayed for the newly widowed man. As Benjamin Douglas noted in 1766, "The sympathy of friends is no small consolation in time of trouble and affliction."[45]

Pain dulled also with the simple passage of time. Thomas Clap of Windham, Connecticut, lost his young wife Mary to consumption and the complications of childbirth in 1736. He had married her when she was fourteen and he twenty-four. She had been pregnant six times by the age of twenty-three when she died. Her death prompted her husband to record his efforts to master his grief. Three months after Mary's death he noted, "All the afflictions which I have ever met with in my whole Life put together are small in Comparison to this. My spirits have been much sunk and my Body Emaciated by it." As a minister, he tried to use her death to further his spiritual journey: "Spent as much of my time in Humiliation Confession Prayer and the like as the Strength of my Body and mind would allow." This work of spiritual reconciliation rather than grieving itself became the focus. "I have Grieved & Mourned more for Sin, and the workings of Corruption in my own Heart than for my outward affliction & Bereavement." He convinced himself that "when I at any time seemed to be the most Distressed, for the want of my Dear Consort and to have the Strongest Desire after her I have thot that if she was now here with me I could freely Leave her to Go to the Enjoyment of God."

After six months, Clap continued in his "Lonely & Melancholly mourning," but he felt that God had compensated him for his loss. "It is Good for me that I have been Afflicted." He nonetheless had wearied of his intense introspection and felt the need "to Curb and Restrain my Grief and to Endeavour to Recover my Spirits to their Natural & usual Order." If his sadness did not abate, he feared he would "not be so Capable of Serving God and Answering the Good End of Affliction." After nine months, he still described himself as "lonely and Melancholly" but had begun to entertain the possibility "of seeking for another Companion."[46]

Although progressively easier to bear, such a loss was not easily forgotten. The wedding anniversary of James Hillhouse, lawyer and public servant of New Haven, Connecticut, became a day of remembrance and devotion. The "precious Memory" of his "dear departed *Wife* . . . will not be in the power of time itself to erase from my Heart."[47] Rev. Mather Byles, formerly of New London, felt a continued affinity toward his dead wife's parents. He asked his sisters in 1780 to, "present my Duty, & assure her that I can never forget the Mother of the amiable Wife of my Youth."[48] "The Wife of my youth," Samuel Sewall remarked in 1728, had "expired Eleven years agoe, it much affected me." He wrote to his son to come dine with him and "join my Condolence."[49] Ebenezer Parkman, minister and farmer in Westborough, Massachusetts, in 1738 noted, "I cannot but remember the Wormwood and the Gall of the Funeral Day Two years agoe and Desire my Soul may still be humbled within me." In 1746, he again remembered "the wormwood and the Gall this Day Ten Years agoe." He complained that visitors had prevented him from keeping his "Retirement." Two years later he still kept this devotion on the day his "dear wife Mary died."[50] Both Sewall and Parkman had remarried, but emotional ties to their first wives remained strong. As Ezra Stiles recorded in 1776: "This day last year my dear Wife died. A day of destress & Sorrow never to be forgotten by me."[51]

Some men created more lasting memorials. Thomas Clap lovingly composed the inscription for his wife's headstone:

Here Lyeth Interred the Body of
Mrs MARY CLAP.
The Consort of the Revd Mr THOMAS CLAP.
She was of a most Amiable Disposition
The Delight & Crown of her Husband.
An Ornament to her Sex
And a Pattern of every Grace and Virtue.
She for a long time Expected Death with Serenity of Mind
And met it with Great Joy and Satisfaction.
She lived Greatly Desired
And Died Universally Lamented,
Augst 9th 1736. In. the 24th Year of her Age.[52]

For the few who kept diaries, a wife's life deserved careful description. When Ezra Stiles lost his dear wife Elizabeth in 1775, he recorded her death adding a loving narrative of her life. He began, "My Wife Elizabeth Stiles was the oldest Daughter of Col. John Hubbard of New Haven & Elizabeth his first Wife, where she was born July 3, 1731, O[ld].S[tyle]." Stiles believed she had inherited the "Sagacity & Sensibility" of her father and the "Nobleness" of her mother. Her parents trained her well for the "Variety of Business of female Life." They married and had eight children. She was an honest woman, "perhaps unexampled for her Love of Integrity." Her religious devotion included private prayer, reading the Bible "thro' 5 Times," raising her children carefully, and various good works. Speaking to his intended audience, Stiles remarked, "it will be an honor to her Posterity to have descended from such an excellent Person."[53] Looking at an even wider constituency, Cotton Mather took the opportunity of his second wife's death in 1713 to publish a sermon prepared earlier, "A CHRISTIAN FUNERAL. *A brief Essay on that Case*, WHAT SHOULD BE THE BEHAVIOUR OF A CHRIS-

TIAN AT A FUNERAL?" He intended to attach "unto a Convenient Number of them, a Memorial of my Departed Consort, which I would present unto her particular friends."[54] These men wanted to assure that their wife's memory would survive.

The crisis over, a man had to settle into his new role of widower. When his precious wife Hannah died in 1717, Samuel Sewall reflected, "God is teaching me a new Lesson; to live a Widower's Life. Lord help me to Learn."[55] For Sewall the transition was particularly trying because he had "not been accustomed to" life alone for forty-one years.[56] He described his plight as his "widowed condition" and "Widowed state." Thomas Clap also spoke of the time after his wife's death in 1736 as his "Widowhood."[57] Cotton Mather thanked God in 1703 for his mercy during "the Time of my Widowhood."[58]

Men pondered the option of life alone. Samuel Sewall explained to a potential matchmaker five months after his wife's death in 1717, "'twas hard to know whether best to marry again or no." He had given the idea some thought. "This morning wandering in my mind whether to live a Single or a Married Life; I had a sweet and very affectionat Meditation Concerning the Lord Jesus; Nothing was to be objected against his Person, Parentage, Relations, Estate, House, Home! Why did I not resolutely, presently close with Him! And I cry'd mightly to God that He would help me so to doe!"[59] The loss of a cherished partner convinced Selleck Silliman in 1775 that remarriage would hold no joy for him. He reflected after the loss of his first wife, "I thought I should never marry again, because I never expected I should find such another."[60]

Thomas Clap in 1737 echoed this sentiment and others in a document he titled "Rev. Thomas Clap's Thoughts on a Second Marriage." He carefully listed "Consideration against entertaining any Prospect of Altering my Condition." First, he

thought it "very unlikely that ever I should be so Pleased &
Satisfied" in marriage again. Even if lucky enough to "meet
with one that was as well or better Qualified" as his former wife
"she would not be the same *to me.*" His grief, in fact, would
be exacerbated by a poor choice. Second, he had "lived scarce
9 years in the married State and it seems to me that I enjoyed
as much satisfaction in it as men generally do in their whole
lives . . . and therefore I am easy and Contented with what I
have already had." Third, he dreaded the possibility of renewed
sorrow. Marriage carried with it the potential for loss. "I have
experienced a great Share of this Kind of Sorrow why should I
desire to be under such Circumstance and to be liable to still a
greater degree of it." Fourth, the death of his wife had "weaned
[him] from the world." Remarriage would mean "another Wife
and more young children, my heart would be engaged to and
for them. I should be loath to part with them, and grow less
tho'tful of and prepared for my own change." Fifth, he worried that young children would require more attention unlike
his "2 children the one about 8 and the other about 5 years
old" who were "in some Degree able to take care of themselves." New children would also need to be settled when they
reached adulthood, stretching his resources and limiting all his
children's portions. All of these issues made Clap hesitant to
alter his "Condition." He pondered that perhaps the ideal was
to "live as much disengaged to this world as possible both as to
the Troubles & pleasure of it." [61]

Despite their protestations, Samuel Sewall, Selleck Silliman,
and Thomas Clap all remarried. A month after Hannah Sewall
died in 1717 Samuel began courting Dorothy Denison. Three
months after this unsuccessful courtship, Sewall pursued the
more willing Abigail Tilley. They married two years after his
first wife's death. Selleck Silliman married in 1775, a year after
his widowhood. Thomas Clap was the only one less anxious for

the altar, marrying some four years after losing the wife of his youth in 1736. Despite their feelings of hopelessness and despair, these men did remarry.

What distinguished widowed men from widowed women was the length of their widowhood. Studying seventeenth-century Wethersfield, John Faragher concluded that widowers remarried more often than widows in this Connecticut town. Over 60 percent of widowers remarried whereas only about 30 percent of widows did so.[62] According to Alexander Keyssar, in eighteenth-century Woburn, Massachusetts, even among the small population of widows and widowers under fifty (those more likely to seek a second marriage), men still remarried more often than women.[63] Susan Grigg, studying remarriage in early nineteenth-century Newburyport, also noted that men were more likely to remarry than women, particularly as both groups aged. Only men over sixty-five lost interest in approaching the altar for a second time.[64] In addition, widowers remarried more quickly than widows. In seventeenth- and eighteenth-century England, most men found a new spouse within a year.[65] In seventeenth-century Wethersfield, men married within a year whereas women waited three.[66] In Newburyport, men remarried on average 1.9 years after the death of a wife; widows married 5.6 years after losing a husband.[67]

Gender specific remarriage patterns are more easily observed than explained. Nonetheless, part of the answer certainly lies in the favorable sex ratio for men in colonial New England. If women survived childbirth they lived longer than men. Particularly in the longer settled areas, marriageable men outnumbered marriageable women. Widowers more often than widows married younger or single partners; expanding the pool of potential mates for widowers even further.[68]

Economic factors also played their part. While the widow of means tended to shy away from remarriage as a result of her economic independence, men who were wealthier were actually more likely to remarry.[69] A man needed the unpaid labor of a wife to keep his household functioning. A woman could, however, take her inheritance, if generous, and keep her family together with the help of her children.[70] For women, such arrangements could be difficult, but for men dependence on children was a bitter pill.[71]

In addition, legal risks accompanied the decision to remarry for women and their children. A return to *feme covert* status, for a woman, put her estate and her children's inheritance at risk.[72] For widows with grown children who had already received their portions or for women who had the foresight and legal assistance to create prenuptial contracts, the stakes were not quite so high.[73] For men, the only hazard of remarriage was the legal necessity to provide for a new family.[74] Despite this reality, John Faragher, for one, uncovered no correlation between family size or age of children and remarriage patterns among widows or widowers in seventeenth-century Wethersfield.[75] Ultimately, demographic, economic, and legal factors explain only part of a widower's or a widow's decision to approach the altar again.[76]

For some men, a deep regard for a first wife pushed them to pursue a second. Their first marriage motivated them to be optimistic about and anxious for a second marriage. Cotton Mather spoke in 1703 of his "Spirit much disposed" toward remarriage. He crowed about his "happy Return to the married state."[77] Samuel Sewall implied that successful remarriage was a sign of God's favor. In 1720, he asked Jeremiah Dummer, Massachusetts's agent in London, to pray for him as he mourned his wife: "I need your Prayers that GOD would sanctify this Stroke to me; and that He would yet again provide such a good Wife for me, that I may be able to say, I have obtained Favour of the LORD."[78]

Men felt remarriage was a sexual necessity, and they confidently pursued a course that would assure them a sexual outlet.[79] In addition, to guarantee social respectability they needed to marry. A man alone was an oddity, a thing to be remedied. An anxious community urged widowers like bachelors to marry.[80]

Cotton Mather fretted over his eagerness to find a wife in 1702/03. "Considering how frequently and foolishly Widowers miscarry, and by their Miscarriage dishonour God, I earnestly with Tears besought the Lord, *that He would please to favour me, so far as to kill me, rather than to leave me unto anything that might bring any remarkable Dishonour unto His Holy Name.*" He thought "the Lord was going to take me at my own Word" when "Within a few minutes" of his prayer he became "very ill." He soon recovered concluding "it was nothing but *Vapours.*" Mather found his resolve tested by a young widow who began to pursue him only three months after his wife's death. Enamored of the newly widowed minister, the forward widow asked Mather "to make her mine." Mather was clearly taken with her. "She is one of rare Witt and Sense; and of a comely Aspect; and extremely Winning in her Conversation." Her age, "not much more than twenty years old," and her reputation as "a very aiery Person" made him cautious. He convinced himself that the match would not enhance either his own reputation or by association his ministry.

Nonetheless, the tenacious woman continued to court him and tongues began to wag. "I sett myself to make unto the L[ord] Jesus Christ, a Sacrifice of a Person, who, for many charming Accomplishments, has not many aequals in the *English America.*" Two months after the romance commenced, "I struck my Knife, into the Heart of my Sacrifice, by a Letter to her Mother." He and his friends concluded that the only way to restore his tarnished name was "by proceeding unto another Marriage." Mather decided to fast and pray for three days, an extraordinary long stretch even for him, on this pressing issue. He prayed for "the Gifts of Purity and Patience." Eventually God rewarded him in summer 1703 with Elizabeth Hubbard, "a Gentlewoman of Piety and Probity, and most unspotted Reputation."[81]

When Samuel Sewall embarked on his hopeless quest to woo Katherine Winthrop in 1720, he learned to "bewail my Rashness in making more haste than good Speed." Their ill-fated courtship revealed that even a man of sixty-nine could long for the marriage bed. He approached Madam Winthrop three months after the shocking and speedy death of his second wife, Abigail Tilley. He wanted Katherine Winthrop body and soul. He asked for permission to remove her glove during one visit. "I told her twas great odds between handling a dead Goat, and a living Lady. Got it off." He spoke to her in the language of romantic love. "Her Kisses were to me better than the best Canary." He focused on her physical appearance and noted as the courtship floundered, "Treated me Courteously, but not in Clean Linen as somtimes." Finally, she made her feelings clear to the mooning Sewall. "I told her I loved her, and was so fond as to think that she loved me; She said had a great respect for me." He finally admitted defeat and took his leave. She called after him to "have a Care." Sewall recorded his final thoughts in terms of his sexual needs: "I did not bid her draw off her Glove as sometimes I had done. Her Dress was not so clean as sometime it had been. Jehovah jireh! [The Lord will provide!]"[82] A few months later, as he continued to search urgently and at times desperately for a wife, he still spoke of his need for physical intimacy: "The truth is, I have little Occasion for a Wife, but for the sake of Modesty, and to cherish me in my advanced years (I was born March 28, 1652) Methinks I could venture to lay my Weary head in her Lap, if it might be brought to pass upon Honest Conditions."[83]

Friends and relations urged a widower to repair his loss and find a new companion. Cotton Mather recorded in 1703, "My Father presses me frequently and fervently, that I would by no means take up Resolutions to continue in my Widowhood."[84] Anna Cutts likewise urged Eliphalet Pearson, her former brother-in-law, to consider the necessity of remarriage in 1784: "I sympathize with you in your inability to performe what I dare say you are convinc'd would be for your domestic interest, I only wish that when you meet with a person whose virtues and abilities come the nearest to those of our dear friend, you would take the matter under consideration."[85] When Samuel Sewall found himself an elderly widower in 1718, his friend Cotton Mather focused on the surplus of widows in his congregation. After giving Sewall a copy of his sermon on the subject he scolded, "But your Honor will allow me now at length, to offer you my Opinion, that all the Regards are not yet paid, which you owe unto the *Widow*, and which are expected of you."

Soon potential mates received particular mention from supporters. Sewall had a visit from Deacon Marion five months after his first wife's death in 1717. Marion informed Sewall that "the Olivers said they wish'd I would Court their Aunt." This Aunt was Katherine Winthrop whom he eventually did court, unsuccessfully. A month later, as he helped the Widow Denison settle her deceased husband's estate, he received some friendly prodding. "Mr. Dorr took occasion in her absence to say she was one of the most dutiful Wives in the world."[86] Sewall took this advice to heart as well, but he found her as reluctant to join him in marriage as the Widow Winthrop. A little more than a month after the death of his second wife, Elizabeth, in

1713 Cotton Mather fretted over the "silly People, inviting my Return to the married State; which it is unaccountable to see, how much they have already begun upon."[87] The same liberty had been taken after the death of his first wife in 1703. "I am extremely Unhappy! My fond Friends take a Liberty of Discoursing about Matches for me. And tho' they are such as I never took any Step about myself, yett presently a Discourse is raised, as if I had been myself concerned in the matters. This hurts me!"[88] The community made single life a difficult alternative for a widower who was hounded with advice and women.

Some men felt the pressure to remarry coming from the grave. Rebecca Douglas "repeated hundreds of times" on her deathbed her desire for her husband, Benjamin, to stay by her side.[89] Her desperation abated only when he slept. After prolonged suffering, she resigned herself to her fate and pondered her husband's future without her. Some of Rebecca Douglas's precious and difficult last words spoke of her husband's widowed state. "She pressed my hand to bear up with fortitude, and to marry again, as soon as I could be happy. urging me to be very carefull in my choice. for as I had been once entirely so, it would be very difficult to be so again. I asked her if I should not chose to marry again it would not be more agreable, than for her to view me anothers She said I must consult my own inclination and happiness it was that she wanted but she rather advised me to Marry &c.[90] Mary Clap told her afflicted husband Thomas in 1736, "I don't want to be your Wife any longer." She had "chosen a better Husband," Christ. She advised him to "get another Wife as soon as you can." With God's help he might find a "Kind Loving and Religious Wife, and one that will be a good Mother to the Children."[91] These words haunted Clap as he contemplated remarriage. "I Remember I used to take a kind of secret Pleasure in Hoping that Divine Goodness would make her Happy in another when I was Gone. I why cant I take that advice to myself which I used to give her. Especially since this was her last and Dying advice to me."[92]

Part of a dying wife's concern was for her children, not her husband. Thomas Clap needed a woman to watch after his children and "Manage the Affairs" of his family, and none could do this so "well and agreably" as one "in the Capacity of a Wife."[93] Cotton Mather lamented in 1703 the "Inconveniencies of a *single State*." "My Family suffers by it, in several Instances." As he approached his marriage to Elizabeth Hubbard in 1703, he comforted himself with the thought "if the Spirit of my departed Consort now in the Kingdome of God, were advized, that her children were falling into the Hands of this Gentlewoman, it would be a Consolation unto her." He prayed that he would "live to see her [Elizabeth Hubbard] illuminating my Family."[94]

Family needs, for some, led to rash choices. Ebenezer Parkman worried in 1745 that his recently widowed brother was "hot in Courtship already" because "the Circumstances of his Family are very Urgent."[95] Eliphalet Pearson felt pressured in 1784 to find his infant daughter Maria "another Parent." His former sister-in-law commiserated with his condition. "With what concern, and often *hidden* anxiety is the mind of a Parent fitted, for the welfare of a Child! I had no Idea of it, till I became a Parent, *you* feel it in its full fourse, having no parental eye, to take the place of yours, when necessaryly taken off."[96] A man needed to remarry, perhaps quickly, because he desperately needed a domestic partner.

Finally, a man remarried because he wanted companionship. James Draper in 1767 wrote to his daughter about his "Lonely Condion" after the loss of her mother.[97] Thomas Clap in 1737 spoke of the "many Inconveniences of a lonely State." Clap and others thought of a new wife as "a Reparation of my loss."[98] Cotton Mather, contemplating his remarriage in 1703, observed of Elizabeth Hubbard, his wife-to-be, "Shee will be a great Gift of Heaven unto me, an astonishing Reparation of my Loss, and Compensation of all the Grief I have mett withal."[99] Thomas Clap concluded in 1737, after penning a long list of reasons for and against remarriage, that, "The principal Reason why I seem to want a Wife is to be an Intimate Spritual Friend & Companion."[100]

Cotton Mather remarked in 1703 "that for the sake of the Lord Jesus Christ, whose I am, a desireable Consort should be bestow'd upon me." Convinced that the Lord would provide he planned to "wait until my heavenly Friend and Father, do more plainly show me, what He would have me to do."[101] Even the less devout saw God's hand at work in their courtship. Selleck Silliman thrilled at the prospect of marriage to Mary Noyes in 1775: "Who but an infidel can neglect to look up and Day by Day give Thanks to God for common Mercies."[102] The reluctant Thomas Clap had to acknowledge in 1737 that the Lord might require his return to the married state. He found it unlikely that he would find another so agreeable as his first wife, but "it may be my Duty to take as much Comfort and Satisfaction as God allows me." Even if, he added, "I should not love her altogether so well and be so entirely pleased and Satisfied as I was in my former." He prayed "(If) thou shall see that to have another Consort will be for the best for me, Dispose and Encline my Heart for such a mercy and let my (mind) be overruled by Depending upon thy Goodness."[103]

The Lord could also provide a man with a specific woman. Thomas Walley planned to go to Boston to procure a wife in 1675. This "tedious Journey" was not a mission he relished, and he finally decided to delay his trip. "I came to a resolve to stay at home and not to look after a wife till the spring." To his surprise, the next morning a Mrs. Clark arrived in the neighborhood, "who had bin motioned by some of my friends the providence of god hath soe ordered it that we are agreed to become one." He marveled, "god hath sent me a wife home to me."[104] As Selleck Silliman assured his beloved Mary in 1775 "this long Chain of Occurences that has thus far rendered our Connexion beyond Expression dear (to me & to You also I hope my Love) should happen by Chance? no surely it cannot be. It is the Hand of Providence."[105]

To follow the hand of providence meant a man had to again venture on to the difficult terrain of courtship. Age and experience made courting the second time around unique for widowers. Widowers were, however, as anxious to get remarried as they had been to marry in the first place. Widows, in contrast, were more reticent. Examining the courtship process, particularly between widowers and widows, illustrates the unique perspectives and differing considerations of men and women as they contemplated a return to the altar.

Much of the courtship between a widower and a financially secure widow, for instance, took the form of negotiation. He had to prove to his reluctant love that she, rather than her estate, was the object of his desire. Richard Bourne of Sandwich, Massachusetts, assured the widowed Ruth Winslow in 1677 that his intentions were honorable and motivated purely by love regardless of what her suspicious relatives thought. "What you have now I doe not desire any of it. but you may please to keep it for your owne improvement and I hope I shall make a suitable addition to that that you have: you may please to remember that I did intimate soe much to you when I was with you though I shall bee willing to advise and helpe if you have occasion, your person and qualifications doth soe far sattisfie mee that I hope wee shall have noe need to improve your estate soe long as I have of my owne for I may truly say that I seeke not yours but you."[106] Dorothy Denison, recent widow of William Denison of Roxbury, Massachusetts, chose not to take the plunge in 1718 despite Samuel Sewall's assurances that she would not suffer financially. "She had better keep as she was, than give a Certainty for an uncertainty."[107] The income from her dead husband's estate assured her future in a way that Sewall's proposal did not.

Katherine Winthrop, widow of Major-General Wait Winthrop, shrewdly bargained with the lovesick Samuel Sewall in 1720. She wanted Sewall to guarantee her status. Such motives clearly marked her insistence that he buy a private coach and a periwig. He considered her suggestions but claimed keeping a coach would land him in "prison for Debt." He declined to wear a wig for different reasons. "My best and greatest Friend [the Lord], I could not possibly have a greater, began to find me with Hair before I was born, and had continued to do so ever since; and I could not find in my heart to go to another." In his attempt to coax the reluctant Katherine to negotiate in earnest he offered her "a Hundred pounds per annum if I dy'd before her." She did not give him a counterproposal but questioned him closely about the inheritance he intended to give his children. Sewall eventually had to concede that the Widow Winthrop did not want him. He noted bitterly while drinking with a friend, "he said: In England the Ladies minded little more than that they might have Money, and Coaches to ride in. I said, And New-England brooks its Name."

The Widow Gibbs received treatment in kind from the sixty-nine-year-old Sewall a few years later. In his negotiations he offered her £50 a year if she outlived him. He wanted £100 from her estate in return and freedom from all obligations of debt incurred by her dead husband. If a man was imprudent enough to marry a widow before her husband's estate was settled, he could become liable for any debt the first husband may have left. Widow Gibbs found these terms and the binding of her children to fulfill such an obligation "hard." She did not want to burden her children and besides "she might dye in a little time." He offered to do without the £100 if her children still agreed to be liable for the debts of their father's estate, but he would lower her yearly stipend to £40. In his courtship of Mary Gibbs, Samuel Sewall made sure that his estate would remain free of entanglements. He insisted that the Widow Gibbs make her children liable for any debts of their father so that he could remain "harmless as to her Administration."[108]

Widowers saw remarriage as a gift extended to their motherless children. If a woman loved him, as Thomas Clap reasoned in 1737, she would love his children: "One that will Love my Children for my sake and wisely and carefully Educate and Govern them with the Authority and Tenderness of a natural Parent that she may always seek and Rejoyce in their Good and find something of the Pleasure and Satisfaction ~~in them~~ of a natural mother, in them. And that they may be Disposed to Love Honour and Obey her and may have reason to Bless God for Providing such a Mother for them."[109] For some this ideal became a reality. Cotton Mather remarked on the death of his second wife, Elizabeth, in 1713, "It comforted her to see that her children in law were as fond of her, as her own could be!"[110] Samuel Sewall was blessed in his old age with a wife that "laboured beyond measure" for his daughter Hannah, crippled by a leg injury that eventually took her life.[111]

Thomas Shepard recalled a less rosy picture of his stepmother: "Father married agayne; to another woman who did let me see the difference betweene my own mother & a stepmother; shee did seeme no to loue me but incensed my father often agaynst me."[112] The possibility that a new wife might not be accepted as a surrogate mother or receive his earlier children as her own was oddly lacking in these widowers' thinking.

Mary Noyes tried to explain to Selleck Silliman in 1775 that his son might resent his remarriage. Although he might put on "an air of chearfull countenance, to welcome, a new inhabitant" his heart might hold a different sentiment. "Here comes one to possess the place of my late dear indulgent *Mamma!*— Did I think, on that fatal day, never to be forgotten; that my dear Pappa, would ever think of another. *My* wound is *recent,* why does it so soon close with *him!* can it be, that another finds a place in his affections, as did *she,* I shall always lament! Ah, he may imagine his loss made up; mine never will be."[113] As it turned out, her fears were unfounded and the two families blended with ease. Children with a new stepmother, however, had emotional issues that needed tending even if their economic future seemed secure. A widower's remarriage could have a profound emotional impact on his children whether he chose to take this into account or not. As Ashley Bowen bitterly remarked about his father's remarriage to the rich Widow Harris in 1741, "To obtain his wish he would separate his own family or anything else."[114]

Children sometimes characterized their father's remarriage as purely selfish. In 1687 Abigail Bush was brought in front of her Westfield, Massachusetts, congregation for ignoring the notion of "Parentall honour" in her characterization of her father's remarriage. She reportedly grumbled: "he married not for Love. And that he was as hot as a Skunk, & the woman as hot as a Bitch." Abigail acknowledged she had "said of my mother too much unchristian here to be mention'd." She, however, never admitted to comparing her father to a skunk in heat. Her church accepted her confession.[115] Even if a father chose well, a child could object to his remarriage. Cotton Mather remarked in 1702 that his wife's spirit had been "extremely broken" as a result of her father's "bringing home a Mother-in-law, tho' he did well in it."[116] For some children no woman could replace a beloved mother, no matter her qualifications or a father's fond hopes.

In addition, widowers rarely dwelled on the financial implications of remarriage for their children. Thomas Clap, an exception, realized in 1737 that his remarriage could hurt his children financially. If he had more children, the portion he could give to each would decline. As a widower with only two children, in contrast, he could guarantee "a Competency for them."[117] The same issue haunted Ann Blackleach Eliot of Stratford, Connecticut. Her husband had two grown children, Jacob and Betty. After the birth of her first child, Joseph, in 1762 Ann began to argue violently with her husband. His assurances that he would not "leave her & her Son to perish for want" fell on deaf ears. According to Jacob, their disagreements often involved Ann "raking up the old Stories about a first & Second Wife, first & Second Children."[118] Her concern was that her own children would be left without resources because settling the older children would absorb her husband's entire estate. Both Clap and Ann Blackleach Eliot had the same concern, but she had less control over the outcome. He could make sure remarriage did not hurt his offspring, whereas she, married and no longer in control of her estate, let alone her husband's, could do little to guarantee the same.

Widows, unlike widowers, approached remarriage with anxious concerns for their children's welfare and little legal ability to protect their interests. Selleck Silliman tried to convince the reluctant Mary Noyes in 1775 that her children would not suffer as a result of her marriage to him. "Give me Leave to ask again, is there no Way my Love in which a second Marriage founded in the Principles of true Love, vertuous Tenderness & pious Friendship can consist with the Good & Happiness of the dear Pledges of a first Love & Marriage?"[119] Mary needed convincing. Her concerns were the same as those of other widowed women. Remarriage meant a risk to both the widow and her children. If the match proved ill advised, the children could suffer economically and emotionally. "Sir, how do I know that You would treat me and my Children in this kind Manner, if You had us in your Power I have Nothing but your Word for it? Very true my Love, I freely own there is a Risque in it; God has endowed us with the noble Powers of Reason, we must in such Cases make the best Use of it to form a right Judgment, and rely upon him for makeing the Event happy. But in such a Case my own Happiness would be so absolutely & inseparably connected with Yours that I could not make You unhappy." He swore to his beloved Mary that he would treat her children "as tho they were my own." [120] But as Mary's father reminded Selleck, such good fortune was rare: "That the Dear Children, of utter Strangers the other day, should, with so much ease; become naturalized to each other, — mutually discover, & treat one another with, the like friendly Temper and Endearments, as if born of the Same Parents; nursd at ye Same Breasts, and had their principles & manners formd by the Same Instructors, Is an Event that rarely happens; & whenever it dos, demands our praise to the *Giver of All*." [121] Mary did finally accept Selleck's proposal.

A widow worried about the legal handicap of *feme covert* status, which took away her independent property rights at marriage and risked the safety of her children's inheritances. A widower courted such women free of similar concerns. As a bachelor, once economic autonomy had been achieved, a man quickly pursued a wife. The young women he pursued also looked to marriage as an opportunity for adulthood. When a widower, a man's need for a domestic partner led him to court with the same urgency. A widow may have also longed for companionship, but she proceeded with caution.

A man became a widower and promptly remarried. This was true among all kinds of men across both centuries in colonial New England. He grieved, sometimes deeply, but this did not hinder his pursuit of a new wife. A single life threatened an unnatural dependence on children. A widower needed companionship, but he also desperately needed someone to care for his children and household. Most men were successful in their search for a new mate. For others, a courtship challenged their powers of persuasion. Remarriage, therefore, was not only desirable but essential to the proper functioning of an adult man's life. Women found emotional fulfillment and economic security with their children. Men found these things only with a wife.

7

"Like an Armed Man": Retirement and Manhood

When Josiah Cotton marked his sixtieth birthday in 1740, he began to withdraw from his work life, beginning with his position as register of wills for Plymouth, Massachusetts. Despite his lobbying efforts, he failed to hold on to his position "a while longer & then to have had some hand in the disposal of it." His goal had been to "be diligent & faithful in my general & particular callings, whilst my time & capacity continue." Now forced to resign his position, Cotton felt bitter and shaken. He lamented, "I find old age coming upon me like an armed man."[1]

Retirement changed the delicate balance of family reciprocity. An interdependent family system required all members to contribute. A man who stopped working no longer made his required contribution.[2] Retirement signaled dependence rather than the familiar interdependence.[3] A dependent old man was equivalent in status to the young, the poor, the mentally ill, and the disabled.[4] Therefore, only the infirm old gave up their labors entirely. Throughout the colonial period, men struggled to be productive until they died.[5]

Avoiding retirement took on a new urgency as demographic and cultural imperatives of the eighteenth century warped traditional family systems. New England was an unusually healthy place in the seventeenth century. People lived longer than they had in Europe, particularly in rural areas. Instead of dying in one's fifties, a man could live into his seventies.[6] Old men, therefore, needed to assure their economic well-being into a prolonged future.[7] An extended, unproductive, old age suddenly seemed a real possibility to these men; they feared dependency. As land became scarce in long-settled areas in the eighteenth century, this fear became acute. A man felt less certain about distributing meager resources to sons eager to start their own interdependent families. Delayed distribution was the only way to guarantee an aging man continued self-sufficiency. Such men clung desperately to their resources. Family members still labored together, but now they worked to maintain an aging household. The result was a skewed family economic system. The father remained independent, but his children remained dependent far into adulthood.[8]

In addition to, or perhaps because of, this new demographic environment, society began to look at the old with an increasingly jaundiced eye. David Hackett Fischer contends that the aged were venerated in the seventeenth century only to be despised by the end of the eighteenth.[9] The wise elder now became the old "geezer."[10] Daniel Scott Smith argues that age no longer defined a man as valuable in the late eighteenth century; instead, wealth, status, and education became paramount.[11] As the colonial period progressed, an aging man faced the end of his work life with fear and caution and in an increasingly hostile environment.

In colonial America, the word "retirement" implied withdrawal from company rather than withdrawal from work.[12] As the health of the seventy-six-year-old Samuel Sewall deteriorated, he found himself obliged to curtail the now burdensome public service that had defined his adult life. "My extraordinary Sickness of Flux and Vomiting . . . quickened me to resign my places of Chief Justice and Judge of Probt." He hoped "that the Retirement and Leisure I am seeking for may be successfully improved in preparing for a better world."[13] His time for reflection was short; he died the following year. Sewall yearned for withdrawal from the world of work not for repose, but to loosen his bond with the corporeal world.

Retirement from company for some meant a welcome seclusion. For example, men retired to their bedchambers. Ministers retired to their studies to pray. Ebenezer Parkman "retir'd from Incumbrance" to contemplate the work of God in his life as the year 1746 began.[14] Jacob Eliot, farmer and minister of Lebanon, Connecticut, used retirement to escape domestic turmoil. He recorded his wife's displeasure with his behavior in 1762. "Sometimes twitted & bantered for Retirement; asked in seeming derision, what is that Closet [small study] is used so much for—is it to say my prayers &c."[15] Retirement meant withdrawal, blessed seclusion, and even disengagement but not idleness. A man stopped laboring in order to retire or withdrawal; he did not retire to stop laboring.

Although a complete departure from productive labor was rare, most men experienced something we would label "phased retirement." For some farmers this process began early, in their fifties, as the labor of grown children allowed them to relinquish some tasks if not give up control of the family enterprise.[16] Nonetheless, as men faced old age they continued to make some contribution if they were physically able. For most, familiar tasks became more difficult. Men noted their disabilities and mourned their loss of serviceableness. Many were forced to cut back in some form. Only extreme infirmity, however, prevented a man from making some financial contribution to the family. Such men were pitied and forced into the dreaded state of dependency.

Like a young man, an aging man wanted to be serviceable and useful.[17] A man ideally would "bring forth fruit in old age" or "Shine with uncommon Brightness even to . . . Decline."[18] Age and infirmity could conspire, however, to deny a man this ideal. On his birthday in 1777, the seventy-three-year-old David Hall of Sutton, Massachusetts, noted, "I find I am not so able to make sermons as years past." Ten years later he still preached although he remarked that while reading "a Considerable part of the Genl. Courts adress to our State" he "thro weakness . . . was not able to go thro' the reading it but Delivered it to ye Deacon and Desired him not to fail of having it read."[19] The Reverend Mr. Thompson of Boston, according to John Hull, "a disconsolate man many years, the sabbath before he died he had some lighting of mind." Thompson decided to go to church and once again take on his responsibilities as pastor in winter 1666. Although he intended "to administer the supper" he found himself unable to leave home on the appointed day. Again descending into melancholy, the Reverend Thompson died nine days later.[20] For both these men, the spirit was willing but the flesh was weak.

The specter of losing serviceableness loomed so large for Increase Mather that he preferred death to retirement. He prayed fervently for his continued usefulness: "How great will the mercy be, If I shall be taken out the world before decayes of age render me useless!" Mather felt it was "a great mercy for a minister not to outlive his work." Poor health and an increasingly poor memory made him wish for death in 1709 on the occasion of his seventieth birthday. "Considering that I feele my selfe under decays by age, so that I am not like to do service for Christ and for his people if I should live much longer because the infirmities of age will grow upon me, I pray with humble submission to the will of God, that this may be my last sinfull birth day." God withheld this blessing until 1723.[21] The ideal was that "usefullness may in some measure continue as long as I do."[22] Lucky, indeed, was Ezekiel Cheever, the famous schoolmaster, who according to Samuel Sewall, worked until his death in 1729/30 at the age of ninety-four: "So that he has Labour'd in that Calling Skillfully, diligently, constantly, Religiously, Seventy years. A rare Instance of Piety, Health, Strength, Serviceableness."[23]

Retirement came when the body gave out. Cotton Mather advised in his 1701 sermon *A Christian at his calling* that "it is not lawful for a Christian ordinarily to Live without some *Calling* or another, until Infirmities have unhappily disabled him."[24] Christian duty required a man to work. Freedom from work was a condition to be pitied.[25] In 1747, at the age of sixty-eight, Josiah Cotton had to now resign from his post as justice of the Inferior Court of Plymouth, Massachusetts. He left because his "growing forgetfulness & decays of mind" forced him "to lay down my commission." He chided himself for his surrender: "I might have held out a little longer."[26] Ebenezer Parkman actively ministered to his flock until fall 1782 when, at the age of seventy-eight, his failing eyesight put his ministry at risk. "I have experienced a grt. Alteration in my *Eyes*. A Cloud has, first more perceptibly at Evenings, arose before each of my Eyes, for I know not how many Months, for it has come on by degrees. But at length Something has so Seizd on my Right, wc always heretofore was my *Best*, Eye, that at length it is a black spot which now intercepts between ye Organ and ye Object. . . . I can't distinguish ye Nose from ye Eyes in a persons Face." With his right eye useless and his left eye providing minimal vision he remarked, "I am much put to it to read or write in ye Eveg. or dark Weather." His inability to read and write sermons took its toll: "My people have paid me no penny for 15 Months, & I know not wt. yy will do."[27] Parkman died the following year. Only disability allowed men to put down their burdens, and then the necessity left them regretful and frustrated.

Struggle though he might to maintain his position, a man gained some comfort from leaving at the right time. At least one's exit could be graceful. Cotton Mather urged his parishioners in 1726 to be "Seasonable" in their retirement. "Be so Wise, as to *Disappear* of your own Accord, as soon and as far as you lawfully may."[28] As Samuel Sewall stepped down from the Superior Court of Massachusetts in 1727, a few weeks before his seventy-fifth birthday, he noted, "I was not capable to do the work, and therefore was not willing to hold the place."[29] Sewall felt this kind of a sacrifice was both prudent and honorable.[30] Earlier, in 1712, when another member of the court had resigned, Sewall noted that he "has given us a further Instance of his Integrity by resigning his place because he apprehended himself incapable of sustaining it by reason of the Infirmities of his Age, (hardness of hearing)."[31] In 1728, Sewall commended Solomon Stoddard, longtime minister of Northampton, Massachusetts, on his ability to "continue your Ministerial Labours on the Sabbath and Lecture, which is wonderfull, yet now it is with much pain; and you hardly expect to live out the winter." Under these circumstances although his "unparalleld constancy of Serviceableness" was undoubtedly a blessing, "When the Set Time comes, I hope you will be enabled joyfully to pronounce Simeon's *Nunc dimittis* [depart in peace].[32]

Less productivity usually meant some decline in resources.[33] Josiah Cotton described his "circumstances" as "precarious" as he faced the potential loss of his position as register of deeds for Plymouth in 1751. Having relinquished his other remaining public post four years earlier due to the infirmities of age, he now depended for the "main part of Support" on his continuation as register of deeds.[34] Joseph Fish gave up his work for the Society for Promoting the Gospel in New England and Parts Adjacent, which ran a school in Charlestown, Rhode Island, for the Narragansett, just before his seventieth birthday in 1776. Committed to—if not overly successful at—converting these Native Americans, he nonetheless felt the necessity to cut back on his ministerial responsibilities even if this meant the loss of "a pretty Resource." This, plus a continuing struggle to "collect My Dues" from a poor and reluctant congregation, not only prevented his usual generosity to his grandchildren, "but we find it even impracticable to get a Sufficiency for our own necessities."[35]

Ministers of all ages complained of their stingy congregations.[36] The elderly, however, had to face their own diminishing capacities and a disgruntled congregation just as their strength for the all-too-familiar struggle waned. The frustration congregations felt toward old sermons and lackluster delivery made them loath to pay an elderly pastor. In 1781, at eighty-two and barely able to complete a Sunday sermon, David Hall found himself "in great trouble for want of My due for Sallery. The Lord be my Slary."[37] Old ministers found their congregations particularly tightfisted—a sore disappointment to men who had served their people for a lifetime.

The parishioners of Ebenezer Parkman had often complained of his dry delivery and familiar sermons; as he aged, they became even less tolerant. Some of the less scrupulous townsfolk exploited his increasing vulnerability. "The Town met to day, partly on acc[oun]t. of ye min[isteria]l. Lot . . . to See whether I would consent to its being sold; and they include also ye min[isteria]l meadow. This latter I consented to (the Interest of ye money being duly paid to me, while I continue in ye ministry). But concer[nin]g the Wood-Lot, I desird to have Time to consider of so import[an]t. an affair as the Selling of it. However, ye Town, I said, might be Sure of it t[ha]t. I Sh[oul]d. not consent to their selling it except they w[oul]d. pass a vote to find me my wood." Parkman struggled for at least a maintenance. He found himself the victim of the "Spoil

& Ravage" of his wood land as locals began to help themselves to the old man's supply. He begged that "Some affect[ive]. care be taken abt. this."[38]

Burdened with financial insecurity and even hostility, men looked for "a Staffe and Comfort" as they aged.[39] For some, aid came from the divine wellspring that had guided them throughout their lives. Benjamin Trumbull of Hebron, Connecticut, urged his grandparents in 1758 to continue to rely on the "Heavenly Friend" of their youth: "While you receive one Smile from your Heavenly Friend and enjoy communion with God and his Son Jesus Christ, you will rejoice with greater Joy even under all the Pains Troubles and Disquietudes of advanced age, that all the Pleasures of Youth and or Vigor can give, even with those yt are peculiar to the Redeamed of the Lord and the Favourites of heaven."[40] John Gates of Stow, Massachusetts, on his seventy-sixth birthday in 1789, prayed to the God of his "Childrenhood and youth and so through Life Even to old age" not to "forsake" him "now Gray hairs and old age are Come on me."[41] The challenges of aging and retirement were simply new trials that could be successfully confronted with divine assistance. God's help was easily asked for and freely given. David Hall noted in 1787, "My God & Father in Christ my Dear Saviour. hath carried me along in this Wilderness More than 82 years. and in my old age he Helpeth me."[42]

Men struggled, however, with requesting and receiving earthly comfort. Physical decline meant an aging man could no longer work, and yet the work, particularly on a farm, still had to get done. What a man could no longer accomplish became the responsibility of a spouse, a servant, a neighbor, or most often, a child. Occasionally men made formal agreements with their children, dubbed by one historian as "agrarian retirement."[43] Lavish in detail, these contracts outlined support for parents in exchange for property. These arrangements were a common way to provide for widows, but men rarely made such living provisions for themselves.[44] Control of family resources, whenever possible, was shared with, but not transferred to, the next generation. More common was a change in what John Demos has called the "self/other" ratio.[45] Men increasingly relied on others to accomplish necessary tasks.

The case of Walter Lee, preserved for posterity in the church records kept by Rev. Edward Taylor of early eighteenth-century Westfield, Massachusetts, provides a revealing glimpse of this shifting balance between work and retirement. Walter did make an agrarian retirement agreement with his son John. He "Covenanted with his Eldest Son, John Lee, & therein cast himselfe upon him as to his mentainance both for himselfe, & Wife, during their Live[s], & in way of recompense bargain'd, & made over by Deed confirm'd according to Law all his in lands & goods, etc., Moveables, & other." Walter's other children protested the arrangement that denied them a share of their father's estate. They went to court claiming their father was not competent to make such an agreement because the "Decays of Age" had made him prone to "Childishne[ss,] Feebleness & Changeableness."

Central to this court action was Lee's capacity to work and support himself. When he became widowed, Walter Lee took up residence with his son John, as they had agreed. He "took his provision with him whi[ch] was a part of a Barrell of pork * * * & I[ndi]an Corn." His son's family, however, began to eat the old man's food. Walter saw that he could soon go wanting. Feeling such behavior indicated a breach of promise, he left and moved in with his daughter and her husband. Walter lived there for five months and then, remarkably, remarried. At this point, he lived on his own although John continued to do his "greate worke" for him. Walter then proceeded to outlive his second wife, a third wife, and even his hapless son. Again, under the necessity of turning to his children, he chose to go to his daughter's home rather than stay with John's widow. He felt unwelcome in John's old home, in part because a sassy granddaughter "told him to his face that he w[as] not worth the Droppings of his nose." Walter stayed with his daughter only eleven weeks when he, "being offended," went to live with John's widow despite his misgivings. His son-in-law, however, wanted to be paid for his trouble. Walter refused and the disgruntled son-in-law brought him to court. The case revolved around whether the old man had the capacity to make his own decisions.

Edward Taylor, as local minister, had testified to Walter's condition without a full awareness, he claimed, of how his testimony would be manipulated by the feuding children. Taylor recorded at length Walter Lee's circumstances to prove to himself and perhaps to posterity that he never thought the old man needed a guardian. Accordingly, Taylor left a remarkable description of phased retirement and the changing self/other ratio for an elderly man in colonial New England. From Taylor's perspective, Lee was "of Sufficient Capacity now to Carry on the Concerns of his Calling answerable to his former carrying out of the same, greate worke onely excepted, & if his wife was alive, he would be beholding to none of them for his tables." Specifically, Taylor outlined the work that Lee still did himself on the farm. "For tho' the man is not able to mannage strong worke as Plowing, Carting, etc., yet when his land is plow'd he plants, Woods, hills, & gathers his Corn: Reaps his Winter grain, pulls his Flax, makes his hay, buys what things he needs, of Merchants, Shoemakers, Taylors, & payes them, is rated in the town, & payes his dues." In other words, he worked and paid his debts. His son John, in contrast, had contributed his share, "plowing, mowing, Carting, & found him wood for 14 or 15 years." Although Taylor felt it wrong for Lee to alienate his land to prevent his son and his descendants from gaining a promised inheritance, he did not think him "in Such a State as required Guardians."[46]

Men relied most often on their children to provide aid but, as Lee's example demonstrates, such help was highly charged. The self/other ratio did not shift without conflict. Family responsibility implied reciprocity. Lee moved in with his son until the loss of his provisions meant their agreement had been broken. Lee moved in with his daughter, but his son-in-law expected payment. All sides had a firm hold on what they thought constituted proper conduct. The shifting boundaries of family obligation chaffed at them all.

Children were obliged to be the props of aging parents. Selleck and Mary Silliman believed, "in the common Course of human Affairs," children were to be "the Props & Supporters of our Hond Parents in their declining Years." They lamented in 1779 their distance from Mary's parents—the young couple in Fairfield and the older pair in Stonington, Connecticut. As Mary's parents aged, their isolation from their only surviving child became poignant.[47] New London minister, Mather Byles, when faced with the terminal illness of his sister in 1763, wrote that his heart was "almost ready to break," particularly "when I consider my Father as so likely to loose one of the principal Props of his declining years." The following year, another sibling died, this time a brother. He wrote to one of his remaining sisters, Mary. "I feel a thousand tender Pangs for my poor Father, under his complicated Distresses, & forsaken of those who, if they had lived, would have rejoyced to have been the Prop of his declining Years. You & my Sister *Katy* must endeavor, as far as you are able, to make up the Loss: & tread in the Steps of your departed Brother & Sister, who were the most shining Examples of Filial Duty & Affection I ever met with." From New London, Byles could do little to help his father in

Boston. He wrote to his sister, "'Tis yours, to rock the Cradle of reposing Age, while your Brother, thro' the Humanity of the Times, can do little more than drop his unavailing Tears at a Distance."[48]

Children ideally supported their parents as necessary, both emotionally and financially.[49] The church reminded even adult children to "Honor thy father and thy mother."[50] In *The Well-Ordered Family,* published in 1712, Benjamin Wadsworth argued, *"Children should be very willing and ready, to Support and Maintain their Indigent Parents."*[51] Public officials tried to force solvent children to live up to their responsibilities. When "father Bulard and His wiffe ware in great nesesity of sum Hellp By reson of Thear age Being vnabell To Hellp Them selves" the selectmen of Watertown, Massachusetts, determined to meet with their son and son-in-law to "see if thay Could not afford Thear aged parents such Hellp as is needfull for them in Thear nesesity." Likewise, "Luis Allin: an aged man of sd town being in a suffering Condition: through age: Infirmity: &: Extream pouerty" found himself without support when his son Ebenezer "under much bodily Infirmity: &: Inconueniancies" himself became "unable to support his aged father any longer at present." His other son, Abel, was "unwilling to take Care of his aged father." The selectmen were convinced that Abel was "in a good mesur able to help to support his aged father: with the help of the town which he hether to hath refused."[52] Public officials tried to force children to be dutiful to their parents, but when necessary they acted the part themselves. When "Ould knap" turned in desperation to the selectmen, they proposed that his children support him in exchange for his estate. But if his children proved truculent, the town would "vndertake the same, apon such tearmes as the children should."[53] Not all children supported their parents in old age, but society modeled such behavior.

In fact, most children were spared this necessity. Some men lost ground economically as they aged, but most successfully maintained their resources. Men over fifty in colonial New England saw some decline in their estates as they settled their children into adulthood, but they also had fewer expenditures.[54] Children left home, diminishing financial outlay, and the few that remained behind provided the labor necessary for the family's continued economic solvency.[55] In eighteenth-century Guilford, Connecticut, one out of three married sons shared a household with their parents.[56] Among preindustrial English families, about one-half of men over sixty-five lived with their unmarried children.[57] Only misfortune left a man dependent or alone in colonial New England.

Pitiful was the man who found that age and poor health deprived him of his ability to work. Such a man became an encumbrance to his family and to society. Joseph Fish, farmer and minister in Stonington, Connecticut, assured his son-in-law and daughter in 1778 that although at times ailing he was still able to work: "What a mercy is it, that our *old age* is not, altogether, cumbersome to ye Earth & Burdensome to our Fellow Men."[58] Josiah Cotton made note of his declining capacities: "I find myself of late under decays; my Eyesight fails considerably, my Memory is less retentive, and my thoughts (tho never very quick & penetrating) are now at farther distance, longer gathering up, & less comprehensive then usual when I have occasion for them &c." He prayed that he not accordingly "become a Cumberer of the Earth."[59] Nothing could be worse than to end one's life like John Ashley of Westfield, Massachusetts, who when he died in 1759 at the age of ninety, had "outlived the expectations of his friends and even the desires of some of his relations."[60]

One of the signs of declining vigor was an increasing inability to travel.[61] When one had trouble riding in a wagon or walking, particularly in poor weather, dependency loomed. This was a poignant demarcation for men. Age and pain might keep a man housebound perhaps for the first time in his life. Samuel Sewall lamented to a friend in 1728, "I am now in a great measure past Travelling, yet still praying to God to correct the Disorders of my Back, to strengthen my weak Hands, and to confirm my feeble Knees."[62] Sewall felt such limitations deserved the label of imprisonment. Speaking of an eighty-year-old friend in 1708, he noted, "Has been a Prisoner in his house almost two years by reason of Sickness."[63] Increase Mather described himself in 1703 as "so stricken in years, as that I am indisposed to travell."[64] Thomas Oliver, a "ruling elder" of his church in Boston, "kept his house, or went very little abroad, for the space of three years before he died" in 1657 at the age of ninety.[65] Confinement to the home limited a man's ability to work and function in the public world. Lack of mobility meant, therefore, both dependency and potentially a redefinition of masculine identity beyond the domestic sphere.

For some, their needs became so pressing that they gave up their homes. Ebenezer Parkman, seventy-eight and blinded by cataracts, turned to a married daughter and her husband for assistance. "My Son & Dauter *Brigham* live in the Same House; He takes Care of ye work on the place; has hird a Man &c." Parkman maintained as much autonomy as possible within the context of this arrangement: "We board in most respects in Comon—in many instances have *peculiarly*."[66] Richard Wilkins, a Boston bookseller, went to live with his daughter in 1704. He was "blind and helpless." He moved into his daughter's home simply "to live and dye." He rode through the streets of Boston and "call'd and took leave as he went along."[67] Wilkins said good-bye to neighbors and friends, but he also bid farewell to his life as an adult male in colonial Boston.

Housebound and finally homeless, an elderly man could lose his ability to provide for his family and for himself. He did not labor at his calling to help support his family; they labored at theirs to support him. He was no longer a productive member of society; he was a mere encumbrance. He was, like a child, no longer able to claim his adult place in the world of work.

Retirement meant loss, not leisure, for colonial New England men.[68] They already faced a prolonged old age in the seventeenth century, and they may have confronted an increasingly hostile social environment as the eighteenth century came to a close. Although men continued to work as long as they were able throughout the colonial period, their quest, therefore, took on a new urgency as the end of the eighteenth century neared. Continued serviceableness remained the goal. Most men entered a stage of phased retirement—working when they could and turning to others when necessary. Children were the cornerstone of a successful old age. Most men, however, avoided total dependence on their offspring. The few unfortunates who found themselves without recourse gave in to dependency. These men felt that they had been robbed of their usefulness.

Conclusion

A man's power and identity originated in the home and like rings in a pond when a pebble is dropped reached to the outer shores. When Roger Wolcott, former governor of Connecticut, died in 1767 at the age of eighty-nine, a sermon given in his honor described the centrality of the domestic world to even such a public figure. Joseph Perry, a minister in Windsor observed:

> Soon after he settled in a family state, he began to emerge from his former obscurity. His worth began to appear, and to be acknowledged first, in a more private manner, among his neighbors and townsmen. They improved him in the business of the town, and at length elected him their representative, at the general assembly. Here he acquitted himself so well, that he began to be noticed in a more public manner. He soon had a commission for the peace; after this, was chosen into the council; then appointed judge of the county court; then one of the judges of the Superior Court; after this, chosen deputy governor; and appointed chief judge of the Superior court, and then chosen governor of the colony of Connecticut.[1]

A man launched himself into the public world from the bosom of his family. A "goodman" first provided service to his family, then his community, and for men like Wolcott, finally the public world beyond.

A man in colonial New England was fundamentally dependent on his family for his sense of self. This made him vulnerable both at home and abroad. His status derived from his own efforts, but also from the efforts of those around him. If his domestic foundation crumbled, a man struggled to maintain not only his proper role within his family, but his reputation in the broader community. Ironically, the domestic world that created such a man also posed the greatest threat to his identity.

These men balanced love with power as husbands and love with discipline as fathers. They shared the economic burden of providing with their families, but as men they held the legal and cultural responsibility for their families' care. These men anxiously and speedily remarried when death ruptured their marriage and threatened their domestic foundations. The constant repetition of these broad patterns marked the terrain of colonial New England manhood and seems strangely familiar today.

A changing demographic environment and a new sentimentalism at the end of the eighteenth century complicated this curious continuity. Men, particularly in eastern New England, found themselves in short supply and, therefore, a valued commodity in the marriage market. They dared to use this new power to pursue, at times rakishly, the wealthy and the fair. At the same time, courting men found the new requirements of sentimentality daunting as they exposed their hearts and reputations on the new playing field of love. The men studied here did speak more freely of their affection toward their wives and children as the colonial period came to a close, but, as before, both love and power remained central. Old men feared the loss of usefulness in both centuries although the increasingly hostile environment for the old as the colonial period came to an end may have pressed them with new urgency to hold their place and shun retirement. During the Revolution, independence from a fatherly king and a motherly country ostensibly drove men to war.[2] Like a young man coming of age, however, interdependence continued to characterize the relations between England and her colonies long after the smoke cleared. Can we then speculate that independence from England may not have been the goal for these colonial men, since national interdependence remained. Maybe these eighteenth-century men were not fighting the War for Independence at all; rather, they put their lives on the line for a War against Dependency? Colonial men were demanding to be "useful" in an imperial system that only valued their economic subordination. Rethinking the birth of our nation and the "fathers" who founded it, in light of colonial concepts of manhood, might yield intriguing new insights.[3]

By the beginning of the nineteenth century, men looked to the world outside their families and immediate communities for self-definition. Domestic concerns gave way to public ones. Men were consigned to the public sphere and women to the private. Men competed with one another in this public domain for status and resources. "Usefulness" became less valued than individual achievement. Such men became so detached from the colonial emphasis on service to family and community that the successful and admired were dubbed "self-made."

Today, a man still agonizes over his career choice, negotiates the perilous terrain of courtship, starts a family, loses a wife, and retires. The roles remain, but the influence of the public world has eclipsed the colonial emphasis on the domestic. Male roles in the family and in the community are, nonetheless, still re-creating themselves. In the late twentieth-century United States, some men have begun to look beyond the work place for self-definition and have increasingly recommitted themselves to their families and communities. Perhaps the twenty-first century will see "useful" men once again return to "domestick concerns."

Notes

A Note on Sources and Methodology

The sources consulted for this study were wide-ranging. Traditional diaries and letters were the most revealing, but court records, church records, and sermons also received attention. I never entirely overcame the inherent bias toward the articulate elite in self-revelatory sources. My method, at first, was to read everything; for example, I read every colonial man's diary in the Massachusetts Historical Society collection. Although I combed carefully through those from the pens of farmers and artisans, journals or diaries with details beyond weather and local news were few and far between. Similarly, any collection that seemed to talk to the issue of class or ethnic balance received special attention. Although very time consuming, this process unearthed some new voices.

The court records proved useful in exposing the common man's perspective. Again, reading everything page by page seemed the only way to approach these records. After a great deal of time and minimal results, I decided to focus primarily on the *Records and Files of the Quarterly Courts of Essex County, Massachusetts*. As other historians have noted, the depositions given by witnesses in the small cases before this court provide invaluable details about daily life and attitudes. In other words, these are not just the voices of deviants, but the views of the community that labeled them as such. In addition, because the records for Essex are published and partially indexed, the needle-in-a-hay-stack kind of research became manageable. One cannot look up "manhood" and find an entry, but one can use existing entries to gain access to relevant documents.

I did not consult probate records or tax lists in part because these documents have already received a great deal of scholarly attention from social historians and have yielded an impressive profile of colonial New England. Instead, I used these studies to set the stage for the drama I saw unfolding in the lives of the men I analyzed. I wanted to contextualize these previous findings by trying to get at the elusive issue of motivation as well as behavior.

Introduction

1. Diary of Peter Thatcher, 26 September 1679, Massachusetts Historical Society, Boston, Massachusetts (hereafter cited as MHS).

2. Samuel Sewall, *Letter-book, Collections of the Massachusetts Historical Society*, vol. 1 (Boston: Massachusetts Historical Society, 1886–88), 108–9.

3. *The Winthrop Papers, Correspondence of Wait Winthrop (continued), Collections of the Massachusetts Historical Society*, vol. 5 (Boston: Massachusetts Historical Society, 1928), 189.

4. Cotton Mather, *Diary of Cotton Mather*, ed. Worthington Chauncey Ford (New York: Frederick Ungar, 1911), vol. 2, 397.

5. John R. Gillis argues a similar point about fathers in early modern England. See Gillis, "Bringing Up Father: British Paternal Identities, 1700 to Present," *Masculinities* 3 (fall 1995): 4–5.

6. Daniel Vickers, *Farmers and Fishermen: Two Centuries of Work in Essex County, Massachusetts, 1630–1850* (Chapel Hill: University of North Carolina Press, 1994); Laurel Thatcher Ulrich, "Housewife and Gadder: Themes of Self-Sufficiency and Community in Eighteenth-Century New England," in *"To Toil the Livelong Day": America's Women at Work, 1780–1980*, ed. Carol Groneman and Mary Beth Norton (Ithaca: Cornell University Press, 1987), 21–34; Bettye Hobbs Pruitt, "Self-Sufficiency and the Agricultural Economy of Eighteenth-Century Massachusetts," *William and Mary Quarterly* 41 (July 1984): 333–64. For early modern England and France, see Louise A. Tilly and Joan W. Scott, *Women, Work, and Family* (New York: Holt, Rinehart and Winston, 1978), pt. 1.

7. Cornelia Hughes Dayton has found a link between manhood and a man's standing as a good neighbor in colonial New Haven. See Dayton, *Women Before the Bar: Gender, Law, and Society in Connecticut, 1639–1789* (Chapel Hill: University of North Carolina Press, 1995), 295–96.

8. The literature on domesticity is vast. The concept has dominated women's history since the 1960s. Some classic works include Barbara Welter, "The Cult of True Womanhood: 1820-1860," *American Quarterly* 18 (summer 1966): 151–66, 171–74; Gerda Lerner, "The Lady and the Mill Girl: Changes in the Status of Women in the Age of Jackson," *Mid-Continent American Studies Journal* 10 (spring 1969): 5–15; Nancy F. Cott, *The Bonds of Womanhood: "Woman's Sphere" in New England, 1780–1835* (New Haven: Yale University Press, 1977); Mary P. Ryan, *Cradle of the Middle Class: The Family in Oneida County, New York, 1790–1865* (Cambridge: Cambridge University Press, 1981). The more recent critiques of this literature include Mary Beth Norton, "The Paradox of 'Women's Sphere,'" in *Women*

of America: A History, ed. Carol Ruth Berkin and Mary Beth Norton (Boston: Houghton Mifflin, 1979), 139–49; Linda K. Kerber, "Separate Spheres, Female Worlds, Woman's Place: The Rhetoric of Women's History," *Journal of American History* 75 (June 1988): 9–39; Linda K. Kerber et al., "Beyond Roles, Beyond Spheres: Thinking about Gender in the Early Republic," *William and Mary Quarterly* 46 (July 1989): 565–85. Colonial historians have tried to shape this paradigm into a useful construct for the earlier period. Kathleen M. Brown has detected a glimmer of a kind of separate spheres ideology as early as the eighteenth century among the Virginia elite. See Brown, *Good Wives, Nasty Wenches, and Anxious Patriarchs: Gender, Race, and Power in Colonial Virginia* (Chapel Hill: University of North Carolina Press, 1996).

9. Mary Beth Norton, *Founding Mothers and Fathers: Gendered Power and the Forming of American Society* (New York: Alfred A. Knopf, 1996), 19–23.

10. The work of Joan Wallach Scott is the starting point for many of these studies. See Scott, "Gender: A Useful Category of Historical Analysis," *American Historical Review* 91 (December 1986): 1053–75 and *Gender and the Politics of History* (New York: Columbia University Press, 1988). Colonial historians who have focused primarily on issues of gender and power include Ramón A. Gutiérrez, *When Jesus Came, the Corn Mothers Went Away: Marriage, Sexuality, and Power in New Mexico, 1500–1846* (Stanford: Stanford University Press, 1991); Susan Juster, *Disorderly Women: Sexual Politics and Evangelicalism in Revolutionary New England* (Ithaca: Cornell University Press, 1994); Steve J. Stern, *The Secret History of Gender: Women, Men, and Power in Late Colonial Mexico* (Chapel Hill: University of North Carolina Press, 1995); Brown, *Good Wives;* Norton, *Founding Mothers and Fathers;* Ann Marie Little, "A 'Wel Ordered Commonwealth': Gender and Politics in New Haven Colony, 1636–1690" (Ph.d. diss., University of Pennsylvania, 1996), 4, 50–84.

11. Gerda Lerner, *The Creation of Patriarchy* (New York: Oxford University Press, 1986), 239. Kathleen Brown defines a more domestic form of patriarchy in early Virginia as "the historically specific authority of the father over his household, rooted in his control over labor and property, his sexual access to his wife and dependent female laborers, his control over other men's sexual access to the women of his household, and his right to punish family members and laborers." See Brown, *Good Wives,* 4–5.

12. An early call for a more nuanced view of "patriarchal New England society" was made by Laurel Thatcher Ulrich in "Vertuous Women Found: New England Ministerial Literature, 1668–1735," *American Quar-*

terly 28 (spring 1976): 40. It must also be kept in mind that the influence of patriarchy itself changed over time. See Dayton, *Women Before the Bar*, 9–10; Brown, *Good Wives*, 140.

13. The division utilized here profited from Joseph F. Kett's work on adolescence. He categorized developmental changes for young men according to notions of dependency, semidependency, and independence rather than age. See Kett, *Rites of Passage: Adolescence in America 1790 to the Present* (New York: Basic Books, 1977). In addition, Toby L. Ditz's idea of independent households, Daniel Vickers's concept of interdependence, and Cornelia Hughes Dayton's new work on dependency helped shape my thinking. See Toby L. Ditz, *Property and Kinship: Inheritance in Early Connecticut, 1750–1820* (Princeton: Princeton University Press, 1986), 117; Vickers, *Farmers and Fishermen;* and Cornelia Hughes Dayton, "Notes from the Archives: Madness, Gender, and Dependency in Early New England," paper presented at the Boston Area Seminar in Early American History, Boston, 1996.

14. Much has been written about life's stages. In the Western world, however, adult life usually included a notion of increase and decline. Stages were marked from the time of Aristotle by life changes more than chronological age. See J. A. Burrow, *The Ages of Man: A Study in Medieval Writing and Thought* (Oxford: Clarendon Press, 1986). The economic cycle of the family was also key. See Michael Mitterauer and Reinhard Sieder, *The European Family: Patriarchy to Partnership from the Middle Ages to the Present* (Chicago: University of Chicago Press, 1982).

15. The domestic world also included servants. The connection between master and servant sometimes resembled that of parent and child; in fact, a servant could be like a child and sometimes was a relative. Still, it is clear that labor dynamics and a sensitivity to racial issues are essential to unraveling this complex connection. Although beyond the scope of this book, the master-servant relationship needs further study with an awareness that gender issues and definitions of manhood are also at the core of this relationship.

16. Edmund S. Morgan, *The Puritan Family: Religion and Domestic Relations in Seventeenth-Century New England,* rev. ed. (New York: Harper and Row, 1966).

17. Joe L. Dubbert, *A Man's Place: Masculinity in Transition* (Englewood Cliffs, N.J.: Prentice-Hall, 1979); Elizabeth H. Pleck and Joseph H. Pleck, *The American Man* (Englewood Cliffs, N.J.: Prentice-Hall, 1980); Michael S. Kimmel, ed., *Changing Men: New Directions in Research on*

Men and Masculinity (Newbury Park, Calif.: Sage Publications, 1987);
Mark C. Carnes, *Secret Ritual and Manhood in Victorian America* (New
Haven: Yale University Press, 1989); Mark Carnes and Clyde Griffen,
eds., *Meanings for Manhood: Constructions of Masculinity in Victorian
America* (Chicago: University of Chicago Press, 1990); Robert L. Gris-
wold, *Fatherhood in America: A History* (New York: Basic Books, 1993);
E. Anthony Rotundo, *American Manhood: Transformations in Masculinity
from the Revolution to the Modern Era* (New York: Basic Books, 1993);
Michael Kimmel, *Manhood in America: A Cultural History* (New York:
Free Press, 1996). A few notable exceptions are Kenneth A. Lockridge,
*On the Sources of Patriarchal Rage: The Commonplace Books of William
Byrd and Thomas Jefferson and the Gendering of Power in the Eighteenth
Century* (New York: New York University Press, 1992); Toby L. Ditz,
"Shipwrecked; or, Masculinity Imperiled: Mercantile Representations
of Failure and the Gendered Self in Eighteenth-Century Philadel-
phia," *Journal of American History* 81 (June 1994): 51-80; Jane Kamensky,
"Talk Like a Man: Speech, Power, and Masculinity in Early New En-
gland," *Gender and History* 8 (April 1996): 22-47. Mary Beth Norton and
Kathleen M. Brown also address manhood, if not exclusively, in *Founding
Mothers and Fathers* and *Good Wives*, respectively. Ann Marie Little and
Mark E. Kann focus on the issue of gender and politics in early America.
See Little, "'Wel Ordered Commonwealth" and Kann, *A Republic of
Men: The American Founders, Gendered Language and Patriarchal Politics*
(New York: New York University Press, 1998).

18. The term "agrarian patriarchy" was first coined by Pleck and Pleck,
American Man, 6-13. Others who use this term include Harry Brod,
"Introduction: Themes and Theses of Men's Studies," in *The Making of
Masculinities: The New Men's Studies*, ed. Harry Brod (Boston: Allen and
Unwin, 1987), 50; Michael S. Kimmel, "The Contemporary 'Crisis' of
Masculinity in Historical Perspective," in *Making of Masculinities*, 126-35;
Carnes, *Secret Ritual*, 109-26; Dubbert, *Man's Place*, 15.

19. Alexander Keyssar, "Widowhood in Eighteenth-Century Massachusetts:
A Problem in the History of the Family," *Perspectives in American History* 8 (1974): 83-119; Nancy F. Cott, "Divorce and the Changing Status
of Women in Eighteenth-Century Massachusetts," *William and Mary
Quarterly* 33 (October 1976): 586-614; Lyle Koehler, *A Search for Power:
The "Weaker Sex" in Seventeenth-Century New England* (Urbana: University of Illinois Press, 1980); Laurel Thatcher Ulrich, *Good Wives: Image
and Reality in the Lives of Women in Northern New England, 1650-1750*

(New York: Alfred A. Knopf, 1982); C. Dallett Hemphill, "Women in Court: Sex Role Differentiation in Salem, Massachusetts, 1636-1683," *William and Mary Quarterly* 39 (January 1982): 164-75; Carol F. Karlsen, *The Devil in the Shape of a Woman: Witchcraft in Colonial New England* (New York: W. W. Norton, 1987); Cornelia Hughes Dayton, "Taking the Trade: Abortion and Gender Relations in an Eighteenth-Century New England Village," *William and Mary Quarterly* 48 (January 1991): 19-49; Marilyn J. Westerkamp, "Puritan Patriarchy and the Problem of Revelation," *Journal of Interdisciplinary History* 23 (winter 1993): 571-95; Gloria L. Main, "Gender, Work, and Wages in Colonial New England," *William and Mary Quarterly* 51 (January 1994): 39-66; Juster, *Disorderly Women;* Dayton, *Women Before the Bar;* Norton, *Founding Mothers and Fathers;* Brown, *Good Wives;* Elizabeth Reis, *Damned Women: Sinners and Witches in Puritan New England* (Ithaca: Cornell University Press, 1997).

20. Judith Butler, *Gender Trouble: Feminism and the Subversion of Identity* (New York: Routledge, 1990). She refines her ideas, in part as a response to various critics, in *Bodies That Matter: On the Discursive Limits of "Sex"* (New York: Routledge, 1993).

21. See, e.g., Morgan, *Puritan Family,* 27.

22. See Roger Thompson, *Sex in Middlesex: Popular Mores in a Massachusetts County, 1649-1699* (Amherst: University of Massachusetts Press, 1986), chap. 4.

23. F. Ivan Nye, "Role Constructs: Measurement," in *Role Structure and Analysis of the Family,* ed. F. Ivan Nye (Beverly Hills, Calif.: Sage Publications, 1976), 17.

24. This is not to say these roles were indicative of sexual behavior. Homosexual behavior, if not the category of "gayness," could be found within and outside these prescribed roles. See Robert Oaks, "'Things Fearful to Name': Sodomy and Buggery in Seventeenth-Century New England," in *The American Man,* ed. Elizabeth H. Pleck and Joseph H. Pleck (Englewood Cliffs, N.J.: Prentice-Hall, 1980), 53-76; Michael Warner, "New English Sodom," *American Literature* 64 (March 1992): 19-47; Richard Godbeer, "'The Cry of Sodom': Discourse, Intercourse, and Desire in Colonial New England," *William and Mary Quarterly* 52 (April 1995): 259-86.

25. F. Ivan Nye and Viktor Gecas, "The Role Concept: Review and Delineation," in *Role Structure and Analysis of the Family,* ed. F. Ivan Nye (Beverly Hills, Calif.: Sage Publications, 1976), 10-11.

26. Tamara K. Hareven, ed., *Transitions: The Family and the Life Course in Historical Perspective* (New York: Academic Press, 1978), 1-16.

27. Included are colonies that were absorbed by Massachusetts and Connecticut by the time of the Revolution, i.e. Plymouth and New Haven.

28. Morgan, *Puritan Family;* John Demos, *A Little Commonwealth: Family Life in Plymouth Colony* (New York: Oxford University Press, 1970); Philip Greven, *The Protestant Temperament: Patterns of Child-Rearing, Religious Experience, and the Self in Early America* (New York: New American Library, 1977); Gerald F. Moran and Maris A. Vinovskis, "The Puritan Family and Religion: A Critical Reappraisal," *William and Mary Quarterly* 39 (January 1982): 29–63.

29. Michael Kimmel has recently argued that the late-eighteenth-century American man rejected not only English notions of aristocratic effete manhood but also the homegrown roles of "genteel patriarch" or alternatively "heroic artisan." The ideal became the "self-made man." Such an American man was "independent, self-controlled, responsible." This new man made his mark in the public sphere. See Kimmel, *Manhood in America,* 8–26.

30. Brown, *Good Wives,* 321. This process actually began in Europe. See Jennifer L. Morgan, " 'Some Could Suckle over Their Shoulder': Male Travelers, Female Bodies, and the Gendering of Racial Ideology, 1500–1770," *William and Mary Quarterly* 54 (January 1997): 167–92; Karen Ordahl Kupperman, "Presentment of Civility: English Reading of American Self-Presentation in the Early Years of Colonization," *William and Mary Quarterly* 54 (January 1997): 193–228.

31. Philip D. Morgan, "British Encounters with Africans and African-Americans, circa 1600–1780," in *Strangers within the Realm: Cultural Margins of the First British Empire,* ed. Bernard Bailyn and Philip D. Morgan (Chapel Hill: University of North Carolina Press, 1991), 157–219.

32. Kupperman, "Presentment of Civility," 194–95; Eve Kornfeld, "Encountering 'The Other': American Intellectuals and Indians in the 1790s," *William and Mary Quarterly* 52 (April 1995): 291; June Namias, *White Captives: Gender and Ethnicity on the American Frontier* (Chapel Hill: University of North Carolina Press, 1993), 86.

33. See, e.g., James Axtell, ed., *The Indian Peoples of Eastern America: A Documentary History of the Sexes* (New York: Oxford University Press, 1981); John Demos, *The Unredeemed Captive: A Family Story from Early America* (New York: Vintage, 1994); William Cronon, *Changes in the Land: Indians, Colonists, and the Ecology of New England* (New York: Hill and Wang, 1983).

34. Namias, *White Captives,* 86.

35. For the conflicted response of New Englanders to Native Americans taking on colonial behavior, see Jenny Hale Pulsipher, "Massacre at Hurtleberry Hill: Christian Indians and English Authority in Metacom's War," *William and Mary Quarterly* 53 (July 1996): 459–86.

36. Long hair suggested Irish as well as Native American savagery. See Brown, *Good Wives*, 36. Even when European fops took on the style the fear of infectious savagery shook those who frowned upon such foolery. See Kupperman, "Presentment of Civility," 197 and 226.

37. For an interesting discussion of this phenomenon, see Timothy J. Shannon, "Dressing for Success on the Mohawk Frontier: Hendrick, William Johnson, and the Indian Fashion," *William and Mary Quarterly* 53 (January 1996): 11–42.

38. Jenny Hale Pulsipher also makes this suggestion in "Massacre at Hurtleberry Hill," 477.

CHAPTER I
A "Business for Life"

1. Simeon Baldwin to unknown friend, n.d., Baldwin Family Papers, Manuscripts and Archives, Yale University Library, New Haven, Conn. (hereafter cited as YUL). The quotes used in this book are as close to the original as possible. Brackets were added only when one word could be mistaken for another.

2. Franklin Bowditch Dexter, ed., *Biographical Sketches of the Graduates of Yale College with Annals of the College History* (New York: Henry Holt, 1903), vol. 4, 178–80.

3. Memoranda of Jeremiah Dummer, 18 October 1709, MHS.

4. Laurel Thatcher Ulrich, *Good Wives: Image and Reality in the Lives of Women in Northern New England, 1650–1750* (New York: Alfred A. Knopf, 1982); Lyle Koehler, *A Search for Power: The "Weaker Sex" in Seventeenth-Century New England* (Urbana: University of Illinois Press, 1980). Cornelia Hughes Dayton, *Women Before the Bar: Gender, Law, and Society in Connecticut, 1639–1789* (Chapel Hill: University of North Carolina Press, 1995), esp. chap. 2.

5. Some of the works that have explored this issue for early America include, Louise A. Tilly and Joan W. Scott, *Women, Work and Family* (New York: Holt, Rinehart and Winston, 1978); Toby L. Ditz, *Property and Kinship: Inheritance in Early Connecticut, 1750–1820* (Princeton: Princeton University Press, 1986), 113–16; Joan M. Jensen, *Loosening the Bonds: Mid-Atlantic Farm Women, 1750–1800* (New Haven: Yale University Press,

1986); Lisa Wilson, *Life after Death: Widows in Pennsylvania, 1750–1850* (Philadelphia: Temple University Press, 1992).

6. Elisha Niles Diary, 1764–1845, 7–9, Connecticut Historical Society, Hartford, Conn. (hereafter cited as CHS).

7. For an overview of the uncomfortable speed with which children arrived, see Daniel Scott Smith and Michael S. Hindus, "Premarital Pregnancy in America 1640–1971: An Overview and Interpretation," *Journal of Interdisciplinary History* 4 (spring 1975): 537–70.

8. Joseph Pease Diary, 1730–94, 11, CHS.

9. Max Weber, *The Protestant Ethic and the Spirit of Capitalism* (New York: Charles Scribner's Sons, 1958); Bernard Bailyn, ed., *The Apologia of Robert Keayne: The Self-Portrait of a Puritan Merchant* (New York: Harper and Row, 1964); Timothy Hall Breen, "The Non-Existent Controversy: Puritan and Anglican Attitudes on Work and Wealth, 1600–1640," *Church History* 35 (September 1966): 273–87; S. N. Eisenstadt, *The Protestant Ethic and Modernization, A Comparative View* (New York: Basic Books, 1968); Benjamin Nelson, "Weber's Protestant Ethic: Its Origins, Wanderings, and Foreseeable Futures," in *Beyond the Classics? Essays in the Scientific Study of Religion,* ed. Charles Y. Glock and Phillip E. Hammond (New York: Harper and Row, 1973), 112–30; Robert M. Mitchell, *Calvin's and the Puritan's View of the Protestant Ethic* (Washington, D.C.: University Press of America, 1979).

10. For a recent discussion of this notion, see Stephen Innes, *Creating the Commonwealth: The Economic Culture of Puritan New England* (New York: W. W. Norton, 1995), chap. 3.

11. Robert S. Michaelsen, "Changes in the Puritan Concept of Calling or Vocation," *New England Quarterly* 26 (September 1953): 332–34; J. E. Crowley, *This Sheba, Self: The Conceptualization of Economic Life in Eighteenth-Century America* (Baltimore: Johns Hopkins University Press, 1974), 76–79.

12. There is considerable disagreement over when this cultural transition occurred, but most historians mark the change. For a gradualist approach, see Richard L. Bushman, *From Puritan to Yankee: Character and the Social Order in Connecticut, 1690–1765* (New York: W. W. Norton, 1967).

13. Michael Kimmel, *Manhood in America: A Cultural History* (New York: Free Press, 1996), 8–26.

14. Stephen Foster argues even the social imperatives of the calling disappeared. See Foster, *Their Solitary Way: The Puritan Social Ethic in the First Century of Settlement in New England* (New Haven: Yale University Press, 1971), 114.

15. William Ames, *The Marrow of Theology*, trans., John D. Eusden (Durham, N.C.: Labyrinth Press, 1968), 32.

16. William Bradford, *Of Plymouth Plantation, 1620–1647*, ed. Francis Murphy (New York: Modern Library, 1981), 248.

17. *The Winthrop Papers, Part IV, Collections of the Massachusetts Historical Society*, vol. 8 (Boston: Massachusetts Historical Society, 1863–92), 202.

18. Samuel Sewall, *The Diary of Samuel Sewall, 1674–1729*, ed. M. Halsey Thomas (New York: Farrar, Straus and Giroux, 1973), vol. 2, 680.

19. Cotton Mather, *A Christian at his calling: Two brief discourses. One directing a Christian in his general calling; another directing him in his personal calling* (Boston, 1701), 37–38; John Robinson, "Diligent Labor and the Use of God's Creature," in *Tensions in American Puritanism*, ed. Richard Reinitz (New York: John Wiley, 1970), 68; Michaelsen, "Changes," 319–20; Foster, *Their Solitary Way*, 99; Breen, "Non-Existent Controversy," 275.

20. Increase Mather, "The Autobiography of Increase Mather," ed. M. G. Hall, *Proceedings of the American Antiquarian Society* 71 (1962): 303.

21. Cotton Mather, *Christian at his calling*, 41; Breen, "Non-Existent Controversy," 277–78; Michaelsen, "Changes," 322; John Robinson made a similar statement about idleness and the importance, particularly for the rich, to make labor a priority not an "accessorie." Robinson, "Diligent Labor," 66.

22. Innes, *Creating the Commonwealth*, 146–47.

23. *Watertown Records* (Watertown, Mass.: Watertown Historical Society, 1894), vol. 2, 18.

24. George F. Dow, ed., *Records and Files of the Quarterly Courts of Essex County, Massachusetts*, 8 vols. (Salem, Mass.: Essex Institute, 1911–78), vol. 2, 34.

25. John Fiske, *The Notebook of the Reverend John Fiske, 1644–1675*, ed. Robert G. Pope, *Publications of the Colonial Society of Massachusetts, Collections* vol. 47 (Boston: Colonial Society of Massachusetts, 1974), 226–27.

26. *Oxford English Dictionary*, 2d ed., (hereafter cited as *O.E.D.*), s.v. "serviceableness"; Cotton Mather, *The Serviceable Man* (Boston, 1690).

27. Cotton Mather, *Diary of Cotton Mather*, ed. Worthington Chauncey Ford (New York: Frederick Ungar, 1911), vol. 2, 280–81. Under the Julian calendar, the first day of a new year began on March 25. Dates falling between January 1 and March 24 of each year appear with two years divided by a slash, for example, 1690/91. The Gregorian calendar that eliminated this system was used in England as of 1752 and slowly took hold in the colonies after this date.

28. Ibid., vol. 1, 487, 470.
29. Increase Mather, "Autobiography," 297.
30. Memoranda of Jeremiah Dummer, 1709-11, MHS.
31. Michael Wigglesworth, *The Diary of Michael Wigglesworth, 1653-1657: The Conscience of a Puritan,* ed. Edmund S. Morgan (New York: Harper and Row, 1946), 94.
32. Josiah Cotton Memoirs, 1726-56, 70, MHS.
33. John Pynchon, *The Pynchon Papers,* ed., Carl Bridenbaugh, *Publications of the Colonial Society of Massachusetts, Collections* vol. 60 (Boston: Colonial Society of Massachusetts, 1982), 108.
34. William Samuel Johnson to Samuel Johnson, 13 June 1747, William Samuel Johnson Correspondence and Papers, CHS.
35. Dwight Foster to Cornelius Lynde, 14 October 1778, Foster Family Papers, American Antiquarian Society, Worcester, Mass. (hereafter cited as AAS).
36. Dwight Foster to Jedediah Foster, 24 September 1778, Foster Family Papers, AAS.
37. Cotton Mather, *Diary,* vol. 2, 124-25.
38. O.E.D., s.v. "usefulness"; Foster, *Their Solitary Way,* 113-14.
39. John Adams, *The Earliest Diary of John Adams,* ed. L. H. Butterfield (Cambridge: Harvard University Press, 1966), 70-72.
40. E. Anthony Rotundo, *American Manhood: Transformations in Masculinity from the Revolution to the Modern Era* (New York: Basic Books, 1993), 13.
41. Cotton Mather, *Diary,* vol. 2, 211.
42. William Samuel Johnson to Samuel Johnson, 13 June 1747, William Samuel Johnson Correspondence and Papers, CHS.
43. Isaac Sherman to Roger Sherman, 8 September 1775, Roger Sherman Collection, YUL.
44. Ezekiel Williams to John Williams, 6 December 1779, Williams Papers, CHS.
45. Ezekiel Williams to John Williams, 14 February 1782, Williams Papers, CHS.
46. William Samuel Johnson to Samuel Johnson, 13 June 1747, William Samuel Johnson Correspondence and Papers, CHS.
47. Jeremy Belknap to Rev. Dr. Rogers, 12 March 1776, Jeremy Belknap Papers, MHS.
48. O.E.D., s.v. "subsistence."
49. O.E.D., s.v. "maintenance."
50. Isaac Sherman to Roger Sherman, 8 September 1775, Roger Sherman Collection, YUL.

51. *Winthrop Papers, Part IV,* 269.
52. *O.E.D.,* s.v. "competency." For a detailed analysis of this concept and early American economic culture, see Daniel Vickers, "Competency and Competition: Economic Culture in Early America" *William and Mary Quarterly* 47 (January, 1990): 3-29.
53. John Davenport, *Letters of John Davenport: Puritan Divine,* ed. Isabel MacBeath Calder (New Haven: Yale University Press, 1937), 16.
54. "Narrative of Joel Stone," n.d., Todd Collection, CHS.
55. Mather Byles [Jr.] and Rebecca Byles to Mather Byles [Sr.], 21 February 1763, Byles Family Papers, MHS.
56. John Hull, "The Diaries of John Hull," *Transactions and Collections of the American Antiquarian Society,* 3 (1857): 142.
57. *O.E.D.,* s.v. "settlement."
58. Ebenezer Parkman, *The Diary of Ebenezer Parkman, 1703-1782,* ed. Francis G. Walett (Worcester: American Antiquarian Society, 1974), 98.
59. Josiah Cotton Memoirs, 1726-56, 34-35, MHS.
60. *Winthrop Papers, Part IV,* 202-3.
61. Josiah Cotton Memoirs, 1726-56, 99, MHS.
62. Diaries Miscellaneous Collection (Peter Pratt), 1 June 1761, YUL.
63. Diary of Joseph Green, 1696-1714, Harvard University Archives, Cambridge, Mass. (hereafter cited as HUA); Clifford K. Shipton, *Sibley's Harvard Graduates* (Cambridge: Harvard University Press, 1933), vol. 4, 229.
64. Sewall, *Diary,* vol. 1, 348.
65. Silas Deane to Samuel B. Webb, 21 December 1772, Samuel Blachley Webb Papers, YUL.
66. Dwight Foster to Joseph Clarke, 29 October 1778, Foster Family Papers, AAS.
67. William Smith to [William Samuel Johnson], 30 October 1747, William Samuel Johnson Correspondence and Papers, CHS.
68. John Adams, *Diary and Autobiography of John Adams,* ed. L. H. Butterfield (Cambridge: Harvard University Press, 1961), vol. 1, 53-55.
69. Samuel Sewall, *Letter-book, Collections of the Massachusetts Historical Society,* vol. 2 (Boston: Massachusetts Historical Society, 1886-88), 112-13.
70. Increase Mather, "Autobiography," 297.
71. Diary of Samuel Chandler, 1751, MHS.
72. Toby L. Ditz makes a similar observation in her discussion of life time transfers. See Ditz, *Property and Kinship,* 117-18.
73. Ezekiel Williams to Mr. Atwater, 1 June 1780, Williams Papers, CHS.

74. Eliphalet Pearsons Promis[e] to his father, 30 October 1769, Park Family Papers, YUL.
75. Diary of Joseph Green, 1696–1714, HUA.
76. Shipton, *Sibley's*, vol. 4, 228.
77. Ebenezer Baldwin Diary, November 1763, Baldwin Family Papers, YUL.
78. Benjamin Trumbull to Parents, 24 November 1765, Benjamin Trumbull Papers, YUL.
79. Sarah Lloyd to Henry Lloyd, 18 June 1749, Cogswell Family Papers, YUL.
80. Increase Mather, "Autobiography," 278.
81. Edward Goddard to Cotton Mather, 19 February 1727, Curwen Family Papers, AAS.
82. Parkman, *Diary*, 35.
83. James Cogswell [Jr.] to James Cogswell [Sr.], 19 September 1781, Cogswell Family Papers, YUL.
84. Ultimately he became a physician in Lebanon, Connecticut. Dexter ed., *Biographical Sketches*, vol. 2, 439.
85. Thomas Williams to Eliphalet Williams, 28 December 1756, Eliphalet Williams Papers, CHS.
86. Eliphalet Pearson to Mrs. Mascarene, 20 August 1782, Park Family Papers, YUL.
87. Josiah Cotton Memoirs, 1726–56, 262–63, MHS.
88. Ezekiel Williams to John Williams, 14 February 1782, Williams Papers, CHS.
89. Ezekiel Williams to John Williams, 24 May 1780, Williams Papers, CHS.
90. Elisha Niles Diary, 1764–1845, 3, CHS.
91. Isaac Sherman to Roger Sherman, 8 September 1775, Roger Sherman Collection, YUL.
92. For the development of this pattern, see Kenneth A. Lockridge, *A New England Town: The First Hundred Years* (New York: W. W. Norton, 1970); Philip J. Greven, *Four Generations: Population, Land, and Family in Colonial Andover, Massachusetts* (Ithaca: Cornell University Press, 1970); Smith and Hindus, "Premarital Pregnancy," 537–70; Robert A. Gross, *The Minutemen and Their World* (New York: Hill and Wang, 1976); John J. Waters, "Patrimony, Succession, and Social Stability: Guilford, Connecticut in the Eighteenth Century," *Perspectives in American History* 10 (1976): 131–60; James A. Henretta, "Families and Farms: Mentalité in Pre-Industrial America," *William and Mary Quarterly* 35 (January 1978): 3–32; Christopher M. Jedrey, *The World of John Cleaveland: Family and Community in Eighteenth-Century New England* (New York: W. W.

Norton, 1979); Bruce C. Daniels, *The Fragmentation of New England: Comparative Perspectives on Economic, Political, and Social Divisions in the Eighteenth Century* (New York: Greenwood Press, 1988); Daniel Vickers, *Farmers and Fishermen: Two Centuries of Work in Essex County, Massachusetts, 1630–1850* (Chapel Hill: University of North Carolina Press, 1994).

93. Parkman, *Diary*, 187.
94. Ibid., 7.
95. Joseph Emerson Diary, 25 February 1749, MHS.

CHAPTER 2
"It Will Not Injure You"

1. Nathanael Greene to Colonel Webb, 4 July 1780, Samuel Blachley Webb Papers, YUL.
2. Kathleen M. Brown makes a similar argument for the eighteenth-century Virginia elite. See Brown, *Good Wives, Nasty Wenches, and Anxious Patriarchs: Gender, Race, and Power in Colonial Virginia* (Chapel Hill: University of North Carolina Press, 1996), 249 and 254.
3. Toby L. Ditz, "Shipwrecked; or, Masculinity Imperiled: Mercantile Representations of Failure and the Gendered Self in Eighteenth-Century Philadelphia," *Journal of American History* 81 (June 1994): 51–80; Cornelia Hughes Dayton, *Women Before the Bar: Gender, Law, and Society in Connecticut, 1639–1789* (Chapel Hill: University of North Carolina Press, 1995), 287, 291, 323–24, and chap. 6. Mark E. Kann suggests that this imperative continued even after death. See Kann, "Manhood, Immortality and Politics during the American Founding," *Journal of Men's Studies* 5 (November 1996): 79–103.
4. Robert Oaks, " 'Things Fearful to Name': Sodomy and Buggery in Seventeenth-Century New England," in *The American Man*, ed. Elizabeth H. Pleck and Joseph H. Pleck (Englewood Cliffs, N.J.: Prentice-Hall, 1980), 53–76; Michael Warner, "New English Sodom," *American Literature* 64 (March 1992): 19–47; Jonathan Katz, *The Invention of Heterosexuality* (New York: Dutton, 1995); Richard Godbeer, " 'The Cry of Sodom': Discourse, Intercourse, and Desire in Colonial New England," *William and Mary Quarterly* 52 (April 1995): 259–86. For a discussion of the bachelor as a sexual threat to social order, see Mark E. Kann, "The Bachelor and Other Disorderly Men during the American Founding," *Journal of Men's Studies* 6 (fall 1997): 1–27.

5. Cornelia Hughes Dayton has suggested that this mandate became less firmly rooted for men in eighteenth-century Connecticut. See Dayton, *Women Before the Bar,* chap. 4.

6. Talking of the French case, Jean-Louis Flandrin argues that celibacy implied fornication. It was not until the seventeenth century that this link was seen as a problem requiring the remedy of marriage. See Flandrin, *Families in Former Times: Kinship, Household and Sexuality* (Cambridge: Cambridge University Press, 1979), 189–90.

7. Cotton Mather, *Diary of Cotton Mather,* ed. Worthington Chauncey Ford (New York: Frederick Ungar, 1911), vol. 1, 107.

8. Ebenezer Baldwin to Mr. Howe, 11 June 1774, Baldwin Family Papers, YUL.

9. Mr. Pitkin to Simeon Baldwin, 28 January 1782, Baldwin Family Papers, YUL.

10. Daniel Allen to sister, 13 March 1714/15, Bromfield Family Papers, MHS.

11. John Dane, "John Dane's Narrative, 1682," *New England Historical and Genealogical Register,* 8 (1854): 150–51.

12. James Cogswell to Alice Cogswell, 19 March 1772, Cogswell Family Papers, YUL.

13. Samuel Crosby to Breck Parkman, 22 November 1775, Parkman Family Papers, AAS.

14. Laurel Thatcher Ulrich and Lois K. Stabler, " 'Girling of It' in Eighteenth-Century New Hampshire," in *Families and Children: The Dublin Seminar for New England Folklife: Annual Proceedings, 1985,* ed. Peter Benes (Boston: Boston University, 1987): 24–36.

15. Dayton, *Women Before the Bar,* 224; Bruce C. Daniels, *Puritans at Play: Leisure and Recreation in Colonial New England* (New York: St. Martin's Press, 1995), 132–34. For New Haven Colony, Ann Little argues this change came about in the mid-seventeenth century. See Little, "A 'Wel Ordered Commonwealth': Gender and Politics in New Haven Colony, 1636–1690" (Ph.D. diss., University of Pennsylvania, 1996), 252–60.

16. Daniel Scott Smith and Michael S. Hindus, "Premarital Pregnancy in America, 1640–1971: An Overview and Interpretation," *Journal of Interdisciplinary History* 4 (spring 1975): 537–70; Daniels, *Puritans at Play,* 129–30.

17. Cathy N. Davidson, *Revolution and the Word: The Rise of the Novel in America* (New York: Oxford University Press, 1986); Dayton, *Women Before the Bar,* 226–30.

18. Ebenezer Baldwin to Betsey Partridge, 21 July 1767, Baldwin Family Papers, YUL.

19. William Smith to William Samuel Johnson, n.d., William Samuel Johnson Correspondence and Papers, CHS.

20. John Adams, *Diary and Autobiography of John Adams*, ed. L. H. Butterfield (Cambridge: Harvard University Press, 1961), vol. 1, 109.

21. Samuel B. Webb to Sally Webb, 21 November 1772, Samuel Blachley Webb Papers, YUL.

22. George Hough to Simeon Baldwin, 8 May 1780, Baldwin Family Papers, YUL.

23. Ulrich and Stabler also found frolics common in early New Hampshire. See "'Girling of It,'" 27.

24. Adams, *Diary and Autobiography*, vol. 1, 172-73.

25. Samuel Crosby to Breck Parkman, 11 November 1775, Parkman Family Papers, AAS.

26. S. Hinckley to Simeon Baldwin, 3 October 1778, Baldwin Family Papers, YUL.

27. M. Byles to Polley Byles, 18 February 1768, Byles Family Papers, MHS.

28. William Smith to William Samuel Johnson, 30 June 1746, William Samuel Johnson Correspondence and Papers, CHS.

29. Adams, *Diary and Autobiography*, vol. 1, 95.

30. Diary of Joseph Hull, 1724, Joseph Hull Papers, AAS.

31. Daniels, *Puritans at Play*, 133.

32. Adams, *Diary and Autobiography*, vol. 1, 195-96.

33. For a discussion of the changing meaning of the word "virtue" in eighteenth-century America, see Ruth H. Bloch, "The Gendered Meanings of Virtue in Revolutionary America," *SIGNS* 13 (1987): 37-58.

34. Bruce C. Daniels notes some similar patterns in his examination of courting behavior. See Daniels, *Puritans at Play*, 138. Historians of England have noticed a similar change in emphasis. See Alan Macfarlane, *Marriage and Love in England: Modes of Reproduction, 1300-1840* (Oxford: Basil Blackwell, 1986), 164-65; and Jeffrey R. Watt, *The Making of Modern Marriage: Matrimonial Control and the Rise of Sentiment in Neuchâtel, 1550-1800* (Ithaca: Cornell University Press, 1992), 79-80.

35. Among the many historians who have traced this trend, see Philip J. Greven, Jr., *Four Generations: Population, Land, and Family in Colonial Andover, Massachusetts* (Ithaca: Cornell University Press, 1970); Alexander Keyssar, "Widowhood in Eighteenth-Century Massachusetts: A Problem in the History of the Family," *Perspectives in American History* 8 (1974): 96-99; K. Kelly Weisberg, "'Under Great Temptations Heed': Women and Divorce in Puritan Massachusetts," *Feminist Studies*

2 (1975): 189; John Demos, "Notes on Life in Plymouth Colony," in *Colonial America: Essays in Politics and Social Development*, ed. Stanley N. Katz and John M. Murrin (New York: Alfred A. Knopf, 1983), 122–42; Jackson Turner Main, *Society and Economy in Colonial Connecticut* (Princeton: Princeton University Press, 1985), esp. chap. 1; Daniel Vickers, *Farmers and Fishermen: Two Centuries of Work in Essex County, Massachusetts, 1630–1850* (Chapel Hill: University of North Carolina Press, 1994), 221–27.

36. Greven, *Four Generations*, 207–22; Kenneth A. Lockridge, *A New England Town: The First Hundred Years* (New York: W. W. Norton, 1970), 74–75, 156–59; Daniel Scott Smith, "Parental Power and Marriage Patterns: An Analysis of Historical Trends in Hingham, Massachusetts," *Journal of Marriage and the Family* 35 (August 1973): 423; Christopher M. Jedrey, *The World of John Cleaveland: Family and Community in Eighteenth-Century New England* (New York: W. W. Norton, 1979), 73–74. John Demos claims, however, there is no real evidence for this kind of interpretation in Plymouth. See Demos, *A Little Commonwealth: Family Life in Plymouth Colony* (New York: Oxford University Press, 1970), 169–70. Similarly, for New Haven, see Little, "'Wel Ordered Commonwealth,'" 197–99.

37. Greven, *Four Generations*; Kenneth A. Lockridge, "Land, Population, and the Evolution of New England Society, 1630-1790," *Past and Present* 39 (April 1968): 62-80; Richard L. Bushman, *From Puritan to Yankee: Character and the Social Order in Connecticut, 1690–1765* (New York: W. W. Norton, 1967).

38. Demos, *Little Commonwealth*, 151; Jedrey, *World of John Cleaveland*, 73; Lockridge, *New England Town*, 66; Daniel Scott Smith, "The Demographic History of Colonial New England," in *The American Family in Social-Historical Perspective*, ed. Michael Gordon (New York: St. Martin's Press, 1973), 406; Greven, *Four Generations*, 34; Douglas Lamar Jones, *Village and Seaport: Migration and Society in Eighteenth-Century Massachusetts* (Hanover, N.H.: University Press of New England, 1981), chap. 5; Bruce C. Daniels, *The Fragmentation of New England: Comparative Perspectives on Economic, Political, and Social Divisions in the Eighteenth Century* (New York: Greenwood Press, 1988), 123.

39. Jones, *Village and Seaport*, 79; Demos, *Little Commonwealth*, 151; Philip Greven found a similar pattern among the women in Andover, Massachusetts, but he is less certain about an explanation, *Four Generations*, 122–23.

40. Genesis 2:18.

41. John Cotton to Mr. Bacheldr., 9 April 1641, Cotton Family Papers, MHS.
42. John Davenport, *Letters of John Davenport: Puritan Divine,* ed. Isabel MacBeath Calder (New Haven: Yale University Press, 1937), 58.
43. Quoted in Laurel Thatcher Ulrich, *Good Wives: Image and Reality in the Lives of Women in Northern New England, 1650–1750* (New York: Alfred A. Knopf, 1982), 106.
44. Cotton Mather, *Diary,* vol. 1, 110.
45. Thomas Shepard, "The Autobiography of Thomas Shepard," *Colonial Society of Massachusetts, Transactions* 27 (November 1930): 373.
46. Laurel Thatcher Ulrich finds a similar shift in attitude. See *Good Wives,* 117.
47. Thomas Clap, "Meditations upon the Death of my Wife," 9 August 1736, Thomas Clap Presidential Records, YRG 2-A-5, YUL.
48. Robert E. Moody, ed., *The Saltonstall Papers, 1607–1815,* (Boston: Massachusetts Historical Society, 1972), vol. 1, 254.
49. Ebenezer Baldwin to Mr. Howe, 11 June 1774, Baldwin Family Papers, YUL.
50. James Cogswell to Alice Cogswell, 19 March 1772, Cogswell Family Papers, YUL.
51. Ulrich, *Good Wives,* 115–16.
52. Henry Livingston to Samuel B. Webb, 28 March 1777, Samuel Blachley Webb Papers, YUL.
53. Ebenezer Baldwin Diary, 10 April 1764, Baldwin Family Papers, YUL.
54. Ebenezer Baldwin to Miss Bethiah Baldwin, 3 May 1773, Baldwin Family Papers, YUL.
55. [Ebenezer Baldwin to Sophia Partridge], 21 July 1767, Baldwin Family Papers, YUL.
56. Adams, *Diary and Autobiography,* vol. 1, 194.
57. Diary of John Jenks, 1774–76, MS N-39, MHS.
58. Register, April 1781, Samuel Benjamin Papers, YUL.
59. William Smith to William Samuel Johnson, 18 July 1748, William Samuel Johnson Correspondence and Papers, CHS.
60. Ebenezer Baldwin to Miss Bethiah Baldwin, 3 May 1773, Baldwin Family Papers, YUL.
61. Ebenezer Baldwin Diary, 10 April 1764, Baldwin Family Papers, YUL.
62. William Williams to [unknown], 1 March 1761, Williams Papers, CHS.
63. William Smith to [William Samuel Johnson], 25 January 1746, William Samuel Johnson Correspondence and Papers, CHS.
64. E. Otis to Eliza Watson, n.d., Bromfield Family Papers, MHS.

65. Daniel Allen to Kath. Allen, 18 July 1714, Bromfield Family Papers, MHS.

66. *The Winthrop Papers, Part IV, Collections of the Massachusetts Historical Society*, vol. 8 (Boston: Massachusetts Historical Society, 1863–92), 491.

67. Richard S. Dunn, *Puritans and Yankees: The Winthrop Dynasty of New England, 1630–1717* (Princeton: Princeton University Press, 1962), 336.

68. William Williams to [unknown], 1 March 1761, Williams Papers, CHS.

69. E. Otis to Eliza Watson, n.d., Bromfield Family Papers, MHS.

70. William Smith to William Samuel Johnson, n.d., William Samuel Johnson Correspondence and Papers, CHS.

71. These men seem to be using the word "sensibility" in the older, Lockean sense of intellect rather than Rousseauian emotional sensibility. See Jay Fliegelman, *Prodigals and Pilgrims: The American Revolution against Patriarchal Authority, 1750–1800* (Cambridge: Cambridge University Press, 1982), 103–4. G. J. Barker-Benfield argues that sensibility was increasingly seen as a female quality by the end of the eighteenth century. See Barker-Benfield, *The Culture of Sensibility: Sex and Society in Eighteenth-Century Britain* (Chicago: University of Chicago Press, 1992), 2.

72. Mr. Perkins to Simeon Baldwin, 3 April 1782, Baldwin Family Papers, YUL.

73. Ebenezer Baldwin to Bethiah Baldwin, 8 May 1770, Baldwin Family Papers, YUL.

74. Ebenezer Baldwin to Bethiah Baldwin, 3 May 1773, Baldwin Family Papers, YUL.

75. [Ebenezer Baldwin to Sophia Partridge], 21 July 1767, Baldwin Family Papers, YUL.

76. Sophia Partridge to Ebenezer Baldwin, 3 March 1768, Baldwin Family Papers, YUL.

77. Sophia Partridge to Ebenezer Baldwin, 27 January 1767, Baldwin Family Papers, YUL.

78. E. Otis to Eliza Watson, n.d., Bromfield Family Papers, MHS.

79. Adams, *Diary and Autobiography*, vol. 1, 194–95.

80. Lawrence Stone found the same pattern among late-eighteenth-century Englishmen. See Stone, *Uncertain Unions: Marriage in England, 1660–1753* (New York: Oxford University Press, 1992), 71.

81. [unknown] to Dear Lady, December 1781, Silliman Family Papers, YUL.

82. Shepard, "Autobiography," 373.

83. Diary of John Page, 1757–80, HUA.

84. Ashley Bowen, *The Journals of Ashley Bowen of (1728–1813) Marblehead*, ed.

Philip Chadwick Foster Smith, *Publications of the Colonial Society of Massachusetts, Collections,* vol. 44 (Boston: Colonial Society of Massachusetts, 1973), 47.

85. Adams, *Diary and Autobiography,* vol. 1, 121.

86. Much ink has been spilled on this question of marital expectation. Lawrence Stone began the debate with his discussion of the aristocratic English family. Historians of Europe and America have continued to test his assumptions. See Stone, *The Family, Sex, and Marriage in England, 1500–1800* (London: Weidenfeld and Nicolson, 1977) and *Uncertain Unions.* Those who agree with some of Stone's general notions if not always with his chronology include Steven Ozment, *When Fathers Ruled: Family Life in Reformation Europe* (Cambridge: Harvard University Press, 1983); Martine Segalen, *Love and Power in the Peasant Family: Rural France in the Nineteenth Century* (Chicago: University of Chicago Press, 1983); John R. Gillis, *For Better, For Worse: British Marriages, 1600 to the Present* (New York: Oxford University Press, 1985); Carol Z. Stearns and Peter N. Stearns, eds., *Emotion and Social Change: Toward a New Psychohistory* (New York: Holmes and Meier, 1988); Martin Ingram, *Church Courts, Sex and Marriage in England, 1570–1640* (Cambridge: Cambridge University Press, 1987); Watt, *Making of Modern Marriage.* Alan Macfarlane has even found examples of romantic love stretching back to the thirteenth century. See Macfarlane, *Marriage and Love in England,* 189. More vehement criticism of Stone's conclusions have come from two works that came out about the same time: Edward Shorter, *The Making of the Modern Family* (New York: Basic Books, 1975) and Randolph Trumbach, *The Rise of the Egalitarian Family: Aristocratic Kinship and Domestic Relations in Eighteenth-Century England* (New York: Academy Press, 1978). The debate also rages in the colonial literature. See Edmund S. Morgan, *The Puritan Family: Religion and Domestic Relations in Seventeenth-Century New England,* rev. ed. (New York: Harper and Row, 1966); Philip Greven, *The Protestant Temperament: Patterns of Child-Rearing, Religious Experience, and the Self in Early America* (Chicago: University of Chicago Press, 1977); Daniel Blake Smith, *Inside the Great House: Planter Family Life in Eighteenth-Century Chesapeake Society* (Ithaca: Cornell University Press, 1980); Helena M. Wall, *Fierce Communion: Family and Community in Early America* (Cambridge: Harvard University Press, 1990). The contrast between seventeenth- and eighteenth-century family patterns might have been less stark for the common sort. See, e.g., Roger Thompson, *Sex in Middlesex: Popular Mores in a Massachusetts County, 1649–1699* (Amherst: University of Massachusetts Press, 1986).

87. Karen Lystra makes the case that romantic love was actually empowering for women. See Lystra, *Searching the Heart: Women, Men, and Romantic Love in Nineteenth-Century America* (New York: Oxford University Press, 1989), 9.

88. Ellen K. Rothman, *Hands and Hearts: A History of Courtship in America* (Cambridge: Harvard University Press, 1987), 32. For an interesting case of a very public "bagging" in Virginia, see J. A. Leo Lemay, ed., *Robert Bolling Woos Anne Miller: Love and Courtship in Colonial Virginia, 1760* (Charlottesville: University Press of Virginia, 1990). I would like to thank Kenneth A. Lockridge for sharing with me an early version of "Robert Bolling, 1738–1775: A Short Life in the Pursuit of Happiness," in *The Human Tradition in Colonial America*, ed. Nancy L. Rhoden and Ian K. Steele (Wilmington, Del.: Scholarly Resources, 1998).

89. William Williams to [unknown], 1 March 1761, Williams Papers, CHS.

90. George Hough to Simeon Baldwin, 8 May 1780, Baldwin Family Papers, YUL.

91. Henry Livingston to Samuel B. Webb, 28 March 1777, Samuel Blachley Webb Papers, YUL.

92. Adams, *Diary and Autobiography*, vol. 1, 74.

93. Oliver Ellsworth to Nabby Ellsworth, 7 August 1781, Oliver Ellsworth Correspondence and Papers, CHS.

94. Asahel Heart to Ebenezer Baldwin, 23 October 1767, Baldwin Family Papers, YUL.

95. The word "friend" may have included other relatives as well. See Richard Adair, *Courtship, Illegitimacy and Marriage in Early Modern England* (Manchester: Manchester University Press, 1996), 136.

96. The best and most thorough work on this topic focuses on early modern Europe. Some of these studies include Gillis, *For Better, For Worse;* Macfarlane, *Marriage and Love in England,* chap. 7; Ingram, *Church Courts;* Stone, *Uncertain Unions;* Watt, *Making of Modern Marriage;* Mary Abbott, *Family Ties: English Families, 1540–1920* (London: Routledge, 1993); Adair, *Courtship, Illegitimacy and Marriage.* The American literature includes Greven, *Four Generations;* Smith, "Parental Power and Marriage Patterns"; Robert A. Gross, *The Minutemen and Their World* (New York: Hill and Wang, 1976), 210n22; Thompson, *Sex in Middlesex;* Lemay, *Robert Bolling Woos Anne Miller;* Lockridge, "Robert Bolling."

97. George F. Dow, ed., *Records and Files of the Quarterly Courts of Essex County, Massachusetts,* 8 vols. (Salem, Mass.: Essex Institute, 1911–78), vol. 1, 180, 225 and 287.

98. Legally, a man could marry without such permission in colonial New En-

gland, unless his lover was underage. See Macfarlane, *Marriage and Love in England*, 124–27. Although the age of these women is uncertain, it is clear that the legal system favored parental consent.

99. John Fiske, *The Notebook of the Reverend John Fiske, 1644–1675*, ed. Robert G. Pope, *Publications of the Colonial Society of Massachusetts, Collections*, vol. 47 (Boston: Colonial Society of Massachusetts, 1974), 209–12.

100. [Unknown] to Benjamin Trumbull, 1771, Benjamin Trumbull Papers, YUL.

101. Sarah was eighteen years old in 1709. See Hermann Frederick Clarke, *John Coney, Silversmith, 1655–1722* (Boston: Houghton Mifflin, 1932), 7.

102. Samuel Sewall, *The Diary of Samuel Sewall, 1674–1729*, ed. M. Halsey Thomas (New York: Farrar, Straus and Giroux, 1973), vol. 2, 614–16.

103. This marriage included alcoholism, infidelity, an illegitimate child, and periodic separations. Sewall, *Diary*, vol. 2, 927–31.

104. Ibid., 948.

105. Ibid., 1066.

106. Franklin Bowditch Dexter, ed., *Biographical Sketches of the Graduates of Yale College with Annals of the College History* (New York: Henry Holt, 1903), vol. 2, 650.

107. Benjamin Douglas to Joseph Fish, 5 October 1762, Silliman Family Papers, YUL.

108. Ulrich and Stabler mark this as a sign that courtship was underway. See " 'Girling of It,' " 28.

109. Lucy Clarke to Sally Bromfield, 5 August 1772, Bromfield Family Papers, YUL.

110. Adams, *Diary and Autobiography*, vol. 1, 119.

111. Ibid., 83.

112. For other angry responses, see Ulrich and Stabler, " 'Girling of It,' " 35; Lockridge, "Robert Bolling."

113. "Joseph Emerson Diary," *Proceedings of the Massachusetts Historical Society* 44 (1911): 272–80.

114. [unknown] to [unknown], 1774, Benjamin Huntington Family Correspondence and Papers, CHS.

115. S. Hopkins to Hannah Edwards, 9 March 1735/36, Jonathan Edwards Papers, Beinecke Library, Yale University, New Haven, Conn. (hereafter cited as BL).

116. John Sergeant to Hannah Edwards, 28 February 1736/37, Jonathan Edwards Papers, 211, BL.

117. John Sergeant to Hannah Edwards, 22 April 1737, Jonathan Edwards Papers, 211, BL.

118. Rough Draught of a Letter to O, Novr.—66 [Ebenezer Baldwin to Sophia Partridge, 22 November 1766], Baldwin Family Papers, YUL.

119. Philomela was "usually with reference to the ancient myth of Philomela metamorphosed into a nightingale." Philander referred to a lover. This word may have begun to acquire some of the negative connotations of modern usage, "to make love, especially in a trifling manner; to flirt; to dangle after a woman." *O.E.D.*, s.v. "philomela," "philander." This reference may also relate to Elizabeth Singer Rowe's, *Poems of Philomela* (1696), which enjoyed some popularity. See Sewall, *Diary*, vol. 1, 418n27.

120. Ebenezer Baldwin to Sophia and Betsey Partridge, ca. 8 April 1767, Baldwin Family Papers, YUL.

121. Sophia Partridge to Ebenezer Baldwin, 30 May 1767, Baldwin Family Papers, YUL.

122. Ebenezer Baldwin to Sophia Partridge, ca. June 1767, Baldwin Family Papers, YUL.

123. Ebenezer Baldwin to Sophia Partridge, 1 November 1767, Baldwin Family Papers, YUL.

124. Sophia Partridge to Ebenezer Baldwin, 3 March 1768, Baldwin Family Papers, YUL.

125. [Ebenezer Baldwin to Sophia Partridge], 18 March 1768, Baldwin Family Papers, YUL.

126. Sophia Partridge to Ebenezer Baldwin, 3 March 1768, Baldwin Family Papers, YUL.

127. Sophia Partridge to Ebenezer Baldwin, 24 September 1768, Baldwin Family Papers, YUL.

128. Asahel Heart to Ebenezer Baldwin, 24 March 1768, Baldwin Family Papers, YUL.

129. [Unknown] Perkins to Simeon Baldwin, 3 April 1782, Baldwin Family Papers, YUL.

CHAPTER 3
A Husband "Well-Ordered"

1. Historians of early modern Europe have made this observation. See Keith Wrightson, *English Society, 1580–1680* (New Brunswick: Rutgers University Press, 1982), 90–104; Ralph A. Houlbrooke, *The English Family, 1450–1700* (London: Longman, 1984), 119; Steven Ozment, ed., *Magdalena and Balthasar: An Intimate Portrait of Life in 16th-Century Europe Revealed in the Letters of A Nuremberg Husband and Wife* (New York: Simon and Schuster, 1986), 163.

2. Like many recent scholars of British history, I have found more continuity than change in the way in which affection appeared and was expressed in marriages in colonial New England in both the seventeenth and eighteenth centuries. See Martine Segalen, *Love and Power in the Peasant Family: Rural France and the Nineteenth Century* (Chicago: University of Chicago Press, 1983); Houlbrooke, *English Family;* John R. Gillis, *For Better, For Worse: British Marriages, 1600 to the Present* (New York: Oxford University Press, 1985); Alan Macfarlane, *Marriage and Love in England: Modes of Reproduction, 1300–1840* (Oxford: Basil Blackwell, 1986); Ozment, *Magdalena and Balthasar;* Martin Ingram, *Church Courts, Sex and Marriage in England, 1570–1640* (Cambridge: Cambridge University Press, 1987); Carol Z. Stearns and Peter N. Stearns, eds., *Emotion and Social Change: Toward a New Psychohistory* (New York: Holmes and Meiers, 1988); Jeffrey R. Watt, *The Making of Modern Marriage: Matrimonial Control and the Rise of Sentiment in Neuchâtel, 1550–1800* (Ithaca: Cornell University Press, 1992).

3. For discussion of the ideal in both the seventeenth and eighteenth centuries, see Laurel Thatcher Ulrich, "Vertuous Women Found: New England Ministerial Literature, 1668–1735," *American Quarterly* 28 (spring 1976): 20–40; Jan Lewis, "The Republican Wife: Virtue and Seduction in the Early Republic," *William and Mary Quarterly* 44 (October 1987): 691–721.

4. Laurel Thatcher Ulrich, *Good Wives: Image and Reality in the Lives of Women in Northern New England, 1650–1750* (New York: Alfred A. Knopf, 1982), chap. 2.

5. G. Selleck Silliman and Mary Silliman to Joseph Fish, 12 December 1776, G. S. Silliman to [Joseph Fish], 7 December 1777, Silliman Family Papers, YUL.

6. Robert C. Winthrop, *Life and Letters of John Winthrop* (New York: Da Capo Press, 1971), vol. 1, 164.

7. Gold Selleck Silliman to Mary Noyes, 19 April 1775, Silliman Family Papers, YUL.

8. John Walley Diary, 17 October 1748, John Walley Papers, MHS.

9. William Dawes to Stephen Salisbury, 1 April 1773, Salisbury Family Papers, AAS.

10. [Tapping Reeve] to Sarah Reeve, 25 September 1773, Reeve Family Papers, YUL.

11. John Walley Diary, 18 September 1748, John Walley Papers, MHS.

12. Cotton Mather, *Diary of Cotton Mather,* ed. Worthington Chauncey Ford (New York: Frederick Ungar, 1911), vol. 2, 255.

13. Joseph Fish to Rebecca Fish, 13 October 1777, Silliman Family, YUL.
14. Eliphalet Pearson to Mrs. Pearson [Sarah Bromfield], 15 October 1785, Park Family Papers, YUL.
15. G. Selleck Silliman to Mary Silliman, 22 May 1780, Silliman Family Papers, YUL.
16. Winthrop, *Life and Letters of John Winthrop*, vol. 2, 390–91, 196–97.
17. [Tapping Reeve] to Sarah Reeve, 25 September 1773, Reeve Family Papers, YUL.
18. William Williams to Mary Williams, 3 September 1776, Williams Papers, CHS.
19. Winthrop, *Life and Letters of John Winthrop*, vol. 2, 380, 391.
20. John Walley Diary, 17 October 1748, John Walley Papers, MHS.
21. Mather Byles [Jr.] to Mather Byles [Sr.], 22 July 1761, Byles Family Papers, MHS.
22. *O.E.D.*, s.v. "tenderness."
23. G. Selleck Silliman to Joseph Fish, 12 December 1776, Silliman Family Papers, YUL.
24. "Humphrey Davenport his testimony," 8 January 1733, Mary Tilden, CHS.
25. "Mary Nicols her Evidence," 25 November 1732, Mary Tilden, CHS.
26. William Henshaw to Phebe Henshaw, 30 January 1776, Henshaw Family Papers, AAS.
27. Benjamin Bangs Diary, 27 January 1764, vol. 4, 37, Bangs Collection, MHS.
28. [Tapping Reeve] to Sarah Reeve, 25 September 1773, Reeve Family Papers, YUL.
29. Winthrop, *Life and Letters of John Winthrop*, vol. 1, 283, 381, and 385.
30. G. Selleck Silliman to Mary Silliman, 21 August 1776, Silliman Family Papers, YUL.
31. For a discussion of the delicate balance between divine and earthly marriage, see Richard Godbeer, " 'Love Raptures': Marital, Romantic, and Erotic Images of Jesus Christ in Puritan New England, 1670-1730," *New England Quarterly* 68 (September 1995): 355–84.
32. Winthrop, *Life and Letters of John Winthrop*, vol. 1, 290, 159.
33. Thomas Shepard, "The Autobiography of Thomas Shepard," *Colonial Society of Massachusetts, Transactions* 27 (November 1930): 374–75.
34. Ezra Stiles, *The Literary Diary of Ezra Stiles*, ed. Franklin Bowditch Dexter (New York: Charles Scribner's Sons, 1901), vol. 1, 517.
35. Diary of John Tudor, 1732–93, John Tudor Papers, 4, MHS.
36. Samuel Sewall, *The Diary of Samuel Sewall, 1674-1729*, ed. M. Halsey

Thomas (New York: Farrar, Straus and Giroux, 1973), vol. 2, 654–55.

37. Cotton Mather, *Diary*, vol. 1, 449.

38. Ebenezer Parkman, *The Diary of Ebenezer Parkman, 1703–1782*, ed. Francis G. Walett (Worcester: American Antiquarian Society, 1974), 141.

39. G. Selleck Silliman to Mary Silliman, 22 May 1780, Silliman Family Papers, YUL.

40. Diary of John Tudor, 1732–93, John Tudor Papers, 40, MHS.

41. John Demos, *A Little Commonwealth: Family Life in Plymouth Colony* (New York: Oxford University Press, 1970), 66, 192–93; Catherine M. Scholten, *Childbearing in American Society, 1650–1850* (New York: New York University Press, 1985), 21–22. Women died in childbirth during the colonial period although the fear of mortality seemed to outstrip the reality. See Maris A. Vinovskis, "Mortality Rates and Trends in Massachusetts before 1860," *Journal of Economic History* 32 (March 1972): 201–14; Daniel Scott Smith and J. David Hacker, "Cultural Demography: New England Deaths and the Puritan Perception of Risk," *Journal of Interdisciplinary History* 26 (winter 1996): 381. Edward Shorter argues that fertile women died earlier than men in part because of the dangers of childbirth but more important because of "overwork" and "undernutrition." See Shorter, *A History of Women's Bodies* (New York: Basic Books, 1982), 241.

42. Scholten, *Childbearing in American Society;* Laurel Thatcher Ulrich, *A Midwife's Tale: The Life of Martha Ballard Based on Her Diary, 1785–1812* (New York: Alfred A. Knopf, 1990).

43. John R. Gillis makes a similar argument for early modern England. See Gillis, "Bringing Up Father: British Parental Identities, 1700 to Present," *Masculinities* 3 (fall 1995): 3–10.

44. Elisha James to Sarah James, 3 June 1777, James Family Letters, MHS.

45. Michael Wigglesworth, *The Diary of Michael Wigglesworth, 1653–1657: The Conscience of a Puritan,* ed. Edmund S. Morgan (New York: Harper and Row, 1946), 96.

46. Parkman, *Diary*, 150.

47. Benjamin Bangs Diary, 25 April 1760, vol. 2, 65, Bangs Collection, MHS.

48. Parkman, *Diary*, 87.

49. Ibid., 56.

50. Diary of Peter Thatcher, 28 February 1682/83, MHS.

51. Sewall, *Diary*, vol. 1, 41.

52. Parkman, *Diary*, 150.

53. Wigglesworth, *Diary*, 96.

54. Sewall, *Diary*, vol. 1, 324.

55. Ibid., 41.
56. Cotton Mather, *Diary*, vol. 1, 307.
57. Sewall, *Diary*, vol. 1, 324.
58. Parkman, *Diary*, 113.
59. Sewall, *Diary*, vol. 1, 41.
60. Mary Silliman to Gold Selleck Silliman, 31 March 1776, Silliman Family Papers, YUL.
61. G. Selleck Silliman to Mary Silliman, 4 November 1776, Silliman Family Papers, YUL.
62. G. Selleck Silliman to Mary Silliman, 12 October 1777, 25 October 1777, Silliman Family Papers, YUL.
63. G. Selleck Silliman to Mary Silliman, 3 October 1776, Silliman Family Papers, YUL.
64. David Waterbury to Mary Waterbury, 6 August 1775, Waterbury Family Papers, YUL.
65. William Henshaw to Phebe Henshaw, 30 January 1776, Henshaw Family Papers, AAS.
66. Toby L. Ditz, "Shipwrecked; or, Masculinity Imperiled: Mercantile Representations of Failure and the Gendered Self in Eighteenth-Century Philadelphia," *Journal of American History* 81 (June 1994): 51–80; Cornelia Hughes Dayton, *Women Before the Bar: Gender, Law and Society in Connecticut, 1639–1789* (Chapel Hill: University of North Carolina Press, 1995), 287, 291, 323–24, and chap. 6; Mark E. Kann, "Manhood, Immortality and Politics during the American Founding," *Journal of Men's Studies* 5 (November 1996): 79–103.
67. M. Byles to Mary Byles, 4 October 1762, Byles Family Papers, MHS.
68. G. Selleck Silliman to Joseph Fish, 12 July 1775, Silliman Family Papers, YUL.
69. Thomas Clap, "Meditations upon the Death of my Wife," 9 August 1736, Thomas Clap Presidential Records, YRG 2-A-5, YUL.
70. John Adams, *Diary and Autobiography of John Adams*, ed. L. H. Butterfield (Cambridge: Harvard University Press, 1961), vol. 1, 65–66.
71. George F. Dow, ed., *Records and Files of the Quarterly Courts of Essex County, Massachusetts*, 8 vols. (Salem, Mass.: Essex Institute, 1911–78), vol. 1, 136.
72. In Massachusetts, such behavior was tolerated only in self-defense. See Roger Thompson, *Sex in Middlesex: Popular Mores in a Massachusetts County, 1649–1699* (Amherst: University of Massachusetts Press, 1986), 119; Roderick Phillips, *Putting Asunder: A History of Divorce in Western Society* (New York: Cambridge University Press, 1988), 329. Wife-beaters

were prosecuted, but their sentences varied according to a wife's provocation. See Phillips, *Putting Asunder,* 336. In Connecticut and other colonies, a man could physically correct his wife with moderation but only as a last resort. See Lyle Koehler, *A Search for Power: The "Weaker Sex" in Seventeenth-Century New England* (Urbana: University of Illinois Press, 1980), 49; Elizabeth Pleck, *Domestic Tyranny: The Making of Social Policy against Family Violence from Colonial Times to the Present* (New York: Oxford University Press, 1987), 21; Phillips, *Putting Asunder,* 325.

73. Dow, ed., *Records and Files of the Quarterly Courts,* vol. 6, 195, 297–98.

74. Mather's brooding over his failure to be appointed as president of Harvard caused a final argument and leave-taking. Lydia returned when news came that Mather's oldest son had died at sea. Kenneth Silverman, *The Life and Times of Cotton Mather* (New York: Harper and Row, 1984), 382–89.

75. Cotton Mather, *Diary,* vol. 2, 749–52.

76. Jacob Eliot Journal, 1762–64, 3–8, MS 56663, CHS.

77. Lawrence Stone, *The Family, Sex, and Marriage in England, 1500–1800,* abr. ed. (New York: Harper and Row, 1979), 316–17; Segalen, *Love and Power,* 45; Phillips, *Putting Asunder,* 351; Richard P. Gildrie, *The Profane, the Civil and the Godly: The Reformation of Manners in Orthodox New England, 1679–1749* (University Park, Penn.: Pennsylvania State University Press, 1994), 129. Mark Breitenberg argues that a social system that defines male honor in terms of female chastity strangely empowers women. See Breitenberg, "Anxious Masculinity: Sexual Jealousy in Early Modern England," *Feminist Studies* 19 (summer 1993): 388.

78. Ulrich, *Good Wives,* 94; Thompson, *Sex in Middlesex,* 128–29, 141–42.

79. Thompson, *Sex in Middlesex,* chaps. 8 and 9; Koehler, *Search for Power,* 149, chart 5.1, 453–59.

80. Stone, *Family, Sex, and Marriage,* 316–17; Jean-Louis Flandrin, *Families in Former Times: Kinship, Household and Sexuality* (Cambridge: Cambridge University Press, 1979), 124–25; Segalen, *Love and Power,* 45–46; Thompson, *Sex in Middlesex,* 142; Phillips, *Putting Asunder,* 350–51; G. R. Quaife, *Wanton Wenches and Wayward Wives: Peasants and Illicit Sex in Early Seventeenth Century England* (New Brunswick: Rutgers University Press, 1979).

81. Dow, ed., *Records and Files of the Quarterly Courts,* vol. 1, 198–99.

82. Ibid., vol. 3, 280–82.

83. Segalen, *Love and Power,* 43–45; Edward Shorter, *The Making of the Modern Family* (New York: Basic Books, 1975), 222–24; Phillips, *Putting Asunder,* 334; Merril D. Smith, *Breaking the Bonds: Marital Discord in*

Pennsylvania, 1730–1830 (New York: New York University Press, 1991), 116–17.

84. Jacob Eliot Diary, 1762–64, MS 56663, 6–8, CHS.
85. Ibid., 18.
86. Ibid., 2.
87. Ibid., 3.
88. Ibid., 4.
89. Ibid., 1–3.
90. Ibid., 9–10.
91. Ibid., 13.
92. Ibid., 7.
93. Ibid., 9.
94. Ibid., 11.
95. Ibid., 16.
96. Ibid., 2.
97. Ibid., 11.

CHAPTER 4
Provider

1. Robert L. Griswold, *Fatherhood in America: A History* (New York: Basic Books, 1993), 10–17; E. Anthony Rotundo, *American Manhood: Transformations in Masculinity from the Revolution to the Modern Era* (New York: Basic Books, 1994), 167–74.
2. M. Byles to Mary Byles, 29 November 1762, Byles Family Papers, MHS.
3. Thomas Shepard, "The Autobiography of Thomas Shepard," *Colonial Society of Massachusetts, Transactions* 27 (November 1930): 392.
4. Cotton Mather, *Diary of Cotton Mather,* ed. Worthington Chauncey Ford (New York: Frederick Ungar, 1911), vol. 1, 405.
5. Josiah Cotton Memoirs, 1726–56, 71, MHS.
6. Theodore Foster to Jedediah Foster, 2 March 1773, Dwight Foster Papers, MHS.
7. Josiah Cotton Memoirs, 1726–56, 49, MHS.
8. Louise A. Tilly and Joan W. Scott, *Women, Work and Family* (New York: Holt, Rhinehart and Winston, 1978); Alice Kessler-Harris, *Out to Work: A History of Wage-Earning Women in the United States* (New York: Oxford University Press, 1982); Lisa Wilson, *Life after Death: Widows in Pennsylvania, 1750–1850* (Philadelphia: Temple University Press, 1992), chap. 4; Claudia Goldin, "The Economic Status of Women in the Early Republic: Quantitative Evidence," *Journal of Interdisciplinary History* 16 (1986):

375-404; Joan M. Jensen, *Loosening the Bonds: Mid-Atlantic Farm Women, 1750-1800* (New Haven: Yale University Press, 1986); Laurel Thatcher Ulrich, *A Midwife's Tale: The Life of Martha Ballard Based on Her Diary, 1785-1812* (New York: Alfred A. Knopf, 1990); Laurel Thatcher Ulrich, "'A Friendly Neighbor': Social Dimensions of Daily Work in Northern Colonial New England," *Feminist Studies* 6 (summer 1980): 392-405.

9. *Watertown Records* (Watertown, Mass.: Watertown Historical Society, 1894), vol. 2, 212.

10. Ashley Bowen, *The Journals of Ashley Bowen (1728-1813) of Marblehead*, ed. Philip Chadwick Foster Smith, *Publications of the Colonial Society of Massachusetts, Collections*, vol. 44 (Boston: Colonial Society of Massachusetts, 1973), 149, 45, and 336.

11. George F. Dow, ed., *Records and Files of the Quarterly Courts of Essex County, Massachusetts*, 8 vols. (Salem, Mass.: Essex Institute, 1912), vol. 2, 57.

12. Marylynn Salmon, *Women and the Law of Property in Early America* (Chapel Hill: University of North Carolina Press, 1986), 76-77.

13. Dow, ed. *Records and Files of the Quarterly Courts*, vol. 2, 304.

14. In both Connecticut and Massachusetts, the most common divorce was *a vinculo matrimonii*, leaving the nonguilty party free to remarry and the wife, if innocent, her dower right in her husband's estate. Less common in Massachusetts and extremely rare in Connecticut was divorce *a mensa et thoro*. As in separation, the parties lived apart and the husband continued to provide some support but neither party could remarry. See Cornelia Hughes Dayton, *Women Before the Bar: Gender, Law, and Society in Connecticut, 1639-1789* (Chapel Hill: University of North Carolina Press, 1995), chap. 3, esp. 110-13; K. Kelly Weisberg, "'Under Greet Temptations Heed': Women and Divorce in Puritan Massachusetts," *Feminist Studies* 2 (1975), 185; Linda K. Kerber, *Women of the Republic: Intellect and Ideology in Revolutionary America* (Chapel Hill: University of North Carolina Press, 1980), 160; George Elliott Howard, *A History of Matrimonial Institutions* (Chicago: University of Chicago Press, 1904), vol. 2, 353; Salmon, *Women and the Law of Property*, 69.

15. Dayton, *Women Before the Bar*, 110, 130; Weisberg, "'Under Greet Temptations Heed,'" 185-87; Lyle Koehler, *A Search for Power: The "Weaker Sex" in Seventeenth-Century New England* (Urbana: University of Illinois Press, 1980), app. 1; Henry S. Cohn, "Connecticut's Divorce Mechanism: 1636-1969," *American Journal of Legal History* 14 (January 1970): 40; Kerber, *Women of the Republic*, 162; Howard, *History of Matrimonial Institutions*, vol. 2, 333-45.

16. Alison Duncan Hirsch, "The Thrall Divorce Case: A Family Crisis in Eighteenth-Century Connecticut," *Women and History* 4 (1982): 43; Edmund S. Morgan, *The Puritan Family: Religion and Domestic Relations in Seventeenth-Century New England,* rev. ed. (New York: Harper and Row, 1966), 37.

17. Dayton, *Women Before the Bar,* 117; Sheldon S. Cohen, " 'To Parts of the World Unknown': The Circumstances of Divorce in Connecticut, 1750–1797," *Canadian Review of American Studies* 11 (winter 1980): 277.

18. Nancy F. Cott, "Divorce and the Changing Status of Women in Eighteenth-Century Massachusetts," *William and Mary Quarterly* 33 (October 1976): 595; Salmon, *Women and the Law of Property,* 68.

19. Cott, "Divorce and the Changing Status of Women," 611; Morgan, *Puritan Family,* 36; Kerber, *Women of the Republic,* 170; Howard, *History of Matrimonial Institutions,* vol. 2, 339; Salmon, *Women and the Law of Property,* 66.

20. Weisberg, " 'Under Greet Temptations Heed,' " 186–89.

21. On the difficulty in estimating the frequency of such occurrences, see Roger Thompson, *Sex in Middlesex: Popular Mores in a Massachusetts County, 1649–1699* (Amherst: University of Massachusetts Press, 1986).

22. Morgan, *Puritan Family,* 130–31.

23. Robert V. Wells, "Illegitimacy and Bridal Pregnancy in Colonial America," in *Bastardy and Its Comparative History,* ed. Peter Laslett, Karla Oosterveen, and Richard M. Smith (Cambridge: Harvard University Press, 1980), 355–56.

24. Ibid., 359; Dayton, *Women Before the Bar,* chap. 4.

25. Alexander Keyssar, "Widowhood in Eighteenth-Century Massachusetts: A Problem in the History of the Family," *Perspectives in American History* 8 (1974): 100–102.

26. Salmon, *Women and the Law of Property,* 143; Wilson, *Life after Death,* 54–55; Toby L. Ditz, *Property and Kinship: Inheritance in Early Connecticut, 1750–1820* (Princeton: Princeton University Press, 1986), 130.

27. Wilson, *Life after Death,* chap. 5; Keyssar, "Widowhood," 99–111; Philip J. Greven, Jr., *Four Generations: Population, Land, and Family in Colonial Andover, Massachusetts* (Ithaca: Cornell University Press, 1970), 84, 137, 240–48.

28. Benjamin Wadsworth, *The Well-Ordered Family* (Boston, 1712), 29; Dow, ed., *Records and Files of the Quarterly Courts,* vol. 6, 101.

29. *The Winthrop Papers, Correspondence of Wait Winthrop (continued), Collections of the Massachusetts Historical Society,* vol. 5 (Boston: Massachusetts Historical Society, 1928), 16.

30. In the court documents their names are variously spelled Edmond Bery, Edmond Berry, Edward Berry, Betteris Berry, Bettrice Berry, Bettorice Berry. See Dow, ed., *Records and Files of the Quarterly Courts,* vol. 6, 194–95, 297–98.

31. Ibid., 297–98.

32. Franklin Bowditch Dexter, ed., *Biographical Sketches of the Graduates of Yale College with Annals of the College History* (New York: Henry Holt, 1903), vol. 1, 30.

33. Samuel Cooke to Brother, 15 May 1745, Thomas Foxcroft Correspondence, CHS.

34. G. Selleck Silliman to Joseph Fish, 13 May 1780, Silliman Family, YUL.

35. Josiah Cotton Memoirs, 1726–56, 119, MHS.

36. Massachusetts Bay passed a law "agaynst excesse in apparrill" in October 1651. "Silke or tiffany hoodes or scarfes, which though allowable to persons of greater estates, or more liberall education, yet we cannot but judge it intollerable in p[er]sons of such like condition." That is "men or women of meane condition, educations, & callinges." See Nathaniel B. Shurtleff, ed., *Records of the Governor and Company of the Massachusetts Bay in New England* (Boston: William White, 1854), vol. 3, 243–44.

37. Dow, ed., *Records and Files of the Quarterly Courts,* vol. 2, 303–4.

38. Ibid., vol. 6, 359–61.

39. John Adams, *Diary and Autobiography of John Adams,* ed. L. H. Butterfield (Cambridge: Harvard University Press, 1961), vol. 1, 352.

40. Josiah Cotton Memoirs, 1726–56, 137–38, MHS.

41. Cotton Mather, *Diary,* vol. 2, 4.

42. Aaron Cleaveland to Samuel Mather, 6 October 1750, Curwen Family Papers, AAS.

43. James W. Schmotter, "Ministerial Careers in Eighteenth-Century New England: The Social Context, 1700–1760," *Journal of Social History* (winter 1975): 249–67.

44. Ebenezer Parkman, *The Diary of Ebenezer Parkman, 1703–1782,* ed. Francis G. Walett (Worcester: American Antiquarian Society, 1974), 173–74.

45. *O.E.D.,* s.v. "groat."

46. Philemon Robbins to 1st Society of Branford, 9 December 1754, Papers of A. R. Robbins and Philemon Robbins, CHS.

47. Dwight Foster to Nabby Foster, 1 April 1777, Dwight Foster, MHS.

48. Ebenezer Baldwin to Bethiah Baldwin, 5 March 1766, Baldwin Family Papers, YUL.

49. For more on this hapless couple, see chap. 2.

50. Cotton Mather, *Diary*, vol. 2, 187.
51. Adams, *Diary and Autobiography*, vol. 1, 358.
52. Cotton Mather, *Diary*, vol. 2, 410; Kenneth Silverman, *The Life and Times of Cotton Mather* (New York: Harper and Row, 1984), 312–13.
53. *Winthrop Papers, Correspondence of Wait Winthrop*, 317.
54. Diary of Benjamin Bangs, 4 October 1762, vol. 3, 96, Bangs Collection, MHS.
55. John Sherman to [Roger Sherman], 24 December 1792, Baldwin Family Papers, YUL.
56. John Sherman to [Simeon Baldwin], 14 July 1792, Baldwin Family Papers, YUL.
57. [John Sherman] to [Simeon Baldwin], 20 December 1792, Baldwin Family Papers, YUL.
58. [John Sherman] to unknown [brother-in-law], n.d., Baldwin Family Papers, YUL.
59. *The Winthrop Papers, Part IV, Collections of the Massachusetts Historical Society*, vol. 8 (Boston: Massachusetts Historical Society, 1863–92), 84.
60. Abigail Graham to Nathaniel Chauncey, [1731], Chauncey Family Papers, YUL.
61. Thomas Shepard, *God's Plot: The Paradoxes of Puritan Piety, Being the Autobiography and Journal of Thomas Shepard*, ed. Michael McGiffert (Amherst: University of Massachusetts Press, 1972), 122.
62. Dow, ed., *Records and Files of the Quarterly Courts*, vol. 6, 328–30.

CHAPTER 5
"Ye Heart of a Father"

1. John Demos, *A Little Commonwealth: Family Life in Plymouth Colony* (New York: Oxford University Press, 1970); Philip J. Greven, Jr., *Four Generations: Population, Land, and Family in Colonial Andover, Massachusetts* (Ithaca: Cornell University Press, 1970); Philip Greven, *The Protestant Temperament: Patterns of Child-Rearing, Religious Experience, and the Self in Early America* (New York: New American Library, 1977); Philip Greven, *Spare the Child: the Religious Roots of Punishment and the Psychological Impact of Physical Abuse* (New York: Alfred A. Knopf, 1991); Michael Zuckerman, *Peaceable Kingdoms: New England Towns in the Eighteenth Century* (New York: Alfred A. Knopf, 1970); In contrast to this perspective is the older work of Edmund S. Morgan, *The Puritan Family: Religion and Domestic Relations in Seventeenth-Century*

New England, rev. ed. (New York: Harper and Row, 1966); For the role of fatherhood, see E. Anthony Rotundo, "American Fatherhood: A Historical Perspective," *The American Behavioral Scientist* 29 (September/October, 1985): 8–10 and John Demos, *Past, Present, and Personal: The Family and the Life Course in American History* (New York: Oxford University Press, 1986), 41–67.

2. For a summary of the literature maligning Puritan parenting, see Ross W. Beales, Jr., "In Search of the Historical Child: Miniature Adulthood and Youth in Colonial New England," *American Quarterly* 27 (October 1975): 379–98. Philip Greven is probably the most outspoken proponent of this perspective in both *Protestant Temperament* and *Spare the Child*.

3. Keith Wrightson has made this argument for early modern England. See Wrightson, *English Society, 1580–1680* (New Brunswick: Rutgers University Press, 1982), 109. Likewise, John R. Gillis argues that fathers were central to child rearing in England before the late eighteenth century. See Gillis, "Bringing Up Father: British Paternal Identities, 1700 to Present," *Masculinities* 3 (fall 1995): 1–27.

4. Carol Gilligan, *In a Different Voice: Psychological Theory and Women's Development* (Cambridge: Harvard University Press, 1982). Gilligan has been criticized as being an essentialist, arguing that differences between men and women are fixed and timeless. See Joan W. Scott, "Gender: A Useful Category of Historical Analysis," *American Historical Review* 91 (December 1986): 1065. This study turns Gilligan's notion of women as innately moral on its head. Men did and do make similarly humane choices. Our misreading of their language, however, precludes this kind of interpretation.

5. Like many recent scholars of British history, I have found more continuity than change in the way affection was expressed in New England families in both the seventeenth and eighteenth centuries. See Martine Segalen, *Love and Power in the Peasant Family: Rural France in the Nineteenth Century* (Chicago: University of Chicago Press, 1983); Ralph A. Houlbrooke, *The English Family, 1450–1700* (London: Longman, 1984); John R. Gillis, *For Better, For Worse: British Marriages, 1600 to the Present* (New York: Oxford University Press, 1985); Alan Macfarlane, *Marriage and Love in England: Modes of Reproduction, 1300–1840* (Oxford: Basil Blackwell, 1986); Steven Ozment, *Magdalena and Balthasar: An Intimate Portrait of Life in 16th-Century Europe Revealed in the Letters of a Nuremberg Husband and Wife* (New York: Simon and Schuster, 1986); Martin Ingram, *Church Courts, Sex and Marriage in England, 1570–1640* (Cambridge: Cambridge

University Press, 1987); Carol Z. Stearns and Peter N. Stearns, eds., *Emotion and Social Change: Toward a New Psychohistory* (New York: Holmes and Meiers, 1988); Jeffrey R. Watt, *The Making of Modern Marriage: Matrimonial Control and the Rise of Sentiment in Neuchâtel, 1550–1800* (Ithaca: Cornell University Press, 1992).

6. Cotton Mather, *A Family Well-Ordered* (Boston, 1699), 22.
7. Cotton Mather, *Family Well-Ordered;* Benjamin Wadsworth, *The Well-Ordered Family* (Boston, 1712). Laurel Thatcher Ulrich notes this pattern for funeral sermons. See Ulrich, "Vertuous Women Found: New England Ministerial Literature, 1668–1735," *American Quarterly* 28 (spring 1976): 39. Alternatively, Jane Kamensky argues "parents" meant "father" and "children" returned to "sons." See Kamensky, *Governing the Tongue: The Politics of Speech in Early New England* (New York: Oxford University Press, 1997), 239n22.
8. Jonathan Edwards to Rev. Benjamin Colman, D.D., 30 May 1735, Edwards Collection, Franklin Trask Library, Andover-Newton Theological School, Newton Center, Mass. (hereafter cited as A-NTS).
9. Benjamin Trumbull to Parents, 24 November 1765, Benjamin Trumbull Papers, YUL.
10. Diary of Samuel Chandler, 1 January 1773, HUA.
11. Cotton Mather, *Family Well-Ordered,* 41.
12. Cotton Mather, *Diary of Cotton Mather,* ed. Worthington Chauncey Ford (New York: Frederick Ungar, 1911), vol. 1, 486.
13. Exodus 20:12.
14. Cotton Mather, *Family Well-Ordered,* 45.
15. The idea of correction expressed in these passages included anything from a reproof to the use of the rod. Philip Greven has a more narrow interpretation in *Spare the Child.*
16. Hebrews 12:6.
17. John Davenport, *Letters of John Davenport: Puritan Divine,* ed. Isabel MacBeath Calder (New Haven: Yale University Press, 1937), 59.
18. G. Selleck Silliman to Joseph Fish, 13 May 1780, Silliman Family, YUL.
19. Increase Mather, "Diary of Increase Mather, 1675–1691," *Proceedings of the Massachusetts Historical Society* 13 (1900): 344.
20. Psalms 68:5.
21. Michael Wigglesworth, *The Diary of Michael Wigglesworth, 1653–1657: The Conscience of a Puritan,* ed. Edmund S. Morgan (New York: Harper and Row, 1946), 50.
22. Cotton Mather, *Diary,* vol. 1, 269.

23. George F. Dow, ed., *Records and Files of the Quarterly Courts of Essex County, Massachusetts*, 8 vols. (Salem, Mass.: Essex Institute, 1911–78), vol. 2, 416–17.

24. M. Sawyer to Rev. Ezra Weld, 18 May 1776, Farnham Family Papers, MHS.

25. The Native Americans involved in this attack on Deerfield were probably the Caughnawaga [French Mohawk] and Abenaki. Richard I. Melvoin, *New England Outpost: War and Society in Colonial Deerfield* (New York: W. W. Norton, 1989), 215–16. For a more detailed analysis of this family's ordeal, see John Demos, *The Unredeemed Captive: A Family Story from Early America* (New York: Vintage, 1994).

26. Alden T. Vaughan and Edward W. Clark, eds., *Puritans among the Indians: Accounts of Captivity and Redemption, 1676–1724* (Cambridge: Harvard University Press, 1981), 179.

27. Cotton Mather, *Family Well-Ordered*, 22–23.

28. Wadsworth, *Well-Ordered Family*, 45.

29. Cotton Mather, *Family Well-Ordered*, 18; Wadsworth, *Well-Ordered Family*, 58.

30. Cotton Mather, *Family Well-Ordered*, 19.

31. Wadsworth, *Well-Ordered Family*, 68.

32. There were no godparents in these ceremonies, rather the community acted as witness. See Daniel Scott Smith, "Child-Naming Practices, Kinship Ties, and Change in Family Attitudes in Hingham, Massachusetts, 1641 to 1880," *Journal of Social History* 18 (summer 1985): 554. Those who could baptize their children in the early years after settlement were church members. After 1662 the Halfway Covenant allowed those who had been baptized but had not become church members to baptize their children as well. The ceremony became increasingly available to all that desired the covenant for their children as the eighteenth century progressed. See E. Brooks Holifield, *The Covenant Sealed: The Development of Puritan Sacramental Theology in Old and New England, 1570–1720* (New Haven: Yale University Press, 1974), 143–59, 169–96.

33. Cotton Mather, *Family Well-Ordered*, 14.

34. John R. Gillis makes a similar argument for early modern England. See Gillis, "Bringing Up Father," 6–11.

35. Samuel Sewall, *The Diary of Samuel Sewall, 1674–1729*, ed. M. Halsey Thomas (New York: Farrar, Straus and Giroux, 1973), vol. 1, 87, 133, 264.

36. John J. Waters makes note of this joint decision-making process briefly in "Naming and Kinship in New England: Guilford Patterns and Usage, 1693-1759," *New England Historical and Genealogical Register* 138 (July

1984): 161; David Hackett Fischer claims the decision was the man's in "Forenames and the Family in New England: An Exercise in Historical Onomastics," in *Generations and Change: Genealogical Perspectives in Social History,* ed. Robert M. Taylor, Jr., and Ralph J. Crandall (Macon, Ga.: Mercer University Press, 1986), 223.

37. Thomas Shepard, "The Autobiography of Thomas Shepard," *Colonial Society of Massachusetts, Transactions* 27 (November 1930): 353-54.

38. Daniel Scott Smith argues that this very common practice reflected high mortality rates and, therefore, the finality of death rather than a lack of awareness of a child's uniqueness as an individual. See Smith, "Child-Naming Practices," 546.

39. James Cogswell [Jr.] to James Cogswell [Sr.], 20 June 1777, Cogswell Family Papers, YUL.

40. G. Selleck Silliman to John Noyes, 24 August 1779, Silliman Family Papers, YUL.

41. Most common of course was the naming of children for parents. See Smith, "Child-Naming Practices," 546-51; Waters, "Naming and Kinship," 172-73.

42. Sewall, *Diary,* vol. 1, 264.

43. Cotton Mather, *Diary,* vol. 1, 307.

44. Sewall, *Diary,* vol. 1, 175; For the Joseph he refers to here, see Ezekiel 37:16-19 and Fischer, "Forenames and the Family," 222.

45. Fischer, "Forenames and the Family," 224.

46. John Ballantine Diary, transcription, 13 June 1762, AAS.

47. Diary of William Cooper, 15 December 1765, MHS.

48. Waters, "Naming and Kinship," 162; Smith, "Child-Naming Practices," 544; Fischer, "Forenames and the Family," 222.

49. Cotton Mather, *Diary,* vol. 2, 59.

50. Daniel Scott Smith, "Continuity and Discontinuity in Puritan Naming: Massachusetts, 1771," *William and Mary Quarterly* 51 (January 1994): 67-91.

51. Cotton Mather, *Diary,* vol. 1, 218.

52. Sewall, *Diary,* vol. 1, 324.

53. Cotton Mather, *Diary,* vol. 2, 251.

54. Numbers 11:12; Isaiah 49:23.

55. For more information on the cultural implications of breastfeeding, see Ross W. Beales, Jr., "Nursing and Weaning in an Eighteenth-Century New England Household," in *Families and Children: Dublin Seminar in New England Folklife: Annual Proceedings 1985,* ed. Peter Benes (Boston: Boston University, 1987), 48-63; Marylynn Salmon, "The Cultural Sig-

nificance of Breastfeeding and Infant Care in Early Modern England and America," *Journal of Social History* 28 (winter 1994): 247-69.

56. Diary of Peter Thatcher, 18 May 1680, MHS.

57. Ebenezer Parkman, *The Diary of Ebenezer Parkman, 1703-1782,* ed. Francis G. Walett (Worcester: American Antiquarian Society, 1974), 56.

58. Diary of Ebenezer Parkman, 20 October 1755, MHS.

59. Sewall, *Diary,* vol. 1, 41.

60. Diary of Peter Thatcher, 19 May 1680, MHS.

61. James Cogswell [Jr.] to James Cogswell [Sr.], 3 August 1777, Cogswell Family Papers, YUL.

62. Diary of Peter Thatcher, 24 September 1679, MHS.

63. Parkman, *Diary,* 100.

64. Sewall, *Diary,* vol. 1, 482-83.

65. Parkman, *Diary,* 14.

66. Eliphalet Pearson to Mrs. Mascarene, 15 March 1783, Park Family Papers, YUL.

67. John Hull, "The Diaries of John Hull," *Transactions and Collections of the American Antiquarian Society* 3 (1857): 149.

68. M. Byles to Mary Byles, 7 May 1766, Byles Family Papers, MHS.

69. Mather Byles [Jr.] and Rebecca to Mather Byles [Sr.], 21 February 1763, Byles Family Papers, MHS.

70. Eliphalet Pearson to Doctor Edward A. Holyoke, 10 June 1782, Park Family Papers, YUL.

71. Eliphalet Pearson to sister, 22 December 1782, Park Family Papers, YUL.

72. Ezra Stiles, *The Literary Diary of Ezra Stiles,* ed. Franklin Bowditch Dexter (New York: Charles Scribner's Sons, 1901), vol. 2, 200.

73. G. Selleck Silliman and Mary Silliman to Joseph Fish, 31 July 1778, Silliman Family Papers, YUL.

74. G. Selleck to Joseph Fish, 20 November 1780, Silliman Family Papers, YUL.

75. Oliver Ellsworth to Nabby Ellsworth, 17 July 1781, Oliver Ellsworth Correspondence and Papers, CHS.

76. G. Selleck Silliman to Joseph Fish, 23 June 1778, Silliman Family Papers, YUL.

77. Mather Byles [Jr.] and Rebecca Byles to Mather Byles [Sr.], 21 February 1763, Byles Family Papers, MHS.

78. G. S. Silliman to [Joseph Fish], 7 December 1777, Silliman Family Papers, YUL.

79. Benjamin Trumbull [Sr.] to Benjamin Trumbull [Jr.], 27 September 1775, Benjamin Trumbull Papers, YUL.

80. Josiah Cotton Memoirs, 1726–56, 162–67, MHS.
81. William Samuel Johnson to Nancy, 25 January 1769, William Samuel Johnson Correspondence and Papers, CHS.
82. William Samuel Johnson to Nancy, 25 January 1769, William Samuel Johnson Correspondence and Papers, CHS.
83. Gen. Samuel McClellan to John McClellan, 30 December 1782, McClellan Papers, CHS.
84. Josiah Cotton Memoirs, 1726–56, 165, MHS.
85. Timothy Edwards to Esther Edwards, 7 August 1711, Edwards Collection, Franklin Trask Library, A-NTS.
86. William Samuel Johnson to Mrs. Johnson, 23 October 1770, William Samuel Johnson Correspondence and Papers, CHS.
87. Ezekiel Williams to John Williams, 6 December 1779, Williams Papers, CHS.
88. "Last Sayings of Rev. Solomon Williams," 26 February 1776, Williams Papers, CHS.
89. Cotton Mather, *Diary*, vol. 2, 265.
90. John Reyner and William Brewster to John Cotton, 24 August 1639, Cotton Family Papers, MHS.
91. Elisha Niles Diary, 1764–1845, 9, CHS.
92. Stiles, *Literary Diary*, vol. 1, 48–49.
93. Benjamin Trumbull [Sr.] to Benjamin Trumbull [Jr.], 27 September 1775, Benjamin Trumbull Papers, YUL.
94. Cotton Mather, *Diary*, vol. 1, 534–37.
95. Ibid., vol. 2, 25.
96. Josiah Cotton Memoirs, 1726–56, [illegible], MHS.
97. Thomas Williams to Ezekiel Williams, 12 March 1776, Williams Papers, CHS.
98. David E. Stannard, "Death and the Puritan Child," in *Death in America*, ed. David E. Stannard (Philadelphia: University of Pennsylvania Press, 1975), 9–29.
99. Benjamin Trumbull [Sr.] to Benjamin Trumbull [Jr.], 27 September 1775, Benjamin Trumbull Papers, YUL.
100. Cotton Mather, *Diary*, vol. 2, 149, 153.
101. Vaughan and Clark, *Puritans among the Indians*, 209–10.
102. "Last Sayings of Rev. Solomon Williams," 26 February 1776, Williams Papers, CHS.
103. Diary of Peter Thatcher, 9 July 1765, MHS.
104. Benjamin Bangs Diary, 30 January 1763, vol. 3, 119, Bangs Collection, MHS.

105. Jonathan Edwards to Timothy Edwards, 1 March 1721, Edwards Collection, Franklin Trask Library, A-NTS.
106. Sewall, *Diary,* vol. 1, 328.
107. T. B. Strandness, *Samuel Sewall: A Puritan Portrait* (East Lansing: Michigan State University Press, 1967), 122.
108. Sewall, *Diary,* vol. 1, 350.
109. Samuel Bradstreet, "Ever Hond. Father," 18 February 1678, Cotton Family Papers, MHS.
110. *The Winthrop Papers, Part IV, Collections of the Massachusetts Historical Society,* vol. 8 (Boston: Massachusetts Historical Society, 1863-92), 419.
111. Cotton Mather, *Diary,* vol. 2, 8-9.
112. Sewall, *Diary,* vol. 1, 89, 145.
113. Cotton Mather, *Diary,* vol. 2, 388.
114. Ibid., vol. 1, 303-5.
115. Ibid., vol. 1, 336-37.
116. Shepard, "Autobiography," 354.
117. Thomas Shepard, *God's Plot: The Paradoxes of Puritan Piety, Being the Autobiography and Journal of Thomas Shepard,* ed. Michael McGiffert (Amherst: University of Massachusetts Press, 1972), 174.
118. Shepard, "Autobiography," 381-82.
119. Thomas Shepard, *Thomas Shepard's Confessions,* ed. George Selement and Bruce C. Woolley, *Publications of the Colonial Society of Massachusetts, Collections,* vol. 58 (Boston: Colonial Society of Massachusetts, 1981), 195.
120. Sewall, *Diary,* vol. 1, 90.
121. Cotton Mather, *Diary,* vol. 1, 382.
122. Job 19:25.
123. Cotton Mather, *Diary,* vol. 1, 164.
124. Ibid., 174.
125. *The Winthrop Papers, Correspondence of Wait Winthrop (continued), Collections of the Massachusetts Historical Society,* vol. 5 (Boston: Massachusetts Historical Society, 1928), 300.
126. *Winthrop Papers, Part IV,* 493.
127. Cotton Mather, *Diary,* vol. 1, 185.
128. Ibid., 376-77.
129. Ibid., 294.
130. Ibid., vol. 2, 389.
131. Ibid., vol. 2, 74.
132. Shepard, "Autobiography," 353-56.
133. Increase Mather to "Sister," 22 January 1676, Cotton Family Papers, MHS.

CHAPTER 6
Widower

1. Clifford K. Shipton, *Sibley's Harvard Graduates* (Boston: Massachusetts Historical Society, 1975), vol. 17, 480; Benjamin Bangs Diary, 25 April 1760, 17 June 1760, 23 June 1760, 12 July 1760, vol. 2, 65, 84, 87, 92, Bangs Collection, MHS.

2. "Widowhood" will be used to indicate the state of "widowerhood." Men of the time used widow and widowhood to refer to their own circumstances.

3. Cotton Mather, *Diary of Cotton Mather*, ed. Worthington Chauncey Ford (New York: Frederick Ungar, 1911), vol. 1, 430.

4. Kenneth Silverman, *The Life and Times of Cotton Mather* (New York: Harper and Row, 1984), 179.

5. Robert Wells argues that for Massachusetts and Connecticut in the late eighteenth century, women outnumbered men in coastal areas on average and men outnumbered women on the frontier. In Connecticut, there were more women than men over seventy everywhere but in New Haven. See, Robert V. Wells, *The Population of the British Colonies in America before 1776: A Survey of Census Data* (Princeton: Princeton University Press, 1975), 85–94; Alexander Keyssar, "Widowhood in Eighteenth-Century Massachusetts: A Problem in the History of the Family," *Perspectives in American History* 8 (1974): 95; Susan Grigg, "Toward a Theory of Remarriage: A Case Study of Newburyport at the Beginning of the Nineteenth Century," *Journal of Interdisciplinary History* 8 (autumn 1977): 196–97. Barry Levy makes a similar connection between the sea and mortality in "Middling Yankee Orphans under Sail: Maritime Death, the Recruitment of Labor, and the Ethos of Salem, Massachusetts, 1770–1820," paper presented to the Boston Area Seminar in Early American History, Boston, 1 February 1996. Widows also outnumbered widowers in seventeenth-century England. See Ralph A. Houlbrooke, *The English Family, 1450–1700* (London: Longman, 1984), 209.

6. John Demos, *A Little Commonwealth: Family Life in Plymouth Colony* (New York: Oxford University Press, 1970), 66, 192–93; Catherine M. Scholten, *Childbearing in American Society, 1650–1850* (New York: New York University Press, 1985), 21–22. Women certainly did die in childbirth during the colonial period, but the fear of mortality seemed to outstrip the reality. See Maris A. Vinovskis, "Mortality Rates and Trends in Massachusetts before 1860," *Journal of Economic History* 32 (March 1972): 201–14; Daniel Scott Smith and J. David Hacker, "Cultural Demogra-

phy: New England Deaths and the Puritan Perception of Risk," *Journal of Interdisciplinary History* 26 (winter 1996): 381. Edward Shorter argues that fertile women died earlier than men because of the dangers of childbirth but more important, because of "overwork" and "undernutrition." See Shorter, *A History of Women's Bodies* (New York: Basic Books, 1982), 241.

7. Widowers married at the same rate as bachelors even into their seventies. See Wells, *Population of the British Colonies*, 95–96; John Faragher, "Old Women and Old Men in Seventeenth-Century Wethersfield, Connecticut," *Women's Studies* 4 (1976): 20; David T. Courtwright, "New England Families in Historical Perspective," in *Families and Children: The Dublin Seminar in New England Folklife: Annual Proceedings 1985*, ed. Peter Benes (Boston: Boston University, 1987), 14. For English patterns, see Houlbrooke, *English Family*, 213–14; Alan Macfarlane, *Marriage and Love in England: Modes of Reproduction, 1300–1840* (Oxford: Basil Blackwell, 1986), 236–38; Randolph Trumbach, *The Rise of the Egalitarian Family: Aristocratic Kinship and Domestic Relations in Eighteenth-Century England* (New York: Academy Press, 1978), 55–56.

8. Benjamin Douglas to Joseph Fish, 9 December 1766, Silliman Family Papers, YUL.

9. Franklin Bowditch Dexter, *Biographical Sketches of the Graduates of Yale College with Annals of the College History* (New York: Henry Holt, 1903), vol. 2, 650–51.

10. Benjamin Douglas to Joseph Fish, 9 December 1766, Silliman Family Papers, YUL.

11. Shipton, *Sibley's*, vol. 13, 47–60.

12. Eli Forbes to Ebenezer Parkman, 17 January 1776, Parkman Family Papers, AAS.

13. Benjamin Douglas to Joseph Fish, 9 December 1766, Silliman Family Papers, YUL.

14. Ezra Stiles, *The Literary Diary of Ezra Stiles*, ed. Franklin Bowditch Dexter (New York: Charles Scribner's Sons, 1901), vol. 1, 565.

15. Cotton Mather, *Diary*, vol. 2, 265. This remark referred to the burial of his second wife, Elizabeth, after she succumbed to measles in 1713.

16. [unknown] to [in-laws], 7 February 1777, Cary Family Papers, III, and Byles Family Papers, MHS.

17. Samuel Sewall, *Letter-book, Collections of the Massachusetts Historical Society* (Boston: Massachusetts Historical Society, 1886–88), vol. 2, 118.

18. E. Forbes to [Ebenezer Parkman], 14 March 1776, Parkman Family Papers, AAS.

19. Eliphalet Pearson to [sister] Mrs. Mascarene, 20 August 1782, Park Family Papers, YUL.

20. Samuel Sewall, *The Diary of Samuel Sewall, 1674–1729*, ed. M. Halsey Thomas (New York: Farrar, Straus and Giroux, 1973), vol. 2, 864.

21. Sewall, *Letter-book*, vol. 2, 82.

22. Eliphalet Pearson to Mrs. Mascarene, 20 August 1782, Park Family Papers, YUL.

23. [unknown] to [in-laws], 7 February 1777, Cary Family Papers, III, and Byles Family Papers, MHS.

24. Benjamin Douglas to Joseph Fish, 9 December 1766, Silliman Family Papers, YUL.

25. Cotton Mather, *Diary*, vol. 1, 457.

26. Stiles, *Literary Diary*, vol. 1, 563.

27. E. Forbes to [Ebenezer Parkman], 14 March 1776, Parkman Family Papers, AAS.

28. Sewall, *Letter-book*, vol. 2, 81.

29. *The Winthrop Papers, Part IV, Collections of the Massachusetts Historical Society*, vol. 8 (Boston: Massachusetts Historical Society, 1863–92), 163.

30. Thomas Shepard, "The Autobiography of Thomas Shepard," *Colonial Society of Massachusetts, Transactions* 27 (November 1930): 391.

31. Nehemiah Hobart to Nicholas Noyes, 29 March 1712, Miscellaneous Manuscripts, AAS. John Langdon Sibley, ed., *Biographical Sketches of Graduates of Harvard University, in Cambridge, Massachusetts* (Cambridge: Charles William Sever, University Bookstore, 1881), vol. 2, 235–38.

32. Benjamin Lord to [unknown], 10 July 1751, Thomas Foxcroft Correspondence, CHS.

33. Stiles, *Literary Diary*, vol. 1, 566.

34. Samuel B. Webb to Joseph Barrell, 21 January 1782, Samuel Blachley Webb Papers, YUL.

35. E. Forbes to [Ebenezer Parkman], 14 March 1776, Parkman Family Papers, AAS.

36. Ibid.

37. James Draper to [daughter], 2 December 1767, Draper-Rice Family Papers, AAS.

38. Samuel B. Webb to Joseph Barrell, 21 January 1782, Samuel Blachley Webb Papers, YUL.

39. Eliphalet Pearson to Mrs. Mascarene, 20 August 1782, Park Family Papers, YUL.

40. [unknown] to [in-laws], 7 February 1777, Cary Family Papers, III, and Byles Family Papers, MHS.

41. Benjamin Douglas to Joseph Fish, 9 December 1766, Silliman Family Papers, YUL.

42. Sewall, *Diary*, vol. 2, 951.

43. Ibid., 872.

44. Ebenezer Williams to Thomas Foxcroft, 17 November 1749, Thomas Foxcroft Correspondence, CHS.

45. Benjamin Douglas to Joseph Fish, 9 December 1766, Silliman Family Papers, YUL.

46. Thomas Clap, "Memoirs of some Remarkable Occurrances," n.d., Thomas Clap Presidential Records, YRG 2-A-5, YUL.

47. James Hillhouse to Abigail Lloyd, 1 January 1780, Cogswell Family Papers, YUL. He married Sarah Lloyd, 1 January 1779. She died in childbirth, 9 November 1780. See Dexter, *Biographical Sketches*, vol. 3, 488.

48. M[ather] Byles to Polly and Kitty Byles, 18 September 1780, Byles Family Papers, MHS.

49. Sewall, *Diary*, vol. 2, 1063.

50. Francis G. Walett, ed., *The Diary of Ebenezer Parkman, 1703–1782* (Worcester: American Antiquarian Society, 1974), 44, 131, and 170.

51. Stiles, *Literary Diary*, vol. 2, 14.

52. Clap, "Memoirs of some Remarkable Occurrances."

53. Stiles, *Literary Diary*, vol. 1, 562–65.

54. Cotton Mather, *Diary*, vol. 2, 256.

55. Sewall, *Diary*, vol. 2, 864.

56. Sewall, *Letter-book*, vol. 2, 74–82.

57. Clap, "Memoirs of some Remarkable Occurrances."

58. Cotton Mather, *Diary*, vol. 2, 495.

59. Sewall, *Diary*, vol. 2, 882–89.

60. G. Selleck Silliman to Joseph Fish, 12 July 1775, Silliman Family Papers, YUL.

61. "Rev. Thomas Clap's Thoughts on a Second Marriage," 9 April 1737, Baldwin Family Papers, YUL.

62. Faragher, "Old Women and Old Men," 18–19.

63. Keyssar found widows were 50.6 years old when widowed whereas widowers were 60.1 years old. See "Widowhood in Eighteenth-Century Massachusetts," 89.

64. Grigg, "Toward a Theory of Remarriage," 202–18.

65. Houlbrooke, *English Family*, 213–14; Macfarlane, *Marriage and Love in England*, 236–38; Trumbach, *Rise of the Egalitarian Family*, 55–56.

66. Faragher, "Old Women and Old Men," 19.

67. Grigg, "Toward a Theory of Remarriage," 217.

68. Wells, *Population of the British Colonies*, 95–96; Grigg, "Toward a Theory of Remarriage," 188–90, 201; For the situation in Europe, see Houlbrooke, *English Family*, 209.

69. Faragher, "Old Women and Old Men," 11–31; Houlbrooke, *English Family*, 213. Susan Grigg argues that economic status was intimately linked to age. See Grigg, "Toward a Theory of Remarriage," 211.

70. Most widowed women, in fact, had some adult children at home. Keyssar, "Widowhood in Eighteenth-Century Massachusetts," 90; Faragher, "Old Women and Old Men," 20; Houlbrooke, *English Family*, 212; Macfarlane, *Marriage and Love in England*, 237; Trumbach, *Rise of the Egalitarian Family*, 57.

71. Keyssar, "Widowhood in Eighteenth-Century Massachusetts," 110–11; For the strain on both mother and children, see Lisa Wilson, *Life after Death: Widows in Pennsylvania, 1750–1850* (Philadelphia: Temple University Press, 1992). For men and their reluctance to depend on their children, see chap. 7.

72. A *feme covert* or married woman by law gave up the right to all her unprotected assets to her husband.

73. Some evidence suggests that widows pursued remarriage more vigorously when their children were young because immediate financial need took precedence over long-term goals. See Grigg, "Toward a Theory of Remarriage," 206.

74. See chap. 4.

75. Faragher, "Old Women and Old Men," 20. Susan Grigg found a weak and contradictory association in Newburyport, Massachusetts. See "Toward a Theory of Remarriage," 203–6.

76. Peter Laslett, *Family Life and Illicit Love in Earlier Generations: Essays in Historical Sociology* (London: Cambridge University Press, 1977), 199–200; Houlbrooke, *English Family*, 212; Macfarlane, *Marriage and Love in England*, 237–38.

77. Cotton Mather, *Diary*, vol. 1, 491–96.

78. Sewall, *Letter-book*, vol. 2, 122–23.

79. Women had the same needs, but polite society preferred to deny this reality. Laurel Thatcher Ulrich, *Good Wives: Image and Reality in the Lives of Women in Northern New England, 1650–1750* (New York: Alfred A. Knopf, 1982), chap. 5; Grigg, "Toward a Theory of Remarriage," 220; Lisa Wilson [Waciega], "Widowhood and Womanhood in Early America: The Experience of Women in Philadelphia and Chester Counties, 1750–1850," (Ph.D. diss., Temple University, 1986), chap. 1.

80. Faragher, "Old Women and Old Men," 21.

81. Cotton Mather, *Diary*, vol. 1, 457–91.
82. Sewall, *Diary*, vol. 2, 960–67.
83. Sewall, *Letter-book*, vol. 2, 133.
84. Cotton Mather, *Diary*, vol. 1, 476.
85. Anna Cutts to Eliphalet Pearson, 27 July 1784, Park Family Papers, YUL.
86. Sewall, *Diary*, vol. 2, 889–92.
87. Cotton Mather, *Diary*, vol. 2, 273.
88. Ibid., vol. 1, 482.
89. Benjamin Douglas to Joseph Fish, 9 December 1766, Silliman Family Papers, YUL.
90. Ibid.
91. Clap, "Memoirs of some Remarkable Occurrances."
92. "Rev. Thomas Clap's Thoughts on a Second Marriage."
93. Clap, "Memoirs of some Remarkable Occurrances."
94. Cotton Mather, *Diary*, vol. 1, 476–94.
95. Parkman, *Diary*, 133.
96. Anna Cutts to Eliphalet Pearson, 27 July 1784, Park Family Papers, YUL.
97. James Draper to Daughter, 2 December 1767, Draper-Rice Family Papers, AAS.
98. "Rev. Thomas Clap's Thoughts on a Second Marriage."
99. Cotton Mather, *Diary*, vol. 1, 491.
100. "Rev. Thomas Clap's Thoughts on a Second Marriage."
101. Cotton Mather, *Diary*, vol. 1, 482–83.
102. Gold Selleck Silliman to Mary Noyes, 31 March 1775, Silliman Family Papers, YUL.
103. "Rev. Thomas Clap's Thoughts on a Second Marriage."
104. [Thomas Walley] to John Cotton, 20 September 1675, Curwen Family Papers, AAS.
105. G. Selleck Silliman to Mary Noyes, 24 April 1775, Silliman Family, YUL.
106. Richard Bourne to [Ruth Winslow], 30 April 1677, Cotton Family Papers, MHS.
107. Sewall, *Diary*, vol. 2, 908.
108. Ibid., 963–93.
109. Clap, "Memoirs of some Remarkable Occurrances."
110. Cotton Mather, *Diary*, vol. 2, 255.
111. Sewall, *Diary*, vol. 2, 1063.
112. Shepard, "Autobiography," 358.
113. Mary Noyes to Gold Selleck Silliman, 20 April 1775, Silliman Family Papers, YUL.
114. Ashley Bowen, *The Journals of Ashley Bowen (1728–1813) of Marblehead*, ed.

Philip Chadwick Foster Smith, *Publications of the Colonial Society of Massachusetts, Collections*, vol. 44 (Boston: Colonial Society of Massachusetts, 1973), 8.

115. Edward Taylor, *Edward Taylor's "Church Records" and Related Sermons*, ed. Thomas M. Davis and Virginia L. Davis (Boston: Twayne, 1981), 188.

116. Cotton Mather, *Diary*, vol. 2, 452.

117. "Rev. Thomas Clap's Thoughts on a Second Marriage."

118. Jacob Eliot Journal, 1762–64, MS 56663, 3–13, CHS.

119. Gold Selleck Silliman to Mary Noyes, 24 March 1775, Silliman Family Papers, YUL.

120. Selleck Silliman to Mary Noyes, 14 March 1775, Silliman Family Papers, YUL.

121. Joseph Fish to G. S. Silliman, 2 August 1776, Silliman Family Papers, YUL.

CHAPTER 7
"Like an Armed Man"

1. Josiah Cotton Memoirs, 1726–56, 274–76, 401, MHS.

2. Thomas R. Cole, *The Journey of Life: A Cultural History of Aging in America* (Cambridge: Cambridge University Press, 1992), 50; Carole Haber and Brian Gratton, *Old Age and the Search for Security: An American Social History* (Bloomington: Indiana University Press, 1994), 148–49.

3. Daniel Vickers, *Farmers and Fishermen: Two Centuries of Work in Essex County, Massachusetts, 1630–1850* (Chapel Hill: University of North Carolina Press, 1994); Howard Chudacoff and Tamara K. Hareven, "Family Transitions into Old Age," in *Transitions: The Family and the Life Course in Historical Perspective*, ed. Tamara K. Hareven (New York: Academic Press, 1978), 217–18.

4. Cornelia Hughes Dayton, "Notes from the Archives: Madness, Gender, and Dependency in Early New England," paper presented at the Boston Area Early American Seminar, Boston, 7 March 1996; Haber and Gratton, *Old Age*, 14–15 and 121. Women were also "dependents" in the legal sense. For a recent discussion of this notion, see Mary Beth Norton, *Founding Mothers and Fathers: Gendered Power and the Forming of American Society* (New York: Alfred A. Knopf, 1996). Although here I discuss economic contribution, it is reasonable to assume that dependency for men also included a real fear of demasculinization.

5. Some age restrictions on military and civil service existed, but most men maintained their positions until disabled by age. See John Demos, *Past,*

Present, and Personal: The Family and the Life Course in American History (New York: Oxford University Press, 1986), 142; Carole Haber, *Beyond Sixty-Five: The Dilemma of Old Age in America's Past* (Cambridge: Cambridge University Press, 1983), 18.

6. John Murrin argues that grandparents were "invented" in colonial New England. See Murrin, "Review Essay," *History and Theory*, 11 (1972): 238; Kenneth A. Lockridge, "Family Structure in Seventeenth-Century Andover, Massachusetts," *William and Mary Quarterly* 23 (1966): 234–56; Kenneth A. Lockridge, "The Population of Dedham, Massachusetts, 1636-1736," *Economic History Review* 19 (August 1966): 318–44; Philip J. Greven, Jr., *Four Generations: Population, Land, and Family in Colonial Andover, Massachusetts* (Ithaca: Cornell University Press, 1970); John Demos, "Notes on Life in Plymouth Colony," *William and Mary Quarterly* 22 (April 1965): 264–86.

7. Life experience rather than chronological age seemed to mark the winter of life in early America. Some historians argue that when a man turned sixty he was old according to tax and militia status changes. See, e.g., Gene W. Boyett, "Aging in Seventeenth-Century New England," *New England Historical and Genealogical Register* 134 (July 1980): 182.

8. Greven, *Four Generations*, chap. 4; Richard L. Bushman, *From Puritan to Yankee: Character and the Social Order in Connecticut, 1690-1765* (New York: W. W. Norton, 1967), chap. 4; Daniel Scott Smith, "Parental Power and Marriage Patterns: An Analysis of Historical Trends in Hingham, Massachusetts," *Journal of Marriage and the Family* 35 (August 1973): 419–28; Haber and Gratton, *Old Age*, 24; David Hackett Fischer, *Growing Old in America* (New York: Oxford University Press, 1977), 52; Linda Auwers, "Fathers, Sons, and Wealth in Colonial Windsor, Connecticut," *Journal of Family History* 3 (summer 1978): 136–49; Christopher M. Jedrey, *The World of John Cleaveland: Family and Community in Eighteenth-Century New England* (New York: W. W. Norton, 1979), 63-64, 73-74; Robert A. Gross, *The Minutemen and Their World* (New York: Hill and Wang, 1976), 75-78.

9. Fischer, *Growing Old*, 40, 78-109. Some have modified this "golden age" notion of old age in the seventeenth century, but most agree that the status of the elderly declined. See Demos, *Past, Present, and Personal*, 179-80; Haber and Gratton, *Old Age*, 7. Brian Gratton, "The New History of the Aged: A Critique," in *Old Age in a Bureaucratic Society: the Elderly, the Experts and the State in American History*, ed. David Van Tassel and Peter N. Stearns (New York: Greenwood Press, 1986), 8.

10. David Hackett Fischer argues that the emergence of derogatory names

for the old illustrated their declining social status. See *Growing Old*, 91–92.

11. Daniel Scott Smith, "Old Age and the 'Great Transformation': A New England Case Study," in *Aging and the Elderly: Humanistic Perspectives in Gerontology*, ed. Stuart F. Spicker, Kathleen M. Woodward, and David D. Van Tassel (Atlantic Highlands, N.J.: Humanities Press, 1978), 292–96.

12. David Hackett Fischer has argued that by the mid-seventeenth century "retirement" took on a modern meaning at times. Fischer, *Growing Old*, 43; *O.E.D.*, s.v., "retirement."

13. Samuel Sewall, *The Diary of Samuel Sewall*, ed. M. Halsey Thomas (New York: Farrar, Straus and Giroux, 1973), vol. 2, 1062.

14. Ebenezer Parkman, *The Diary of Ebenezer Parkman, 1703–1782*, ed. Francis G. Walett (Worcester: American Antiquarian Society, 1974), 129.

15. Jacob Eliot Journal, 1762–64, MS 56663, CHS.

16. Vickers, *Farmers and Fishermen*, 75–76.

17. Edward H. Thompson has found similar patterns among modern men facing unemployment or retirement. See *Older Men's Lives* (Thousand Oaks, Calif.: Sage, 1994), 106.

18. J[ohn] Cotton to Josiah Cotton, 13 January 1755, Curwen Family Papers, AAS; Benjamin Trumbull to grandparents, 18 August 1758, Benjamin Trumbull Papers, YUL.

19. David Hall Diary, 16 August 1777 and 13 January 1787, Hall Collection, MHS.

20. John Hull, "The Diaries of John Hull," in *Transactions and Collections of the American Antiquarian Society* 3 (1857): 223.

21. Increase Mather, "The Autobiography of Increase Mather," ed. M. G. Hall, *Proceedings of the American Antiquarian Society* 71 (1962): 352–54.

22. Josiah Cotton Memoirs, 1726–56, 73, MHS.

23. Sewall, *Diary*, vol. 2, 600.

24. Cotton Mather, *A Christian at his calling: Two brief discourses. One directing a Christian in his general calling; another directing him in his personal calling* (Boston, 1701), 39.

25. A number of historians have noted this imperative to work until disabled. See Demos, *Past, Present, and Personal*, 142, 156; Fischer, *Growing Old*, 4, 44; Haber, *Beyond Sixty-Five*, 15.

26. Josiah Cotton Memoirs, 1726–56, 372, MHS.

27. Ebenezer Parkman, Natalitia #20, 5 September 1781, Parkman Family Papers, AAS.

28. Cotton Mather, *A Good Old Age* (Boston, 1726), 28.

29. Sewall, *Diary*, vol. 2, 1051.

30. Historians have studied this notion of an honorable retirement. See Haber and Gratton, *Old Age*, 147; Fischer, *Growing Old*, 43; Haber, *Beyond Sixty-Five*, 18-19.

31. Sewall, *Diary*, vol. 2, 695.

32. Samuel Sewall, *Letter-book, Collections of the Massachusetts Historical Society*, vol. 2 (Boston: Massachusetts Historical Society, 1886-88), 259; Luke 2:29.

33. Lillian E. Troll, "The Family of Later Life: A Decade Review," *Journal of Marriage and the Family* 33 (May 1971): 266; Demos, *Past, Present, and Personal*, 161-63; Boyett, "Aging in Seventeenth-Century New England," 191-92.

34. Josiah Cotton Memoirs, 1726-56, 404, MHS.

35. Joseph Fish to G. Selleck Silliman, 25 January 1776, Silliman Family Papers, YUL; John Langdon Sibley, *Biographical Sketches of Graduates of Harvard University, in Cambridge, Massachusetts* (Cambridge: Charles William Sever, University Bookstore, 1885), vol. 3, 422.

36. James W. Schmotter, "Ministerial Careers in Eighteenth-Century New England: The Social Context, 1700-1760," *Journal of Social History* 9 (winter 1975): 249-67.

37. David Hall Diary, 20 January 1781, Hall Collection, MHS.

38. Ebenezer Parkman, Diary, 1 January 1773, MHS.

39. Sewall, *Letter-book*, 266.

40. Benjamin Trumbull to grandparents, 18 August 1758, Benjamin Trumbull Papers, YUL.

41. Diary of John Gates, 25 October 1789, John Gates Collection, MHS.

42. David Hall Diary, 13 January 1787, Hall Collection, MHS.

43. Fischer, *Growing Old*, 54; Cole, *Journey of Life*, 12; Haber, *Beyond Sixty-Five*, 9.

44. Lisa Wilson, *Life after Death: Widows in Pennsylvania, 1750-1850* (Philadelphia: Temple University Press, 1992); Daniel Scott Smith, "Old Age and the 'Great Transformation,'" 296.

45. Demos, *Past, Present, and Personal*, 169-70.

46. Edward Taylor, *Edward Taylor's "Church Records" and Related Sermons*, ed. Thomas M. Davis and Virginia L. Davis (Boston: Twayne, 1981), 208-12.

47. G. S. Silliman and Mary Silliman to Joseph Fish, 12 January 1779, Silliman Family Papers, YUL.

48. Mather Byles [Jr.] to Mather Byles [Sr.], 8 May 1763, Mather Byles to Mary Byles, 26 June 1764, Mather Byles to Kitty Byles, 18 August 1783, Byles Family Papers, MHS. It is hard to know from the existing documentation whether Byles was relieved that the burden did not fall to him.

We do know that during this period he struggled mightily with a disruptive group of Sabbatarians known as the Rogerenes who ultimately forced him to leave New London. See Clifford K. Shipton, *Sibley's Harvard Graduates* (Cambridge: Harvard University Press, 1965), vol. 13, 9–15.

49. Haber and Gratton, *Old Age*, 24; Boyett, "Aging in Seventeenth-Century New England," 188.

50. Exodus 20:12.

51. Benjamin Wadsworth, *The Well-Ordered Family* (Boston, 1712), 99.

52. *Watertown Records* (Watertown, Mass.: Watertown Historical Society, 1894), vol. 2, 20, 169.

53. Ibid., vol. 1, 49.

54. Troll, "Family of Later Life," 266; Demos, *Past, Present, and Personal*, 161–63; Boyett, "Aging in Seventeenth-Century New England," 191–92; Bettye Hobbs Pruitt, "Self-Sufficiency and the Agricultural Economy of Eighteenth-Century Massachusetts," *William and Mary Quarterly* 41 (July 1984): 347; Jackson Turner Main, *Society and Economy in Colonial Connecticut* (Princeton: Princeton University Press, 1985), 233–34.

55. Fischer, *Growing Old*, 56; Haber, *Beyond Sixty-Five*, 11; Haber and Gratton, *Old Age*, 22–25; David I. Kertzer, "Toward a Historical Demography of Aging," in *Aging in the Past: Demography, Society, and Old Age*, ed. David I. Kertzer and Peter Laslett (Berkeley: University of California Press, 1995), 372.

56. John J. Waters, "Patrimony, Succession, and Social Stability: Guilford, Connecticut, in the Eighteenth Century," *Perspectives in American History* 10 (1976): 150.

57. Richard Wall, "Elderly Persons and Members of Their Households in England and Wales from Preindustrial Times to the Present," in *Aging in the Past: Demography, Society, and Old Age*, ed. David I. Kertzer and Peter Laslett (Berkeley: University of California Press, 1995), 81–106.

58. Joseph Fish to G. Selleck Silliman [and Mary Silliman], 1 January 1778, Silliman Family Papers, YUL.

59. Josiah Cotton Memoirs, 1726–56, 172, MHS.

60. John Ballantine Diary, 17 April 1759, AAS.

61. Kathleen M. Brown makes a similar link between manhood and mobility in colonial Virginia. See Brown, *Good Wives, Nasty Wenches, and Anxious Patriarchs: Gender, Race, and Power in Colonial Virginia* (Chapel Hill: University of North Carolina Press, 1996), 277.

62. Sewall, *Letter-book*, 257.

63. Sewall, *Diary*, vol. 1, 605.

64. Increase Mather, "Autobiography," 352.

65. Hull, "Diaries of John Hull," 182.

66. Ebenezer Parkman, Natalitia #20, 5 September 1781, Parkman Family Papers, AAS.

67. Sewall, *Diary*, vol. 1, 512.

68. Bruce C. Daniels, *Puritans at Play: Leisure and Recreation in Colonial New England* (New York: St. Martin's Press, 1995), 190–92.

Conclusion

1. Joseph Perry, *The Character of Moses illustrated and improved: in a Discourse Occasioned by the Death of the Honorable Roger Wolcott, Esq.* (Hartford, 1767).

2. Scholars who have explored this link include Jay Fliegelman, *Prodigals and Pilgrims: The American Revolution Against Patriarchal Authority, 1750–1800* (Cambridge: Cambridge University Press, 1982); and Edwin G. Burrows and Michael Wallace, "The American Revolution: The Ideology and Psychology of National Liberation," *Perspectives in American History* 6 (1972): 167–306.

3. Mark E. Kann, a political scientist, has tried to tackle this complex issue from a political perspective. A focus on the domestic context of colonial manhood would alter his conclusions about the primacy of male independence and patriarchal power. See Kann, *A Republic of Men: The American Founders, Gendered Language and Patriarchal Politics* (New York: New York University Press, 1998).

INDEX

calendar, 198n. 27

calling: and family imperatives, 26–35; general, 16–17, 171; idleness in, 17; inward, 16; and the ministry, 16; outward, 16; parental control challenged, 32–34; particular, 16–17, 171; and wealth, 25, *See also* service

celibacy: and fornication, 203n. 6; as marriage alternative, 38–40

Chackswell, John (witness in Laurence Turner case), 93

Chandler, Benjamin (actor in William Beale case), 93–94

Chandler, Samuel: and ministerial salary, 26; and parents, 116–17

Chauncey, Charles, 33

Chauncey, Nathaniel (relative of Abigail Graham), 113

Cheever, Ezekiel: serviceable into old age, 174–75

childbirth: and death of wife, 151; and husband's fear of loss, 83, 143–44; husband's role in, 83–86; and tending a sick child, 134

clap, 44

Clap, Mary (wife of Thomas Clap), 151; and headstone, 153; and remarriage of husband, 161

Clap, Thomas: and angry wife, 89; ideal qualities in a wife, 47–48; and memorial to dead wife, 152–53; and remarriage, 154–56, 161–62, 163; and remarriage and children, 166, 168; and widower, resolution of grief, 151; and his widowhood, 154

Clark, Mrs. (love interest of Thomas Walley), 163–64

Clarke, Joseph (friend of Dwight Foster), 25

Clarke, Lucy (gossiped about courting), 63

Cleaveland, Aaron: providing and family size, 108

clerk, 33

Cogswell, James: and breastfeeding, 123; and brother's calling, 30–31; and ideal wife, 48; lovesick, 40; and naming, joint role in, 121

Cogswell, Mason (brother of James Cogswell): and calling, 30–31

Cole, Mr. (Providence lawyer), 20

college education, 27–31

competency, 23, 51, 52

Cooke, Samuel: and providing needful items, 104–5

Cooper, John (son of town clerk, William Cooper, second by that name), 121

Cooper, Judith Sewall: courtship of, 61

Cooper, William (Boston town clerk): and naming as form of instruction, 121

Cooper, William (minister, sonin-law of Samuel Sewall), 61

Copley, Mrs. (courting man directed to ask her about interest), 63

Cotton, John: and meet help, 47

Cotton, Josiah, 100; and calling, 171; calling and family imperatives, 32–33; and dependence in old age, 183; and family prayer, 131; and living within means, 105; old age and declining re-

Mayhew, Thomas: and minister's salary, 112–13
McClellan, Samuel: and teaching children, 128
merchant, 13, 16, 24–25, 30–31
minister, 29–30, 33–34; ordination, anniversary of, 35–36; salary and aging, 175–78. *See also under* calling
minister's salary, 24–26, 108–9, 112–13. *See also under* calling
Mirick, Thomas: poor providing, alcohol, and marital discord, 111–12

naming. *See* father
Native American: as Caughnawaga, or Macquas [Mohawk], 118; as other, 6–7
needful. *See* providing
Nicols, Mary (witness in Mary Tilden case), 78–79
Niles, Dorcas Bechwith (stepmother of Elisha Niles), 33
Niles, Elisha, 14–15; and family prayer, 130; ministry vs. military, 33–34
Niles, Mary Sexton (mother of Elisha Niles), 33
Niles, Nathan (father of Elisha Niles), 33
Norcross, Richard, 17
Nursing the sick; by women, 133–34

Oddingsall, Thomas, 17
old age: children as props of, 181–83; chronology vs. life experience, 236n. 7; cultural perspective on, 172; and declin-

ing resources, 176–77; demographic realities, 171–72; God as comforter in, 178; and inability to travel, 183–84; and loss of home, 184–85
Oliver, Thomas (housebound old man), 184

Page, John: on ideal wife and money, 56
painter, 32
parenting: and mutual obligation, 117. *See also under* father
Parkman, Ebenezer, 15; old age and loss of home, 184; and breastfeeding, 122–23; calling and family imperatives, 30; and childbirth, 83, 84, 85–86; farm for son, 35; and minister's salary, 108–9; old age and declining resources, 177–78; and remarriage, 162; and retirement, meaning of, 173; and retirement and physical disability, 175; and settlement, 23; and weaning, 123; and wedding anniversary, 81–82; and widower, anniversary of loss, 152; and widower, resolution of grief, 149
Parkman, Elias (brother of Ebenezer Parkman), 30
Parkman, Mary Champney (wife of Ebenezer Parkman), 15, 152
patriarchy, 2–3
Partridge, Betsey (sister of Sophia Partridge), 41; courtship of, 70
Partridge, Sophia, 41, 110; beauty of, 49; courtship of, 67–71; intellect of, 53–54. *See also* Philomela

Pearson, Eliphalet: calling and family imperatives, 27-28, 32; and grief over wife's death, 147; and monitoring development of children, 124; and remarriage, 160, 162; and weaning, 123-24; and widower, resolution of grief, 149; and wife as friend, 76-77

Pearson, Marie (daughter of Eliphalet Pearson): and father's remarriage, 162; and weaning of, 123-24

Pease, Joseph, 15

Pease, Mindwell King (wife of Joseph Pease), 15

Perkins, Mr. (friend of Simeon Baldwin): ideal wife and intelligent companion, 53

Perry, Joseph (minister at Roger Wolcott's funeral): and domestic world, 186

Philander, 67-69, 211n. 119

Phillips, Justice (involved in joke played on Nat Hurd), 44

Philomela, 67, 211n. 119

Plymouth, Mass., 129-30

power relations, 2, 7

Prey, Richard (abusive husband), 90

private sphere, 2

providing: adequacy judged by other men, 109-11, 114; after death, 102-3; and alcohol's effect on, 106, 111-12; and children, 106-7; and divine mandate, 103; and future needs, 107-8; and illegitimate births, 102; and keeping wife like her father did, 106-7; lifecycle and family size, 108-9; and living within means, 105; male responsibility for, 101; needful items for, 104-5; shared with family, 99-101

public sphere, 2, 5

Punderson, Mrs. (nurse to Rebecca Douglas), 145

Puritanism, 5

Pynchon, Joseph: and service, 19

Quincy, Hannah (love interest of John Adams), 63

rake, 41-42

Randall, Nurse (worked for Samuel Sewall); as wetnurse, 123

Reeve, Sarah [Sally] (wife of Tapping Reeve), 76, 77, 79

Reeve, Tapping: and love for wife, 77; and passion for wife, 79; and wife as friend, 76

remarriage. See divorce; widow; widower

retirement: agrarian, 178-81; age of, 235-36n. 5; meaning of, 172-73; phased, 173, 180-81; and physical disability, 175; as pitiful, 183; and self/other ratio, 179-81; and timing of, 175-76

Robbins, Philemon: and minister's salary, 108-9

Rockwell, Matthew: anger and bag of, 65-67

Rogerenes. See Byles, Mather

Role analysis, 4-5

sailor, 13, 32-33, 143

Salisbury, Stephen, 76

Salter, Theophilus (courting without parental permission), 59